COMPLEXITIES
iN SOCiƎL WORK

COMPLEXITY iN SOCiƏL WORK

RICK HOOD

Los Angeles | London | New Delhi
Singapore | Washington DC | Melbourne

Los Angeles | London | New Delhi
Singapore | Washington DC | Melbourne

SAGE Publications Ltd
1 Oliver's Yard
55 City Road
London EC1Y 1SP

SAGE Publications Inc.
2455 Teller Road
Thousand Oaks, California 91320

SAGE Publications India Pvt Ltd
B 1/I 1 Mohan Cooperative Industrial Area
Mathura Road
New Delhi 110 044

SAGE Publications Asia-Pacific Pte Ltd
3 Church Street
#10-04 Samsung Hub
Singapore 049483

Editor: Kate Keers
Editorial assistant: Talulah Hall
Production editor: Katie Forsythe
Copyeditor: Mary Dalton
Proofreader: William Baginsky
Indexer: Gary Kirby
Marketing manager: Camille Richmond
Cover design: Wendy Scott
Typeset by: C&M Digitals (P), Ltd, Chennai, India
Printed in the UK

First published 2018

Library of Congress Control Number: 2017955328

British Library Cataloguing in Publication data

A catalogue record for this book is available from
the British Library

ISBN 978-1-4739-9380-8
ISBN 978-1-4739-9381-5 (pbk)

At SAGE we take sustainability seriously. Most of our products are printed in the UK using FSC papers and boards.
When we print overseas we ensure sustainable papers are used as measured by the PREPS grading system.
We undertake an annual audit to monitor our sustainability.

For Vicki and Finn

Table of Contents

ABOUt the AUthOR

Rick Hood is a registered social worker and Associate Professor in the Department of Social Work and Social Care at Kingston University and St Georges, University of London. Rick has over ten years' experience of statutory social work, mainly in the fields of child protection and looked after children. His interests lie in the application of systems ideas to people-centred services, particularly in relation to children and families. He has undertaken research into interprofessional expertise, complexity in child protection work, relationship-based practice, performance indicators and inspection in children's social care. His work has been published widely in the areas of interprofessional care and social work.

iNTRODUCtiON: What is COMPLEXity?

CHAPTER SUMMARY

This introductory chapter will define and explain the concept of complexity. It starts with a discussion of what makes social work complex and the difference between complex and complicated problems. Characteristics of complex systems are then explained along with some of the main principles of complexity theory. The links between concepts of complexity and risk are discussed. The chapter concludes with a précis of the structure and layout of the book.

iNTRODUCtiON

Social workers are constantly aware of complexity. Their professional remit, after all, is the messy reality of life. To practise as a social worker is to deal with the uniquely problematic interface between each individual and the world around them. Most social workers would say their work is far from predictable and often bears scant resemblance to academic models and theories. Experience teaches them to accept uncertainty and to tolerate risk without becoming panicked or paralysed.

Social workers are regularly asked to find solutions to intractable situations, navigate ethical and legal dilemmas, and provide services to those who do not want them. To accomplish these and many other tasks, they draw on an eclectic body of knowledge that stretches beyond their own academic discipline to incorporate elements of psychology, sociology and bio-medical science, as well as the law. So – one might indeed say that social work is a complex undertaking!

But what does complexity really mean? And is the complexity of their work something social workers need to know more about? These two questions underlie the topics covered in this book. Its focus is on thinking about complexity in practice rather than explaining scientific and mathematical theories in great detail. However, it will be important for readers to grasp some of the basic principles of complexity in order to understand fully the connections and applications made in later chapters. This introductory chapter will therefore seek to define and explain complexity, starting with conventional understandings of the term before exploring insights from theories of complex systems. The chapter concludes by outlining the topics covered in the rest of the book.

What Do We Mean By Complexity?

Conventional understandings of the term 'complex' tend to stress the idea of difficulty. However, when we look more closely at how the term is used, we can begin to see what it is about complexity that makes things difficult.

Wicked problems

Most social workers will be able to highlight certain pieces of work that they regard as especially complex. When practitioners are asked what makes their cases complex, often they point to the difficulty of solving the problem, or more likely the set of problems, with which they are presented. 'There's so much going on it's hard to know where to start' is one way of paraphrasing this sentiment. It could be argued that social workers in these cases find themselves confronted with what Rittel and Webber (1973) call 'wicked problems'. According to Hood et al. (2016a) such problems are characterised as follows:

- They have no definitive formulation
- They relate to multiple issues, so it may be difficult to recognise when an end-point has been reached
- They have a unique configuration, so a 'solution' may not work in other cases

Arguably, all problems in social work conform to this description; some situations just make us more aware of their 'wicked' characteristics than others. This is an important point that we shall return to later in the chapter.

Complex or complicated?

One way of understanding complex problems is to think about what makes them different from a complicated technical problem. An example of a technical problem that many people have experienced is a car engine that refuses to start. Unless it is something relatively straightforward, such as a dead battery, a car engine is too complicated for most people to repair on the spot. They will need the help of a car mechanic. The mechanic should be able to obtain all the necessary information to understand what is wrong with the engine, and formulate what needs to be done. There is a clear measure of success and an end-point to the intervention, i.e. the car should start and not cut out. If the solution works, then it should apply to all similar problems in the future. These points all differ fundamentally from the characteristics of wicked problems that were identified above.

What is it about the car engine that makes it a complicated rather than a complex problem? In essence, an engine is an intricate assembly of components, whose properties and connections to each other are largely determined by the laws of physics. The individual parts of an engine do not move independently or decide how to interact with each other. If they change the way they behave, it is through wear and tear or accidental damage rather than because their intentions have changed or because of an unconscious shift in attitudes. In other words, car engines cannot feel, think or reflect on what they do. They can neither adapt to their environment nor evolve new ways of performing their function. All this means that an engine should behave predictably as long as our theoretical model of how it works is accurate *and* we have comprehensive information about its current state.[1]

In contrast, consider a complex human problem that all social workers will come across at some point in their work (as well as in their personal lives), which is the experience of loss (Currer, 2007). Most obviously there is great variation both in the nature and perception of loss as well as our response to it. The significance of any loss is unique to the person and their circumstances at a particular time and in a given social and cultural context. In order to find out what a loss means to someone, discussion and dialogue are needed, not to say considerable interpersonal skills on the part of the professional. Equally, the professional's own experience of loss will have a bearing on how she is able to work with and relate to the service user. While there are certainly theories that help professionals to recognise and think about these issues, no social worker could use them to try and 'repair' a grief-stricken human being in the same way as a car engine.

Interactions and dynamics

Complex situations, unlike complicated ones, tend to come up with unusual or unexpected types of behaviour, or behaviour that is hard to understand in its current context.

---

[1]This is not to say that fixing a car engine is easy – on the contrary complicated problems are also difficult, which is why car mechanics are rarely short of work.

That brings us to another aspect of complexity that social workers often deal with, namely the patterns or 'dynamics' of relationships between people. This issue can be interpreted and understood in various ways. For example, interactions between certain members of a family may be very antagonistic, so that social workers worry about an escalation of abuse or violence. On the other hand, there may be collusion and resistance to professional scrutiny, which presents an altogether different set of challenges. Whatever the specific situation, the importance of these patterns tells us that complexity in social work is often about relationships. These are rarely predictable and may not correspond to the information that professionals have. Moreover, as soon as they start working with people, social workers become part of the dynamics they are trying to understand and influence.

REFLECTIVE EXERCISE 0.1

- Think about a complex piece of work that you have undertaken recently. Jot down three or four things that made it complex.
- Do you see any parallels between what you wrote and the points made in this chapter so far?

Systems

At this point it may be worth recapping where we have got to with our initial definition of complexity. So far, we know that when people use the word 'complex' they often refer to situations in which it is difficult to state exactly what is going on or to predict what will happen next. In other words, the relationship between cause and effect is not entirely clear. We also know that this has a lot to do with interactions between people who are free to act and think independently but are also closely connected to each other in various ways, e.g. in families, communities, and societies.

Some readers may already be thinking that this sounds a lot like systems theory. And indeed it is! The rest of this introductory chapter will clarify the relationship between complexity and systems ideas, with an unsurprising focus on theories of complex systems. Our working definition of complexity is as follows:

> Complexity is a set of principles about social events and behaviour that derive from scientific theories of complex adaptive systems. These principles help to explain the challenges of working with complex human problems, and therefore point towards appropriate professional and organisational approaches.

The next step in our exploration of complexity is therefore to outline and critique some basic ideas from systems theory before considering how complex systems differ from other types of system.

Basic systems ideas

On a basic level, systems can be conceptualised in terms of structure, processes, feedback loops, and states.

- *Structure*: Systems are structured as a network of interconnected components (or 'agents') that exchange energy and information within a boundary. If nothing can pass across the boundary then the system is said to be 'closed', whereas if the boundary is permeable then the system is 'open'.
- *Processes* are the characteristic ways in which energy is transferred, not only between parts of the system but also between the system as a whole and its environment. For example, 'inputs' are absorbed from the environment into the system, whereas 'outputs' pass out of the system into the environment.
- *Feedback loops* occur when the system's output affects the environment, which in turn provides the system with information about the results of its activity. A simple example of a feedback loop is when a thermostat switches on the radiator in a room that has got cold. As the room warms up, the thermostat responds to information from its sensors and turns the heating off again when the desired temperature has been reached.
- *State*: The feedback loop described above keeps the room in a 'steady state', i.e. not too warm and not too cold. In this sense, 'state' refers to how the system as a whole changes or stays the same over time. Note that this type of feedback is called 'negative feedback' because its purpose is to alert the system to any deviation (above or below) from the desired state.

A key assumption in many systems theories is that systems try to maintain a steady state or 'equilibrium'. If we conceive of living beings as systems, then 'state' may be more appropriately thought of in terms of health, wellbeing, identity, or purpose. These are holistic concepts that are hard to define purely in terms of their individual components, however many we try to list. The whole system is therefore more than just the sum of its parts – the principle of 'non-summativity' (Payne, 2015: 145). Furthermore, since all the parts of a system interact with each other, changes in one part of the system will affect all the others. This means that feedback loops can also occur within a system, so that a system can change through its internal processes as well as in response to its environment. For example, a physical injury may have psychological effects and eventually lead to a change in perceived wellbeing. This is an important issue in complex systems, as we shall see.

Systems ideas have had great influence on social work practice, notably through theories of ecological systems (Bronfenbrenner, 1979), helping systems (Pincus and Minahan, 1973), and family systems (Minuchin, 1974). Their contribution has been to focus attention on interactions and patterns of relationships, both within and outside of the family, as well as highlighting the importance of environmental context for people's development through the life-course (Gitterman and Germain, 2008). Systems theories have therefore helped to balance the psychodynamic emphasis on behaviour as determined by inner psychological drives. Social workers are encouraged to accept that there are multiple pathways for people to achieve a given outcome, and that similar circumstances can lead to divergent outcomes for different people (Baltes, 1987).

Critique of systems theory

These are all important insights. Nonetheless, there are some problematic assumptions inherent in many variants of systems theory, which are relevant to our understanding of complexity.

First, it is often assumed that systems tend towards equilibrium. Achieving and maintaining stability therefore becomes an implicit aim of intervention. This applies even when the goal is change, e.g. in a family's patterns of behaviour, since the idea is that a desirable equilibrium is substituted for an undesirable one. A key problem with this assumption, as we shall see shortly, is that complex systems operate 'far from equilibrium' and will therefore confound our expectations of stability. The emphasis on stability also makes it hard to understand how and why new patterns of behaviour emerge; many applications of systems theory therefore fail to provide a satisfactory account of creativity and innovation (see Stacey, 2007).

Another objection to 'standard' systems theory concerns the assumption that a system's parts should all contribute to its overall function or purpose. A breakdown in the cohesive relationship between the parts and the whole is seen as detrimental to the system's functioning, e.g. when an organ fails the body falls ill. While this 'functionalist' perspective seems straightforward in a physical or biological context, such as the human body, when applied to social settings it arguably downplays the existence of competing interests and the significance of power relationships and conflict in human societies. Indeed, from a functionalist perspective, disorder and conflict are seen as problematic because they disrupt equilibrium. While this is understandable in many respects, disturbance of some kind is often a prelude to change in the positive sense; for example, a short-term crisis in the life of a drug addict may prompt them to seek treatment for their addiction, which could have long-term benefits. Episodes of turmoil are therefore characteristic of systems that adapt and evolve (Prigogine and Stengers, 1984). There may also be hidden ideological content to the notion that individuals are part of a social system whose stability is paramount (see Dominelli, 2002, on 'maintenance approaches' to social work).

Finally, the idea that systems have boundaries implies that the characteristics and behaviour of a given system can be observed from an objective standpoint outside that boundary (Stacey, 2007). There are reasons to be sceptical of this assumption, particularly in social contexts where it may be hard to identify where one system stops and another begins. Social ecological theories such as Bronfenbrenner's (1979) conceive of individuals as being embedded in a series of 'nested' systems that represent different aspects of their environment. Although such frameworks emphasise openness and interconnection, they also imply that individuals are contained and stabilised at the heart of this nested structure so that analysis is directed at the system itself. The problem is that there is no vantage point outside of the system from which to observe and assess what is going on 'inside'. On the contrary, any would-be observer is herself involved in and contributing to what she is purporting to analyse. In everyday terms, the abstract notion of 'the system' or 'systems' tends to collapse into the messy dynamics of social interaction (Stacey, 2007).

complex systems

Having outlined and critiqued some of the basic principles of systems theory, we are now in a position to explore the characteristics of complex systems. Before doing so, it is important to note that complexity is a diverse, multi-disciplinary field that encompasses mathematics and the natural sciences, as well as social sciences and applied disciplines such as social work. What follows is necessarily a concise summary and readers who are interested in finding out more about complexity theory are directed towards the writers cited below.

Starting point: Equilibrium systems

Mowles (2014) draws on Stacey (2007) and Allen (1998) to outline how theoretical models of systems have gradually incorporated complexity. His starting point is the 'equilibrium system' that has already been discussed above and which derives from classical physics. The basic model of such a system is a bit like a pocketless billiards table with some balls on it (see Figure 0.1). All the entities in the system have the same characteristics, i.e. all the balls are the same shape and weight. Cause and effect are linear so that a given input leads to a direct and measurable change in system behaviour, i.e. players can more or less predict what will happen when they strike one of the balls with a cue.[2] Without further inputs from the environment, the system will move towards equilibrium, i.e. the balls will come to a halt.

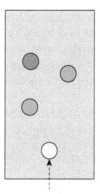

Figure 0.1   Example of an equilibrium system: balls on a billiards table

---

[2]Nonetheless, it would be impossible even for the most well-informed billiards player to predict *exactly* where the balls will end up.

Stage One: Non-linear systems

The first step away from this classical model of a system is to take away the assumption of equilibrium. Instead, the results of one interaction feed into the next interaction in a cumulative fashion. This leads to 'non-linear' behaviour, which Elliot and Kiel (1997: 66) define as 'feedback in which internal or external changes to a system produce amplifying effects'. It is as if the balls on the billiards table, once set in motion, do not come to a rest but continue moving around the table in a way that constantly builds on their own speed and direction. Note that this constitutes 'positive feedback' as opposed to negative feedback: it is as if a thermostat were set to turn up the heating when the temperature rises!

Mathematical equations that model non-linear dynamics show that small changes in their original state (e.g. the position of the balls or the force of the cue strike) can significantly affect outcomes, a characteristic known as sensitivity to initial conditions, or the 'butterfly effect'. Such equations explore what is known as 'mathematical chaos' and their significance lies in the nature of the iteration itself, i.e. the values that govern feedback within the system. Some values produce stable, predictable patterns of movement, whereas others lead to wildly fluctuating, unpredictable behaviour. However, certain values create movement that is paradoxically *both* stable *and* unstable, and this is seen as characteristic of complex systems, whose non-linear behaviour is not chaotic but lies 'at the edge of chaos' (Waldrop, 1994).

Stage Two: Self-organising systems

According to Mowles (2014), the second step towards modelling a complex system is to remove the assumption that interactions between entities can be calculated as a statistical average. This is because non-linearity applies not only to the interaction between entities within the system but also to how the system interacts with its environment. Systems that are far from equilibrium move towards a critical state of disorderly change, at which point they can suddenly shift to a new and orderly pattern of behaviour.

An example from the field of thermodynamics is the way molecules in a layer of silicone oil behave when heat is carefully applied under laboratory conditions; as the temperature exceeds a critical value, a honeycomb pattern of convection currents forms where previously there was only a featureless liquid (Coveney and Highfield, 1995: 155). Going back to our billiards analogy, imagine that balls in one half of the table were sent whizzing round randomly and suddenly all of them moved together into a hexagon! Such orderly structures are said to 'self-organise' out of the disorder created by an influx of energy from outside the system. Ilya Prigogine called them 'dissipative structures' because the system can only maintain its critical distance from equilibrium by dissipating a minimum amount of energy into the environment (Prigogine and Lefever, 1973: 125).

Stage Three: Complex adaptive systems

The final stage in modelling a complex system is to simulate the behaviour of agents who have intention and volition. Imagine, for example, that the balls on our billiards table actively tried to get out of each other's way. The challenge then is to understand how local interactions between agents give rise to wider global patterns of behaviour. As an illustration of this process, Reynolds (1987) designed a computer program in which individual bits of code (called 'boids') are given three simple rules of interaction:

- Separation: maintain an equal distance from neighbouring boids
- Alignment: match the velocity and direction of local boids
- Cohesion: move towards where the population of boids is densest

More sophisticated rules can also be added, such as steering to avoid obstacles or away from predators. When the program is presented visually, the result is flocking behaviour that closely resembles that of birds in the natural world.[3] The crucial point here is that the global flocking pattern is not programmed or designed in any way, but emerges from the local interactions of individual agents (boids) following their rules. This is the principle of *emergence*, defined by Jeffrey Goldstein as 'the arising of novel and coherent structures, patterns, and properties during the process of self-organization in complex systems' (Goldstein, 1999: 49).

Agent-based models such as the boids program, which exhibit emergent properties, are examples of 'complex adaptive systems' (CAS). However, a key limitation of the systems considered so far is that all the agents are homogenous, i.e. they all share the same characteristics, whether they are molecules in a liquid or boids in a flocking simulation. As Mowles (2014) points out, this limits their applicability to social life, 'where all human beings are unique, and even the simplest rules are open to misinterpretation' (Mowles, 2014: 166). More sophisticated versions of CAS therefore assume heterogenous agents, i.e. with distinct characteristics and behaviour. Such systems have a high degree of interconnection *and* differentiation, which enables them to transform and evolve in creative and unexpected ways. CAS models of Darwinian evolution, for example, have shown how group processes such as competition and cooperation emerge from the conditions that drive natural selection (Ray, 1992). It has therefore been argued that social systems in the natural world, such as termite colonies, but also in the human world, such as stock market fluctuations, are real-life examples of complex adaptive systems (Coveney and Highfield, 1995).

---

[3]You can see a video and explanation of the boids flocking simulation here: www.youtube.com/watch?v=QbUPfMXXQIY

Summary

In summary, complexity theory can be understood as a conceptual framework for the behaviour of complex systems. Its origins lie in mathematical chaos models developed in the natural sciences to explain non-linear behaviour in a range of phenomena. However, complex systems are not chaotic. They are composed of a large number of interconnecting parts, which between them generate a constant flux of interactions and feedback that generates instability. Unlike 'classical' systems,

Table 0.1 Principles of complexity

Principle	Meaning	Implications
Non-linearity	The relationship between cause and effect is disproportionate, e.g. a small change in one variable can have a very large effect on outcomes.	Change is unpredictable and cannot be controlled and manipulated simply by changing a known variable to produce a particular outcome. Lack of predictability does not mean that we cannot explain complex behaviour, but cause and effect may only be evident with hindsight. Interventions are likely to have unintended consequences.
Self-organisation	At critical points of instability, systems may spontaneously organise themselves into new structures and behaviours that could not have been predicted from their previous state.	Seemingly minor events and incidents may escalate situations and lead to sudden and unexpected changes in behaviour. Apparent order and stability may disguise the potential for volatile change. A period of heightened instability and uncertainty may be necessary for fundamental change to occur.
Emergence	Self-organising local interactions produce global patterns of behaviour without this being at all planned or designed.	The key drivers of change are relationships and interactions on a localised, everyday level, rather than grand designs implemented on a global scale. Since structural change emerges through processes of interaction and feedback, agents can exert influence through their relations with others. However, the exact nature and degree of this influence cannot be known in advance.
Evolution	Systems operating far from equilibrium periodically experience upheaval and transformation as a way of adapting to their environment and avoiding decay and obsolescence.	Novelty and innovation are the hallmarks of complex change, and often emerge in conditions of instability and disorder. Interventions can give rise to creative outcomes that they were not intended to produce.

complex systems do not settle into equilibrium, but continually adapt and evolve, organising themselves in a state of critical disorder that is 'far from equilibrium' (Cilliers, 1998: 4). The behaviour of such systems is explained in Table 0.1 in terms of four key principles: non-linearity, self-organisation, emergence, and evolution.

COMPLEXITY IN THE SOCIAL WORLD

Scientific theories of complex systems have met with considerable interest within the social sciences (Byrne, 1998; Kiel and Elliot, 1996; Stewart, 2001; Eve et al., 1997). However, applying complexity principles to social contexts raises a number of issues. It cannot be assumed that societies can simply be modelled as the same type of complex adaptive systems found in physics or biology, nor that such behaviour can be observed and represented using the same methods (Carter and Sealey, 2009).

A crucial way in which social systems differ from systems in the natural world is in the role played by human subjectivity, intention, and agency. As Harvey and Reed (1996) point out, there is a risk of 'treating humanly produced conventions, institutions and historically complex events as though they were natural objects governed by recurrent processes and universal laws' (Harvey and Reed, 1996: 314). Furthermore, we cannot stand outside society to decipher its underlying rules, since we are part of society.[4] Understanding the social world involves a greater degree of reflexivity and self-awareness than does the physical world, not just because of the onus on interpretation but also because of the capacity of social actors to shape the world around them (see Chapter 5).

What Waldrop (1994) called the 'emerging science' of complexity has contributed to various philosophical and methodological debates around social research (Harvey and Reed, 1996). Writers such as Cilliers (1998, 2005) and Byrne (1998, 2009b) have presented complexity theory as a challenge to positivist social science, with its focus on generalisable causal laws, empirical regularities, and the objective, value-free scientist. Cilliers (1998), for example, argues that complexity could be seen as a paradigm shift towards a new kind of 'postmodern' science that emphasises reflexivity, interconnection and distributed networks of meaning. Some researchers, including the author of this book, have advocated a 'complex realist' approach to the study of social phenomena (Hood, 2012; Byrne, 2009b; Harvey and Reed, 1996). This approach views complexity through the lens of scientific realism, which explains scientific method as a search for the causal mechanisms that generate events. Configurations of cause and effect are constantly variable and interactive, so that the outcomes of an intervention are never entirely predictable: mechanisms produce only 'tendencies' that can be counteracted by others. The realist approach to research is discussed further in Chapter 7.

---

[4]Indeed quantum theory has shown that similar effects apply in the physical world of subatomic particles, where the act of observation itself helps to constitute the reality that is observed (see Barad, 2007).

complexity and technical rationality

The principles of complexity tell us that there are limits to the extent to which we can predict and control events – both in the natural world as well as in human affairs. This insight contributes to a critique of 'technical rationality', an approach to knowledge and practice that continues to be very influential in social work as well as in other applied disciplines (Schön, 1991). Technical rationality is character- ised by:

- A linear view of causality in terms of proximal cause and effect, the nature of which can be identified through scientific method
- The reduction of complex situations into a series of technical problems, whose solution is to be found in formal scientific knowledge
- An emphasis on detailed procedures and practice guidelines, in order to ensure consistent application of knowledge to problem-solving and decision-making

Each of these elements is problematic from a complexity perspective. The assump- tion of linear causality ignores important system effects such as feedback, self-organisation, and emergent properties. A narrow emphasis on individual or isolated problems ignores the way in which multiple elements interact and combine to produce system events. Finally, seeing professional practice purely in terms of systematically solving 'well-formed instrumental problems' (Schön, 1987: 3) mis- understands the way that human problems as well as solutions are negotiated and socially constructed, and the extent to which professional expertise is built on prac- tical experience as well as theoretical knowledge (Hood et al., 2016a). Going back to our discussion of wicked problems at the beginning of the chapter, is it appropri- ate to go about understanding and alleviating the distress of a bereaved client in the same way as one might work out how to fix a car engine?

According to Kinsella (2007: 104), 'the technical-rational approach to decision- making is normative in professional life in Western society'. It tends to be associated with managerial control of professional activity (Freidson, 2001), and as such is often contrasted with approaches that put more emphasis on professional expertise, reflexivity, and discretion (Webb, 2001; Schön, 1991). In a well-known metaphor, Schön describes the 'high hard ground' of technical rationality as overlooking the 'swamp' of real-life situations:

> On the high ground, manageable problems lend themselves to solution through the application of research-based theory and technique. In the swampy lowland, messy, confusing problems defy technical solution. (Schön, 1987: 3)

Complexity theory provides a useful conceptual framework to understand this apparent dichotomy. For example, Hassett and Stevens (2014) draw on complexity ideas to criticise what they see as largely linear approaches to child protection over the past 50 years, including an 'increasing emphasis on controls and procedural- ised responses' (Hassett and Stevens, 2014: 97). A more detailed analysis is found in Munro (2010), who uses systems theory to explain why excessive prescription of child protection practice ends up constraining the expertise needed to carry out complex work. In the field of youth justice, Case and Haines (2014) have criticised the tendency to explain young people's offending behaviour as the 'linear, proportional and deterministic outcome of exposure to "risk factors"', ignoring the 'unpredictability, context-dependence and multidimensionality of the young people and behaviours targeted by the [Youth Justice System]'. They argue that a simplistic understanding of risk factor research in turn leads to a static and decontextualised risk assessment process (Asset) based largely on the aggregation of rating scales (see Chapter 3).

The point of this type of critique is not just to expose the flaws in current approaches but to highlight more appropriate ones. For example, Case and Haines (2014) go on to describe a revised assessment framework (AssetPlus) developed by the Youth Justice Board to allow a more dynamic and flexible assessment of a young person's life circumstances. The chapters in Part 1 of this book focus on a number of practice issues for working with complexity in social work. Other applications of complexity theory discussed in this book include research and evaluation (Chapter 7), organisational structure and management (Chapter 8), and the analysis of policy systems (Chapter 9).

COMPLeXity, RiSK aNd UNCeRTaiNty

Since the concept of risk is central to assessment and intervention in social work (see Chapters 3 and 4), it is worth noting some important distinctions and connections between complexity and risk in professional practice. Complexity is bound up with causal relationships, i.e. how events and behaviour arise out of a given set of conditions. An important consequence of complexity is that there are limits to how well we can *predict* what future events and behaviour will look like. Any predictions we make have an element of uncertainty, which is unavoidable no matter how good our information and which rapidly increases over time. This is illustrated by a familiar example of predictive difficulty, the weather forecast, which these days is facilitated by an array of sophisticated technology including complex computer models of weather systems. Despite this, while we might consider the forecast to be fairly reliable for tomorrow, most people would have little or no confidence in predictions for a month's time.

Uncertainty about the future is obviously important when it comes to risk, which is about predicting the *probability* and *severity* of a given outcome in the future. Usually risk predictions are about adverse events although this is not necessarily the case. For example, a gambler may bet money on getting a double-six on his next roll of two dice. His probability of success is 1/36, which is a formal expression of how many times one could expect a double-six to appear in successive rolls of the dice. Severity in this instance is represented by the gain for guessing correctly or the loss incurred by betting on the wrong result. A crucial point here is that the calculations of probability and severity, which lie at the heart of most risk analysis, assume a linear approach to reducing uncertainty. We know each die has six sides and rolls in a random way and so our predictions can rely on statistical averaging over time. However, this is not really feasible in complex systems – imagine if after a certain number of rolls we suddenly see the dice clumping together or evolving additional sides!

Complexity therefore inserts an extra element of uncertainty into risk analysis, which cannot be reduced to statements of probability. It therefore undermines conventional ideas about prediction. This is disconcerting for frontline practitioners, who are frequently tasked with two kinds of risk calculations: first, to predict what type of (usually negative) outcomes are likely to happen if nothing is done about a situation, and second to know what type of (hopefully positive) outcomes will result from an intervention. Linear risk models, based on correlations between risk factors and outcomes in large populations, are designed to help professionals compensate for the cognitive biases that affect 'intuitive' decision-making in conditions of uncertainty (Munro, 2008; Kahneman et al., 1990). However, such models do not (nor do they pretend to) predict outcomes in individual situations because they are based on correlational findings rather than causal explanations (see Chapter 7). Arguably this distinction is ignored by technical-rational approaches to risk, as discussed in Chapter 3.

CRITIQUE OF COMPLEXITY THEORY

Complexity ideas have been contested in various ways. In particular, the assumption that society can be understood in terms of complex systems has attracted criticism. Stewart (2001) argues that social processes and phenomena cannot be modelled as some sort of complex adaptive system, and so most complexity models, 'while having validity for some analytic tasks, cannot substantially account for the events and particularities of the social world' (Stewart, 2001: 341). Furthermore, Stacey (2007) points out that the concept of a social system adopts contradictory ideas about human cognition and volition: behaviour 'inside' the system is considered to be determined by systemic processes but these processes can be deciphered by rational individuals on the 'outside'. Stacey argues instead that social complexity should be understood in terms of responsive processes of human interaction and identification (see Chapter 8).

Complexity theory can be criticised for lacking explanatory power, given the limits it places on predicting and controlling behaviour in complex systems (Thelen and Smith, 1994; Nybell, 2001). In positivist terms it appears more useful as a tool of hindsight than as a way of generating testable hypotheses. There also continues to be debate about how readily the conceptual language of complexity (non-linearity, emergence, and so on) can be transferred to social contexts. Gerrits and Verweij (2015) suggest that the complexity sciences are 'more a set of ideas than a theoretical framework', ideas which furthermore are difficult to operationalise, i.e. turn into properties and behaviour that can be observed and measured. Thrift (1999) suggests talking about 'complexity metaphors' rather than complexity theory, pointing out ways in which these metaphors have already influenced scientific and cultural discourse in the Western world.

Structure of this book

Complexity lends itself both to a 'micro' and a 'macro' perspective; social workers deal on an individual level with complex cases, while managers, policymakers, and researchers deal with complex systems on a wider scale. The book is therefore divided into two parts. The six chapters in Part 1 examine some of the key challenges of working with complex cases in social work. The three chapters in Part 2 explore some of the implications of complex systems in the broader context of research, policy, and service delivery.

Chapter 1 considers the concept of need, which is central to many areas of social work practice. It starts by discussing how need is generally understood by professionals, with reference to Maslow's hierarchical model, and explores some dilemmas around identification and response. The chapter then examines the significance of complex needs, which usually take the form of multiple problems that intersect with each other and pose a challenge for services designed around professional specialisms. Some comments are made on the link between need and risk, before focusing on implications for social work assessment. Case studies are used to illustrate the importance of constructing hypotheses and exploring competing explanations of need.

Chapter 2 explores the nature of uncertainty and change in complex cases. It begins with the process of change, which underlies the aims and outcomes of social work interventions. Two principal areas of uncertainty are then considered. First, complexity undermines the extent to which we can predict what will happen either with or without a given intervention. Second, the critical instability associated with complexity can produce volatile dynamics that are challenging to manage, or a frustrating sense that underlying issues are being allowed to drift. The chapter proceeds to examine the most prevalent response to these issues, which is to reduce uncertainty by reframing complex situations as a series of solvable technical problems. Finally, attention is drawn to the importance of developing professional expertise and resilience in order to work with complexity.

Chapter 3 considers the challenges associated with making judgements and decisions in social work. The question of what constitutes a justifiable decision is discussed in terms of rationality, ethicality, and reasonableness. Analytic and intuitive approaches to decision-making are compared before exploring some of the cognitive biases that can unwittingly affect professional judgement, including confirmation bias, hindsight error, and the rule of optimism. The discussion then moves on to judgements about harm, which involve a probabilistic analysis based on predictive risk factors and draw a combination of clinical, consensus-based, and actuarial approaches to risk assessment. Finally, there is a discussion of bounded rationality, which suggests that heuristic models continue to be useful in complex situations where there is pressure to make decisions quickly and with limited information.

Chapter 4 focuses on the relationship between social workers and their clients. Initial considerations include the significance of relationships within the social work role and the skills required to build and maintain relationships with people in order to help them to achieve positive change. These ideas are integrated into an account of the 'helping relationship' drawing on the counselling theories of Rogers and Egan.

The chapter then outlines some key psychodynamic concepts for understanding the underlying dynamics of practitioner – client interactions and behaviour, including transference and counter-transference, containment, and holding. There follows a discussion of complexity in relationship-based practice, which includes working with strong feelings, understanding and addressing resistance, and managing dilemmas and transitions in long-term work.

Chapter 5 examines the role of reflection in helping social workers to understand and manage complexity. It begins with some overarching theories and concepts from the work of John Dewey and Donald Schön before exploring what is meant by reflective practice and critical reflection in social work. There follows an account of key areas for reflection, such as emotions, ethical dilemmas, and power dynamics, with common applications and tools designed to help practitioners to think about these issues. The chapter concludes by putting the reflective process in a wider institutional context, outlining the concept of the learning organisation and the importance of supervision for reflective practice.

Chapter 6 examines interprofessional working as a response to complex needs. It starts by outlining the policy context to specialisation and professionalisation in the welfare state, and the move towards greater managerial control of professional work along with efforts to foster partnership and integration across agency boundaries. Theories of collaboration are then explored, including interprofessional education, continuum and gestalt models, ecological and organisational perspectives, and teamwork. Approaches to interprofessional ethics are followed by a discussion of conflict and consensus in collaborative contexts. Psychodynamic concepts are then applied to the role of anxiety in shaping patterns of communication and collaboration in institutional contexts. The chapter concludes by exploring some key areas of interprofessional expertise for social workers, including knowledge, communication, negotiation and reflective practice.

Chapter 7 considers the challenges faced by researchers and evaluators in producing scientifically robust explanations of complex social phenomena. Social work is described as an applied field of practice and research, which draws eclectically from a range of academic disciplines and approaches to the pursuit of knowledge. This leads to a consideration of research paradigms, of which scientific realism is argued to be the one that engages most comprehensively with the problem of complexity. The main principles of realist research are outlined and linked to a critique of the dominant positivist paradigm, before proceeding to discuss some of the methods commonly employed in realist designs. Particular attention is given to realist evaluation and realist synthesis, which provide an alternative to experimental field trials and meta-analysis as the standard approach to 'what works' in social work and related fields. The chapter concludes by examining some limitations of the realist approach and alternative ways of researching complexity.

Chapter 8 turns to the implications of complexity for the management and administration of social services. Such services are accountable to a number of stakeholders, including taxpayers and elected officials. However, their ultimate purpose is to address the needs of their users. Demand for a service will tend to have a predictable and unpredictable element, and the challenge is to organise services to meet both types of demand as quickly and efficiently as possible. In systemic terms, services need to have the 'requisite variety' to deal with the complexity of demand. Effective provision means trying to place the expertise needed to solve problems near the 'front' of the system where users first come into contact with services.

Chapter 9 broadens the scope of analysis to consider what complexity means for social policy. It begins by exploring non-linear effects in a range of policy areas, including housing, social care, and public health interventions. The chapter then turns to the development of risk regulation regimes, which are increasingly important in social work. Proceduralisation and blame culture are linked to a growing preoccupation with institutional risk, particularly among statutory agencies, driven in part by a scandal–reform cycle in politically sensitive areas such as child protection. Different policy approaches to human error are compared, drawing on the ideas of socio-technical systems to explore the interface between policy and research evidence. The chapter concludes with a discussion of top-down and bottom-up approaches to policy implementation and the importance of stimulating innovative solutions to complex social problems.

The final chapter looks ahead to the future of social work in a fast changing policy and practice environment. Some broad implications are drawn from the topics discussed in the book. Complex problems often create a sense of disconnect between citizens, social workers, managers, and policymakers. This is partly because paradoxical patterns of interaction and intention are a feature of complex behaviour. It is argued that current models of policy and practice have become highly intolerant of paradox and are skewed towards analytic approaches that rely on processing ever greater quantities of data. Shifting the balance towards systems thinking may prove a difficult culture shift in many social work settings but is essential for a people-centred profession.

PART 1

WORKING WITH COMPLEX CASES

UNDERSTANDING COMPLEX NEEDS

1

CHAPTER SUMMARY

This chapter considers the concept of need, which is central to many areas of social work practice. It starts by discussing how need is generally understood by professionals, with reference to Maslow's hierarchical model, and discusses some dilemmas around identification and response. The chapter will then examine the significance of complex needs, which usually take the form of multiple problems that intersect with each other and pose a challenge for services designed around professional specialisms. Some comments are made on the link between need and risk, before focusing on implications for social work assessment. Case studies are used to illustrate the importance of constructing hypotheses and exploring competing explanations of need.

INTRODUCTION

The concept of need is central to policy and practice in social work. Statutory duties to provide services are often based on need, such as the 'children in need' defined by Section 17 of the 1989 Children Act, or the duty to meet adults' care and support needs set out by Section 18 of the 2014 Care Act. Assessing need is one of the core tasks of social work, particularly in statutory settings where social workers may act as gatekeepers, referrers and care coordinators, as well as undertaking reports for court. The activity of assessment has increasingly blurred the distinction between need and risk, as will be discussed later in the chapter. Furthermore, need itself has become categorised, with the significance of 'complex needs' becoming ever more prevalent in the health and social care literature (Carney, 2005; Easton, et al. 2012; Keene, 2001; Law et al., 2011; Limbrick, 2004; Rankin and Regan, 2004). Before examining what complexity of need might mean for social workers, it is worth taking a closer look at professional usage of the term.

What do we mean by 'needs'?

When social workers talk about someone's needs, they are generally referring to whatever is necessary for someone to live a healthy, happy, and fulfilled life. Needs refer both to our inner attributes – what we want and desire – but also to our dependence on the environment, including social resources such as support, care, and nurture. Need is therefore an ambiguous concept, reflecting positive, life-affirming impulses but also the potential for constraint and suffering – 'life's desperate attempt to become itself', as Carl Rogers put it (Van de Luitgaarden, 2009: 119).

Most social workers are familiar with Maslow's hierarchy of needs (Maslow, 1970), which distinguishes between two different kinds of need:

- Those which are oriented towards survival, including basic physiological needs but also the urge to feel safe, experience love and belongingness, and gain the esteem and respect of others
- Those which are oriented towards fully realising one's potential – what Maslow calls 'self-actualisation'

The distinction is important for Maslow because while fulfilling basic needs can be seen purely in terms of reducing or removing a deficient state (e.g. quenching one's thirst, or countering a threat), activities that relate to self-actualisation are about personal growth and satisfaction (e.g. learning to play an instrument). Needs that are lower down in the hierarchy must be satisfied before the higher ones can be attended to, and this reflects the evolutionary development of the human species. In other words, striving for 'self-actualisation' is a uniquely human trait that is bound up with our individual and social identities.

Normative vs relative needs

The more basic needs tend to have a clearer basis in normative frameworks. For example, gauging whether someone is eating the right kinds of food requires some knowledge of nutritional science and the signs and symptoms of malnutrition. In contrast, the 'higher' needs are linked to people's motivations, personalities and life histories, and are correspondingly more difficult to standardise. There is also a social and cultural dimension to need; what people regard as sufficient or necessary for a fulfilled or dignified life changes over time and between contexts. Social workers therefore have to integrate what individuals tell them – how they perceive and interpret their own needs – with evidence from various sources about what helps people in certain circumstances to recover, thrive, or succeed. Furthermore, the distinction between basic and higher needs is not necessarily straightforward, as we shall see in our discussion of housing below.

Developmental pathways

Human development is both multi-directional and multi-dimensional, so that life outcomes are the result of a complex interplay of developmental factors (Baltes, 1987). There are many pathways to get to the same outcome and similar circumstances can lead to very different results. This presents something of a quandary for social workers, who are often tasked with a one-off analysis of need but know that the experience and significance of different needs will vary over time.

Ethics of need

Social workers are often placed in a difficult ethical position when it comes to responding to need. What Miller (2013) calls the 'ethics of need' can be seen from two perspectives:

- a Kantian 'duty of care', in which moral agents are obliged to respond to the needs of others
- a utilitarian calculation of what (and whose) needs assume priority given scarce resources

As avowedly 'caring professionals' (Abbott and Wallace, 1990), social workers' first instinct is often to adopt the former stance, i.e. to advocate for their client's needs to be met. Yet social workers generally do not have resources of their own; they are employed by organisations, who have limited budgets and are accountable to other stakeholders (governments, taxpayers, donors) for how their money is spent. This means that the decision whether or not to provide a service will always involve some form of utilitarian trade-off, even if social workers prefer to leave this aspect of the job to their managers! The existence of resource constraints makes it even more important for practitioners to correctly understand and articulate need when they first come into contact with service users (see Chapter 8).

COMPLEX NEEDS

There are arguably two ways of understanding complex needs in social work. The first is perhaps the most obvious, which is to recognise that all human needs are complex in their own right. This applies even to basic needs, which in advanced industrialised societies have acquired layers of significance that often blur the distinction between the 'levels' proposed by Maslow.

Consider the need for 'shelter', which is shared by all living things. Human beings may seek shelter, for example, when they are caught outside in a sudden downpour. But the main purpose of the structures in which we spend our time sleeping, eating, working, and socialising, is not to keep the rain off our heads but to facilitate human behaviour and interaction. We need the places we live to provide us with comfort, security, dignity, and self-worth. People who are homeless are often able to find shelter but they still feel they have nowhere to live. Houses, flats, and workplaces are also powerful signifiers of social and cultural information – they 'say something' about the people inside. Even the term 'housing' is not a neutral word but is often used (in the UK) to denote state-subsidised accommodation and services for people with a 'housing need'.

POINT FOR REFLECTION

Where accommodation is available for someone with a need for housing, is the need addressed if the person does not want to live there? What kind of assumptions about need (e.g. normative vs relative, Kantian vs utilitarian) underlie your answer?

A second way of understanding complex needs is as a distinct type of demand for services. A distinction can be made between needs that are part of general everyday life, and more specific needs that are experienced by some people at certain points in their life. The former are addressed by universal public services, such as schools and GP surgeries, which are available to everyone. The latter are catered for by specialist services, which usually need a referral, for example from a GP to a consultant in a particular field of medicine. Within this group, there may be some people with a range of specialist needs. Their needs do not fit entirely in the remit of any single service or professional group because of the requirement for multiple specialisms.

These distinctions are illustrated in Figure 1.1. As we shall see in Chapter 6, this pyramidal model of need is implicit in the provision of health and social care services in the UK. Superficially it resembles Maslow's hierarchy of needs, which is also usually presented as a pyramid. Complexity in Maslow's model emerges from the dynamic interplay of physical, psychological, social, and spiritual needs, all of which are implicated in the goal of human self-actualisation. The focus appears to be on the individual but this is misleading. Self-actualisation is a social as well as individual project, since people can only fulfil their goals and aspirations with and for others, and as part of a historical and cultural context. Needs are simultaneously a product of individual difference – ability, health, affluence – but also of the social structures and institutions that allocate resources and opportunities.

Figure 1.1 illustrates this symbiotic relationship; need here refers to the need for *services*. Complex needs are those that straddle various professional domains, and therefore present a particular problem in terms of coordination and collaboration (see Chapter 6). This view of complexity tends to highlight two attributes:

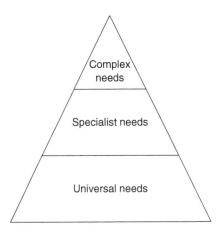

Figure 1.1   Universal, specialist and complex needs

- **Multiplicity** – the presence of multiple needs that require a range of specialist support
- **Intersectionality** – the difficulty of treating needs separately because they all seem to affect each other

---

CASE STUDY 1.1

Clive

Clive is a 40-year-old unemployed man who has a long history of alcohol dependency. He has several convictions relating to criminal damage, assault, and theft, and has served two prison sentences. He was recently arrested and charged with being drunk and disorderly outside a football ground. Clive suffers from alcohol-related liver disease, and he has been advised by his GP to stop drinking. He is also well known to community mental health services in his local area and has been treated in the past for bi-polar depression. However, he rarely attends appointments but instead turns up at the clinic or at A&E in a state of crisis and often intoxicated. He has a 12-year-old daughter, who lives with her mother in Cornwall and whom he has not seen for five years. As a child, Clive experienced physical and emotional abuse from his father, who was an alcoholic and violent towards Clive and his mother. He says he drinks to 'get away' from his father, who died ten years ago but whom he still hears sometimes as a voice in his head.

Questions

- What would you say were Clive's main needs?
- How do these different needs affect each other?

The case study of Clive illustrates these attributes. Clive is experiencing a high level of need in multiple domains, including alcohol misuse, physical and mental health problems, estrangement from close family, unemployment, criminality, and a family history of abuse. Each one of these problems is serious enough to have a significant impact on Clive's welfare. The combination of several such problems presents a challenge to specialist services, who generally only have expertise in a single domain. The challenge is compounded by the fact that it is not easy to separate one need from the other. For example, the co-existence of substance misuse with some form of mental disorder makes it difficult to diagnose and treat the latter while the former is entrenched. The impact of Clive's experience of abuse as a child also seems to present an underlying therapeutic need. There is uncertainty about a range of possible causes and effects that all seem to intersect with one another. Cases like this can also create anxiety for practitioners because they seem to present a high degree of risk without a clear pathway to addressing need.

Need and Risk

Are complex needs inherently more risky? If we define complex needs in terms of multiple and intersecting problems that require specialist support, it seems reasonable to argue that such cases often incur a higher level of risk, i.e. a greater likelihood of serious consequences. For example, co-morbidity of substance misuse and severe mental illness – often termed 'dual diagnosis' – is associated with a range of negative outcomes including higher rates of relapse, perpetrating and being a victim of violence, imprisonment, homelessness, and serious infections such as HIV (Taylor, 2010: 470). However, this is not to say that risk can simply be evidenced by providing a long list of needs. Certain needs – along with other variables such as demographic characteristics – *may* be risk factors in the sense of increasing the probability of particular outcomes. The question of which needs are associated with which risks can only be answered through careful research and statistical analysis (see Chapter 7).

The relationship between need and risk can be conceptualised in various ways. In England, a child with a disability is considered in the 1989 Children Act to be automatically 'in need', i.e. entitled to local authority services to help her or him attain a reasonable standard of health and development. However, the child would not be considered at risk of (significant) harm unless there were also concerns about the standard of parental – or institutional – care. In this sense, risk implies an escalation of need, which can be exacerbated by the actions or omissions of others. Elsewhere, need may be associated with vulnerability, i.e. risk to self, but possibly also as a source of dangerousness, i.e. risk to others. For example, young people with complex needs may be particularly vulnerable to abuse and exploitation as well as exposure to and engagement in antisocial and criminal behaviour (Ungar et al., 2012; Carter et al., 2016). Social workers often deal with cases where one person's needs may present a risk to others as well as to themselves. Going back to our case study, what risks would be involved in re-establishing contact between Clive and his daughter?

Social workers should nonetheless be careful about assuming that need necessarily implies risk unless they are able to specify both the risk factor and the associated outcome. It is also a good idea to check the evidence base for that particular link, bearing in mind that there could be other variables that mediate (strengthen or weaken) the link. In relation to dual diagnosis, for example, Kessler (1993) discusses the complexity of causal links that could be said to 'predict' the development of mental disorders in combination with substance misuse. As outlined in the introductory chapter, complexity makes it harder for professionals to predict outcomes, and therefore risks, in any given case. Nonetheless, this is often what social workers are expected to do in their assessments.

Needs assessments

Needs and risk assessment are perhaps the two main types of assessment carried out by social workers (Toulmin, 1958; Ward and Rose, 2002; Doueck et al., 1993; Ryan et al., 2005; Youth Justice Board, 2005). They may labelled one or the other but in practice are interlinked. Social workers conducting needs assessments are usually expected to indicate the probable consequences of unmet needs for the person in question, as well as the impact on other people such as carers or dependants. Likewise, risk assessments are usually based on the presence (and absence) of risk and protective factors that often correspond to needs of some sort. It could be argued that social workers first have to understand someone's needs before they can reach a judgement on risk (see Chapter 3).

Holistic assessment

Understanding and addressing complex needs is often said to require a holistic way of working (Danvers et al., 2003; Kirk, 2008; Kinman and Grant, 2011; Ruch, 2005; Boddy et al., 2006). In this context, the term 'holistic' basically means 'pertaining to the whole', and suggests that all aspects of a person's life should be explored and integrated into an overall account of their needs. Rather than focusing on the most pressing area of need, such as a serious illness or problematic type of behaviour, practitioners are encouraged to ask for information in a range of developmental domains: physical, psychological, emotional, behavioural, social, and spiritual. By considering these factors together, professionals should be able to make more appropriate referrals and avoid unnecessary duplication of work.

Since people and their problems rarely come in isolation, a holistic approach to need may start with an individual but through their significant relationships will often end up considering the needs of others. Whenever there are children involved, a social worker would normally consider the family as a whole (Kendall et al., 2010). Moreover, families, carers, and support networks are also a fundamental part of needs assessments undertaken with adults (Mainstone, 2014). Holistic approaches therefore tend to expand the sphere of inquiry, i.e. to a wider range of developmental concerns but also to a larger number of people.

A consequence of this broad approach is that holistic assessment and intervention often requires expertise that is held in several different professionals and agencies (see Chapter 6). For example, the complex needs experienced by Clive (above) might lead to involvement of a psychiatrist, psychologist, substance misuse specialist, social worker or possibly a probation service officer. In some cases, social workers have the role of coordinating all this activity, but first have to collate and synthesise information from a number of sources in order to make their assessment as holistic as possible.

Assessment frameworks

Nowadays, most social workers are guided by some sort of assessment framework (e.g. Brehmer, 1999), which consists of a template for information-gathering, and sometimes a tool for analysing risk factors (e.g. Youth Justice Board, 2005). Increasingly, this work is being done on electronic forms linked to computer databases, which facilitate the collation and sharing of information as well as managerial oversight of the process (Shaw et al., 2009). However, improvements in information technology are only a support and not a substitute for social work skills, such as working in partnership with people to understand and solve their problems. One result of having to spend lots of time filling in lengthy forms on sophisticated IT systems is that this activity in itself starts to seem equivalent to 'doing' an assessment. In turn, as many social workers will tell you, completing assessments actually takes them away from the people they are meant to be working with.

Detailed and prescriptive assessment templates are also commensurate with a rational-technical approach to social work (see Introduction). What this means in the context of needs assessment is splitting a complex human problem into smaller individual issues that can each be matched to the appropriate intervention. However, as we saw in the case study of Clive, the intersectional nature of complex needs makes it hard for even the most experienced practitioner to address a single type of need without considering the others. In practice, complex cases tend to involve collaboration between many different agencies, which creates additional opportunities and challenges (see Chapter 6).

Assessing complex needs

The emphasis on procedures in contemporary social work has been linked to another type of risk, namely the institutional and professional risk of getting things wrong. Demonstrating that procedures are followed dutifully and comprehensively is one way that agencies and practitioners can protect themselves from being blamed in the event of a tragic and unforeseen outcome. Complex cases tend to be associated with uncertainty and unpredictability, which can raise anxieties about this sort

Table 1.1   Elements of needs assessment (adapted from Hood, 2016a)

Knowledge and awareness	Methods and activities
• Knowledge of the legislative framework, relevant policies, and procedures • Background information from the referral and any case files, including previous assessments • A clear idea of the purpose of the assessment and the interprofessional context in which it is to be carried out • Choice of a general social work approach and theoretical framework • Considering how issues of diversity and difference will shape the assessment process • Awareness of research evidence in relation to the main areas of assessment	• Plan and prepare the work to be done • Engage and build a working relationship with service users and other relevant people • Liaise with other agencies and professionals who are working with the individual and/or family • Gather information from a number of sources, using a range of methods, e.g. interviews, observations, questionnaires • Interpret and analyse information, and test hypotheses • Explore potential resources and interventions • Make decisions and recommendations • Write and share the report

of risk (see Chapter 3). However, these are exactly the sort of cases where a professionally defensive, tick-box approach to needs assessment is unlikely to work well. On the contrary, they will require careful attention to all elements of the assessment process, as summarised in Table 1.1.

All these elements are discussed in greater detail in Hood (2016a), and readers are also advised to review the literature on assessment in their specialist area. However, in trying to understand the challenges presented by complex needs, it is worth considering the following issues:

- **Scope** – is need being considered at the level of the individual, family, or other social unit?
- **Priority** – what and who should be given priority when the needs of several people are relevant to the situation, or when a person has multiple needs, or when several different explanations of need are plausible?
- **Impact** – what will intervening or not intervening to address need mean for the person's wellbeing, and what might be the unintended consequences?
- **Reliability** – how much confidence can we put in the information we possess or the hypotheses we have at this stage?
- **Sustainability** – assuming that only some needs can be targeted at a time of stress or crisis, which are likely to produce sustainable improvements?

Some of these issues are apparent in the case study of Yusuf and Faduma below. Take the time to read the case study and consider the questions posed underneath.

CASE STUDY 1.2

Yusuf and Faduma

Yusuf Osman and Faduma Ahmed live with their four children, aged 2, 4, 7, and 12, in a two-bedroomed flat on the sixth floor of a tower block in central London. Both parents moved to the UK from Somalia 15 years ago and have leave to remain. Yusuf used to have a part-time job as a taxi driver but has not worked for eight months. He is often absent from the home and regularly chews khat (a stimulant drug) when socialising with friends. Faduma suffered from post-natal depression after the birth of her youngest child and still finds it hard to leave the house. Recently some racist graffiti was sprayed on the wall near their front door, and Faduma says she has received racist abuse when she goes out. She does not let the children play outside as she is worried about the amount of gang activity and drug-related crime on the estate. The health visitor has made a referral to children's social care services in relation to the two-year-old girl, who lags behind her peers in terms of language and motor skills, and has not been taken to her immunisation appointments. The health visitor has observed the mother to be quite unresponsive and 'flat' in her interactions with her children and is concerned about their lack of stimulation, unkempt appearance, and the overcrowded home environment. When a social worker visits the home, the parents are adamant that all their problems would be solved by moving to a bigger flat in a better area.

Questions

- What would you say were the family's main needs, and the most important to solve right now? Do you agree with the family?
- What cultural and socio-economic factors might contribute to the way need is perceived and constructed in this case?
- What issues other than housing might a social worker want to explore with the family?
- Is there any information that might not be known at this stage but you would want to check on?

How do we approach this case study? One possible starting point is to observe that there are a range of different needs in this family, and that while each family member may have different needs they are interconnected. For example, Faduma's emotional and psychological wellbeing may be affected by aspects of her relationship with her husband, such as his frequent absences or drug use. Her mental health may also affect how well she is able to respond to her children's needs. It is often the case that people's welfare is bound up with their relationships – including ones in the past. This is important to consider even if (or especially if) someone lives on their own and appears to have little in the way of social support. So it is not really possible to consider one aspect of need in isolation from others. The cultural context of need is often apparent in the way activities are interpreted within and outside of communities. For example, chewing khat may be seen as a form of substance misuse by the professional but as a normal pastime by the person concerned; coming to a mutual understanding on this issue will require dialogue and negotiation. Social work assessments have been found to downplay environmental factors such as deprivation, employment, housing, and discrimination in favour of evaluating individual strengths and deficits in relation to children and families (Jack and Gill, 2003). Bringing together these ideas contributes to a 'holistic' approach to need, as discussed above.

Working with hypotheses

However, achieving a holistic understanding of need clearly involves more than just compiling a list of every piece of relevant information about every significant person. Analysis is what enables the professional to state what is important and why. It means moving beyond description towards explanation, trying to decipher complexity rather than ignoring it or becoming paralysed by it. One way of doing analysis involves the construction of hypotheses. A hypothesis is a kind of working theory, based on currently available information, which can be explored and tested in the real world. Constructing a hypothesis about need will initially involve:

- Defining the problem
- Identifying the causes
- Predicting the consequences
- Questioning the evidence

It is important to bear in mind that a hypothesis is only a starting point for investigation. It is not a pre-formed answer that we seek to justify with supporting evidence, as doing so will undermine our analysis and potentially lead to mistakes in our judgements (see Chapter 3). For this reason, social workers are encouraged to work with more than one hypothesis and keep an ongoing record of their analysis. It is also why social workers have to question the evidence for their hypotheses, so that they know what other information may be needed to test its validity. When they have settled on their main hypotheses, they will need to consider other questions, such as how to define and measure change, and what types of intervention are most likely to produce that change (see Chapter 2).

As an example, two initial hypotheses about need are presented below in relation to Yusuf and Faduma:

The hypotheses presented in Table 1.2 explore much of the same information but frame it in different ways. The first hypothesis sees the problem in terms of possible child neglect, most likely caused by diminished parenting capacity in the light of a range of stress factors. It is important to note that this hypothesis does not *assume* that there is neglect but suggests there is enough evidence to gear an initial assessment around this concern. The hypothesis is then questioned as to whether there is enough evidence of parental neglect and the stress factors responsible. In contrast,

Table 1.2 Initial hypotheses about need

	Hypothesis 1	Hypothesis 2
Problem definition	Child neglect – inconsistent parental care and stimulation, particularly in relation to youngest child.	Inadequate living conditions – overcrowded and poor quality housing, combined with high levels of deprivation, crime, and racist attitudes in local area.
Main causes	Faduma's parenting capacity may be affected by mental health issues, linked to her post-natal depression, social isolation, and lack of support from her husband. Yusuf seems to lack involvement with his children, and may have a drug dependency. The family home is overcrowded, and the children lack opportunities to play.	There is an acute shortage of social housing in London, and much existing stock is of poor quality. To have any chance of a bigger home, families are often told they would have to move to a different part of the country. There are social and institutional barriers for people from ethnic minority and asylum-seeking backgrounds, which make it harder for them to meet their basic needs and achieve their goals.
Predicted consequences	For all the children, continuing neglect will have an impact on their physical, emotional, and social development. Effects may be particularly severe for the two-year-old child, who is more vulnerable at a young age and is at home full time.	Overcrowding, isolation, and racist abuse are taking their toll on Faduma's mental health and affecting her ability to look after her children. If the family are not assisted to move house, the emotional and psychological welfare of the parents and children will suffer.
Evidence	The health visitor's referral contains evidence from home visits and observation of mother–child interaction. Do other professionals involved with the older children share concerns about neglect, e.g. schools, GPs? Have things got worse recently? E.g. father's unemployment, more frequent absence, drug use?	Unfortunately, many families in London are living in overcrowded conditions. Have things got worse for this family recently, and if so why? Has the family ever lived elsewhere and was the situation better there? What steps have the parents taken to mitigate the effects of overcrowding, e.g. routines, one-to-one time, activities outside the home?

the second hypothesis focuses on the family's lack of suitable housing, which is attributed largely to structural factors outside of the family's control. Individual concerns, such as Faduma's mental health or the children's welfare, are seen as a consequence of the family's basic needs not being met. The hypothesis is then questioned in terms of whether this is a sufficient explanation or whether other factors are at play.

REFLECTIVE EXERCISE 1.1

Consider the two hypotheses outlined in Table 2.1 in the light of the case study of Yusuf and Faduma:

1. Which of these hypotheses seems more convincing to you? Why? Do you have an alternative explanation?
2. What kind of hypothesis might the following practitioners be likely to adopt?

   i. Social worker
   ii. Psychologist
   iii. Housing officer
   iv. Substance misuse worker

3. What hypothesis do you think the parents might have?

The two hypotheses could be seen as complementary because they are using different parameters to define the problem. This is partly about the scope of analysis. Yusuf and Faduma can be considered on a number of levels: as individuals, as a married couple, as a nuclear family with their children, as part of an extended family with other relatives, as part of an ethnic Somali community living in London and other parts of the UK, as part of a local community incorporating many different ethnicities, and as part of a society shaped by broad cultural, historical, and political trends. Relationships and interactions within all these different contexts contribute to people's behaviour. Family characteristics, including standards and perceptions of 'good enough' parenting, are also shaped by structural issues such as inequality, racism, discrimination, deprivation, and (the fear of) crime.

Focusing the analysis

Social workers are sometimes criticised for putting too much emphasis on individual factors rather than the social and environmental context in which families live (Evans, 2003; Jack and Gill, 2003). The reason for this is partly about scope – social workers have limited time and resources to conduct their inquiries and address the problems they find. But it is also about priorities – social workers are expected to decide what is important in such complex situations and what should be done about it. This task is often formulated in terms of risk, i.e. which needs are likely to produce the most negative outcomes, and also vulnerability, i.e. who is most likely to suffer the most harm if nothing is done. As we saw in our hypotheses, prediction depends on how we understand cause and effect in relation to a defined problem.

How we define that problem will depend on a number of factors: personal preferences, professional training and experience, theoretical frameworks, models of practice, and our professional role and remit.

Of these factors, the nature of our professional involvement is perhaps the most influential. Social workers often work in secondary or tertiary services, such as community mental health teams within the NHS, or social care teams within local authorities. These services work with individuals and families who are referred from universal services such as schools or GP surgeries. In other words, social workers often become involved with people who are going through a period of stress, transition, and crisis. The nature of these urgent problems tends to determine which service is referred to and this in turn shapes the way the overall situation is defined. In the case of Yusuf and Faduma, for example, the health visitor has made a referral to children's social care, whose job is to focus on the children's needs and explore any safeguarding concerns.

The tendency for social workers to be analysing need at a time of crisis (or incipient crisis) imposes certain constraints on the scope of their analysis. This is illustrated in Figure 1.2, which shows the effects of various risk factors that may have contributed to a crisis. The timeline serves to contrast longer-term, cumulative needs, such as overcrowded and poor quality social housing (A), with more recent developments that may have escalated the situation, such as maternal depression (C) or paternal drug use (D). As Sparrow (2008) points out, preventing harm means choosing where to intervene in its particular chronology, with concomitant trade-offs between efficacy and risk. The longer agencies wait to act the more efficiently they can target proximal causes – but the consequences of failure are higher because the crisis point has almost been reached. Universal services have a preventative remit for the population as a whole; they intervene early on in the chronology of harm. Specialist services, on the other hand, arrive relatively late in the day. Their job is to focus on the immediate and most salient concerns, while understanding the configuration of events, histories, personalities, relationships, and interactions that have given rise to them.

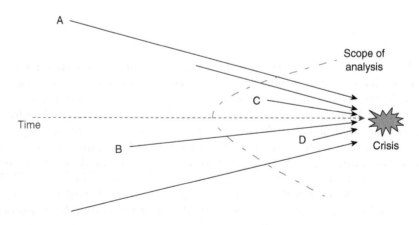

Figure 1.2   Constraints on the analysis of complex needs (adapted from Sparrow, 2008: 137)

Assessing complex needs therefore requires social workers to remain open to multiple causal explanations but also to identify the factors that are most critical to preventing harm. This creates a dilemma because the pressures of the job – workload, deadlines, the expectations of service users and managers – can push social workers into concentrating just on the latter. However, there are good reasons for coming to terms with uncertainty (White, 2009). For one thing, it is worth maintaining a certain scepticism about our own hypotheses and the reliability of the information that sustains them. Psychological research has shown that human beings have a 'confirmation bias' that makes them interpret evidence in ways that justify their existing beliefs or expectations (Stanovich and West, 2000; see Chapter 3). There may be risk factors that we do not know about yet, as represented by the unlabelled arrows in Figure 1.2. Medium-term factors that seem to fall just outside the scope of analysis (arrow B in Figure 1.2) may in fact prove crucial, perhaps because they indicate a period when the family was coping better or a tipping point when things started to get worse.

Openness to explanation also allows social workers to think more creatively about change, Complex needs are difficult to tackle in isolation because they are interconnected. Any intervention designed to address a single aspect of need will have an unpredictable impact on the overall situation. Similarly, if the underlying causes of a crisis are not addressed, then any changes achieved may be short-lived. And since change is about the future, not the past, social workers may be able to introduce a new element into the situation that was not there before. In this respect, it is important to remember that feelings, thoughts, motivations, and perceptions are causal factors every bit as important as incidents and events. It is one reason why relationships are so emphasised in social work practice, because they enable practitioners to understand and empathise with the people they work with. All of these issues will be explored in subsequent chapters.

CONCLUSION

This chapter has explored the challenges of understanding complex needs. Social workers are often required to piece together a picture of multiple needs and multiple causes of need. Because needs tend to intersect with each other, they cannot be treated as a set of individual issues to be tackled separately. Complex needs may be associated with a higher risk of negative outcomes, although social workers should be careful about assuming that all needs are risk factors without checking the evidence first. In assessing complex needs, social workers are advised to take a holistic view of people's welfare and use assessment frameworks in a thoughtful and critical way. This means working with hypotheses and being open to competing explanations. Social workers in specialist services will have to prioritise the most urgent needs but also work towards sustainable change.

MANAGING UNCERTAINTY. VOLATILITY. AND DRIFT

2

CHAPTER SUMMARY

This chapter explores the nature of uncertainty and change in complex cases. It begins with the process of change, which underlies the aims and outcomes of social work interventions. Two principal areas of uncertainty are then considered. First, complexity undermines the extent to which we can predict what will happen either with or without a given intervention. Second, the critical instability associated with complexity can produce volatile dynamics that are challenging to manage, or a frustrating sense that underlying issues are being allowed to drift. The chapter proceeds to examine the most prevalent response to these issues, which is to reduce uncertainty by reframing complex situations as a series of solvable technical problems. Finally, attention is drawn to the importance of developing professional expertise and resilience in order to work with complexity.

INTRODUCTION

The previous chapter highlighted some of the challenges involved in understanding complex needs. Yet like all professionals, social workers are also in the business of change – helping people to meet their needs, to achieve their goals in life, and to keep themselves and others safe from harm. Often the nature of this task is conceptualised in terms of outcomes (Devaney, 2004; Glendinning et al., 2008; Toulmin, 1958; Mukamel et al., 2006; Mullen, 2001). Depending on their approach, social workers often try to agree clear aims and objectives for working together with service users (Doel and Marsh, 1992), and focus on solutions rather than restating historical problems (Turnell and Edwards, 1999). Assessment frameworks and care plans (see Chapter 1) also require practitioners to be explicit about the intended results of actions and interventions, so that progress can be monitored and reviewed. Focusing on outcomes therefore encourages professionals and their agencies to work in partnership with, and be accountable to, the people for whom they provide services.

From a complexity perspective there are some pitfalls with using outcomes as a proxy for change. Most obviously, outcomes represent 'desirable' change, a fixed endpoint to be reached from an existing state of affairs. Complex problems, on the other hand, are not at all fixed; they emerge from configurations of cause and effect that may be significantly or subtly different in each case. As we saw in the introductory chapter, even the smallest difference in initial conditions can result in huge disparities in outcomes. Change in complex systems is therefore unpredictable and correspondingly hard to control. Things may get worse rather than better, and since we can never know 'enough' about a complex situation to predict exactly how it will turn out, new information can – and in some cases should – change our minds about what to do. These issues remind us that as well as having a clear idea of where we want to end up, we also need to keep a close eye on where we are now and where that seems likely to take us. It may be that our journey produces an entirely new set of problems, or an unanticipated diversion, or seems to have no clear end in sight.

JOURNEYS OF CHANGE

Conceptualising change in social work involves many of the same considerations that were explored in the last chapter. At the outset, much depends on how problems are defined, explained, and prioritised. Individuals may be supported to change their attitudes and behaviour in order to achieve certain goals, which could include changing the patterns of interaction within families. Over time, the effects of such changes ripple outward, helping to shape the life of communities, and even society as a whole. It would be a brave profession that would claim to foresee such wide-ranging consequences. Yet the task of predicting individual futures, let alone those of entire families, is scarcely less complex. Social workers are not fortune-tellers; instead they accompany people in a painstaking and often circuitous journey of change. Such journeys are subject to uncertainty in a number of areas, three of which will be examined below: consensus, agency, and emergence.

Consensus

Consensus here refers to the level of agreement between those responsible for initiating and managing change in a situation. The more complex the situation, the less likely there is to be consensus. In a social work context, contributing factors may include:

- **Stakeholders** – service users, their families, carers, professionals, managers, and any other involved parties, e.g. commissioners and budget-holders
- **Hypotheses** – theories about the nature of the change required and the best methods of achieving it
- **Goals** – ideas about what constitutes a successful outcome, and how to demonstrate or measure it
- **Sustainability** – what conditions are necessary to avoid a recurrence of the original problem

As Stacey (2007) points out, complex situations are often characterised by disagreement about such issues within groups, organisations, and teams. Since there is also uncertainty about cause and effect, technical expertise alone is unlikely to resolve any disagreement. An objectively superior course of action is usually unclear at the outset – although may become clearer with hindsight. Moreover, while those involved might be able to negotiate an initial agreement about what to do, consensus may well be short-lived if events develop in unexpected ways. Instead, practitioners must also be willing to experiment, innovate, and learn from experience, rather than conforming rigidly to a pre-determined blueprint for success.

The potential for disagreement inherent in complex situations is exacerbated by the sensitive, sometimes controversial areas of public and private life in which social workers operate. Their work is often characterised by legal, ethical, and political dilemmas such as care and control, advocacy and allocation, abuse and protection, capacity and best interest. In these contexts it is important for social workers to acknowledge and understand the power dynamics that are an inevitable part of conflict and disagreement in human affairs (see Chapter 5). It is also important to note that social workers are not neutral arbiters in such disagreements but – once involved in people's lives – become part of them.

CASE STUDY 2.1

Agatha

Agatha is 77 years old and since her husband died ten years ago has lived alone in a three-bedroom house in central Birmingham. Following a bad fall in her bathroom six months ago, she has become physically more frail and sometimes struggles to get upstairs. Over the same period, she has also had occasional episodes of memory loss, in which she has gone shopping but then forgotten how to get home. Agatha's daughter, Sophie, lives 20 minutes' drive away, works full-time and has three children of her own. She sees her mother most days, and helps with the household as much as she can. However, she is worried about coming under pressure to assume a more comprehensive caring role, as Agatha has often expressed horror at the prospect of being forced to leave her home. Sophie has an older brother, David, who lives in another part of the country and is often difficult to contact. He has said he is unable to provide much help and that social services should either provide home care or move Agatha to a care home.

- What do you think are the barriers to consensus in this case?
- Is it clear what Agatha's needs are or are different hypotheses plausible?
- Consider the goals and motivations of the different family members and how these may or may not be aligned with the outcome of a social work assessment.

Agency

Agency concerns our capacity to exert power and influence in our social environment. In one sense, social workers are agents because they carry out duties and functions conferred on them by the organisations ('agencies') they work for. However, they are also agents in their own right, for example as professionals who deploy their knowledge and skills in the service of others. When facilitating change in people's lives, social workers are sometimes perceived as 'change agents' (Haidt, 2008), a term adopted by Pincus and Minahan (1973) in their theory of social work systems. They conceptualised social workers and their organisations as 'change agent systems', and the people, families, and communities they work with as 'client systems' (Pincus and Minahan, 1973). Although this terminology is rarely used nowadays, the underlying concepts continue to be influential in how we think about systemic change in social work. This applies both to the idea of promoting change in society, which is an important aspect of social work (Dominelli, 2002), as well as furthering the welfare of individuals and their families.

If social workers are change agents, a difficult question arises: who exactly is changing whom? A chemical analogy might be to view social workers either as *catalysts* or as *reactants*. A catalyst is able to precipitate an event or process while remaining unchanged itself. A reactant, on the other hand, takes part in and undergoes change itself. Arguably, the prevailing view of professional expertise tends more towards the catalytic interpretation, emphasising objectivity and rationality as opposed to involvement and reaction. This may be so if we take the medical or legal professions as our role model, although empathetic communication is central to their work too (Hawton et al., 2013; Heath and Tindale, 2013; Kemp et al., 2008). Social work, on the other hand, largely depends on relationships (Ruch et al., 2010). Social workers have to engage people, often in their own homes, and establish a connection with them, often in stressful and sometimes adversarial circumstances. Such work is all but impossible to carry out in a dispassionate, uninvolved way, and in that sense is bound to produce a reaction. This aspect of social complexity demands a degree of reflection, self-awareness, and attention to the ethical dimension of practice (see Chapters 4 and 5).

Such factors mean that a social worker's agency – their power to influence and shape events – is itself a source of uncertainty. Any social work intervention, including the act of turning up at someone's door, instigates complex social dynamics consisting of mutually responsive processes of communication, interaction, and relational understanding (Stacey, 2007). The outcomes of such processes are unpredictable, even when the social worker is a seasoned practitioner complying with the latest evidence-based guidelines. On the surface, this may seem a rather dispiriting conclusion – most professionals would choose stability and control over uncertainty and unpredictability. However, complex change is always characterised by the latter, even if the result turns out as intended.

Emergence

Emergence is one of the key principles of complexity (see Introduction). It describes how local interactions give rise to overall patterns of behaviour without the latter being planned or designed. In social work, this means that outcomes emerge from a host of everyday interactions, some of which social workers can influence directly but most of which they cannot. Instead, they become part of a unique configuration of social and relational dynamics, which may or may not correspond to what was planned or intended. Social workers contribute to emergent change – but then again so does everyone else. The difference is that social workers deploy their professional knowledge and skills to try and steer change in particular directions.

Emergence therefore imposes constraints on agency in the sense discussed above, i.e. the capacity of individual practitioners – and their organisations – intentionally to bring about a given outcome. As Stacey (2007) points out, this does not mean that things happen entirely by chance but rather that intentionality itself gives rise to complex social dynamics of participation and mutual response:

> All that *everyone*, no matter how powerful, can do is to continue participating with intention and continually negotiate and respond to others who are also intentionally doing the same. (Stacey, 2007: 150)

The fundamentally social nature of human agency, and the uncertainty it produces, puts pressure on notions of professional competency and accountability. Since the principle of emergence invokes the causal power of multiple agents and intentions, outcomes can be argued to be uncertain but *not* random, which weakens but does not entirely dispel the idea that individuals (and their organisations) can be held responsible for the way things turn out. Expectations in this respect are raised if specialist practitioners lay claim to causal agency as part of their professional project (Larson, 1977) or have it conferred on them by dint of carrying out an organisation's duties and functions. In turn, this has implications for the management of performance and risk. Organisational approaches to dealing with uncertainty are compared later in the chapter.

A final point about emergence concerns the potential for sudden, unexpected, and wholesale change. This is analogous to the 'dissipative structures' found in thermodynamic systems, in which an influx of energy builds up critical instability leading to spontaneous self-organisation into a new state (Prigogine and Stengers, 1984). Not only is the new state qualitatively different from the original one, i.e. it cannot be extrapolated from earlier activity, but the transformation itself can be quite sudden and unexpected. This aspect of complex change presents distinct challenges for social workers, which are discussed in the next section.

Volatility and Drift

So far, this chapter may have given the impression that complexity is about constant change and transformation. After all, complex systems exist on the edge of equilibrium and so by definition never settle into a stable state. Yet while such systems perhaps exhibit the constant *potential* for change, which could be triggered by the most minor of events, from the perspective of participants it may seem for long periods as if not much is changing at all. The troubling co-existence of stasis and fluctuation, order and disorder, is one of the hallmarks of complexity, and is perceived by social workers in very different ways (Hood, 2015a).

To explore this point further, we will explore the connections between two seemingly unrelated concepts: volatility and drift. Both are usually perceived as negative in a social work context. Volatility tends to be ascribed to situations – and sometimes people – that appear dangerously unstable, likely to explode suddenly into action, and raise professional anxiety about safety and vulnerability. When dealing with volatile situations, social workers tend to be on high alert and geared up for unexpected developments. They are often the cases that keep social workers up at night and make them dread opening their emails in the morning. This is because volatility is associated with higher risk; Brandon (2009) for example, points to the importance of recognising and acting on volatile family dynamics in child abuse cases.

CASE STUDY 2.2

Rachel

Rachel is 17 years old and has survived an abusive relationship with Gerald, 35, a heavy drinker whose violence towards her escalated during her pregnancy and nearly resulted in a miscarriage. Rachel is currently staying in a women's refuge and her five-month-old son, Reece, is the subject of a child protection plan. Rachel is supported by her older sister, Anya, who attends meetings and helps her look after her baby. Anya rings the child's

(Continued)

social worker to tell her that she has found out her sister is still in touch with Gerald on social media and she is worried Rachel may have told him where she is staying.

Questions

- What is volatile about this situation?
- How should the social worker respond to Anya's concerns?
- How might this incident affect long-term care planning?

Drift, on the other hand, refers to a kind of slow-moving negative spiral or state of paralysis, in which progress seems to be short-lived and prone to repeated setbacks. Such cases do not seem to provoke the same sensation of acute angst, but instead incur a sense of frustration and helplessness in the face of an apparently intractable state of affairs. Social workers feel 'stuck' and wonder whether there is anything more they can do. The case is allocated and then reallocated and each new social worker starts again in a spirit of optimism (Dingwall et al., 1983). Eventually 'drift' is identified, perhaps because managers become aware that an individual or family has had a long history of involvement with secondary and tertiary services, which are designed for complex and acute cases of need rather than ongoing support and maintenance (see Chapter 1).

It could be argued that volatility and drift are part of the same phenomenon, i.e. complexity and how it is experienced by practitioners in particular cases at particular times. Volatility, of course, may well be a feature of emergent change as instability reaches a critical point and gives way to fluctuation and 'orderly disorder'. As noted in the previous chapter, social workers often become involved when situations are escalating towards crisis, where issues previously in the background suddenly come to the fore and can no longer be ignored. Furthermore, as discussed above, since professional involvement brings new energy to a situation already in the process of change, volatility is not necessarily reduced. In some cases, social workers engage in 'fire-fighting', or constant crisis management, and so feel unable to make progress with the 'real' underlying problems because as soon as one emergency is dealt with the next one arises. Even periods of relative calm cannot be trusted because of the sense that the next crisis is 'bubbling' beneath the surface (Hood, 2015a). Indeed, volatility can look a lot like drift, once we step back from the fire-fighting.

CASE STUDY 2.3

Simon is an 11-year old White British boy who experienced neglect and emotional abuse in his early childhood and has been in public care since the age of seven. During that time he has been placed with nine different foster families. He has unsupervised contact with his mother on Saturday afternoons, and sees his younger siblings at a contact centre after school once every two weeks. He has been with his current foster carers for six months. They describe him as a bright and caring boy who loves animals and enjoys outdoor activities; he also presents as temperamental and impulsive, prone to temper tantrums when he is told 'no', and can be easily led astray by his peers. He has recently started truanting from school and staying out late with a group of friends. Last week he was caught shoplifting and given a warning by the police. His foster carers report that his angry outbursts are becoming more violent, and he has damaged the furniture in his room. He has had numerous changes in social worker and is often reluctant to take part in pre-arranged visits or meetings. Simon's foster carers have told his current social worker that they would like him to stay but are finding his behaviour increasingly difficult to manage. This has been a recurrent pattern in previous placement breakdowns.

Questions

- As Simon's social worker, what would be your main concerns about his care and welfare?
- Would you describe the situation as volatile or drifting?
- What would positive change look like in the short and long term?
- What do you think are the biggest areas of uncertainty?

Case Study 2.3 illustrates some of these issues in its account of Simon's turbulent family life. It is known that multiple placements for looked after children are a risk factor for poor outcomes in later life, yet finding a solution to the cycle of breakdown, containment, and transition can prove difficult. The pattern of comparative stability following a placement move, followed by escalating problems and a sudden eruption into crisis, will be unhappily familiar to many social workers. As Nybell (2001) points out, our experience of such dynamics also affects the way we regard vulnerable children and young people, i.e. as inherently volatile and unstable, prone to unruly and disruptive behaviour, and in ever-greater need of boundaries. The result is a paradoxical combination of paralysis and crisis that is perpetuated, not alleviated, by our efforts at containment and control.

Careful analysis and reflection is required before we can make progress in such cases, not least because of our own contribution to the dynamics that are keeping them stuck (Molin, 1988). One of the reasons that chronologies and case summaries are so valued in social work is that they help practitioners to identify underlying patterns and take a step back from the immediate exigencies of the situation. Newly allocated workers are encouraged to resist 'start again syndrome' (Brandon et al., 2008) and make sure they have a longitudinal perspective on what has been tried in the past and what might help break the cycle of crisis and intervention. That is easy enough to say (or write) but in practice social workers must somehow carve out space for such activity while being inundated with urgent demands on their time.

Professional and managerial support is therefore essential to help social workers deal effectively with complex phenomena such as uncertainty, volatility, and drift (see Chapter 5). In the next section, we will explore two contrasting approaches to this important issue.

APPROaches to maNaGiNG UNCeRtaiNty

For the reasons explored above, the experience of working with complex cases – and feeling accountable for their outcomes – can be stressful and anxiety-provoking for frontline practitioners and their managers. In politically sensitive areas such as child protection and mental health, such cases also serve to heighten institutional anxiety about risk, i.e. the prospect of being blamed if things go wrong (Munro, 2009; Rothstein et al., 2006). The response is often a defensive one, relying on technical rationality to reduce uncertainty and procedural compliance to limit the repercussions of unforeseen outcomes (Hood et al., 2001). The procedural approach does have its disadvantages, however, as will be discussed shortly. An alternative is for organisations to understand and accept uncertainty, and the risks that go with it, developing instead the professional resilience and expertise to deal with it (see below, and Chapter 5).

The procedural approach

The procedural approach is associated with technical rationality, which was discussed in the Introduction. Its way of dealing with complex problems is to reduce them to a series of technical tasks that can be allocated to relevant specialists. In the case of Simon, for example (Case Study 2.3), one could expect to see him referred to a number of professionals, each with a remit to tackle specific issues such as educational achievement, school attendance, self-esteem, consequential thinking, positive activities, counselling, and so on. He might be diagnosed with a medical condition amenable to treatment, such as ADHD, or his behaviour could be ascribed to psychological issues such as attachment. Every six months, a formal meeting will be held with Simon and all of the professionals working with him, in order to review his care plan and agree tasks and targets for the next review. Gradually, incrementally, all the specialists do their work and the overall result is progress (see Chapter 6).

The problem – in our hypothetical example – is that all this carefully choreographed activity is not working. Simon's foster placement is close to breaking down; he is absconding from school, which presumably is affecting his learning; he is being drawn into petty crime and antisocial behaviour and may be vulnerable to exploitation by older peers; he is also disinclined to engage with yet another social worker who is unlikely to stick around. It is a frustrating state of affairs, for which the usual explanations are:

1.   The care system 'fails' children by not properly meeting their needs, e.g. because of high turnover of social workers, or shortage of therapeutic services

2. Intervention did not come early enough, so that the developmental conse-
    quences of childhood abuse and neglect cannot be entirely mitigated
3. Other factors interfere with provision, e.g. cuts to services, excessive bureau-
    cracy, organisational 'churn', and political interference

While all these factors may play a role, what is often not considered is that technical
rationality itself may be the problem, rather than flaws in the way it is implemented. From a complexity perspective, the fundamental flaw in trying to 'split
up' complex problems is that it often increases complexity (see Chapter 6). Each
professional necessarily works with the whole person, not a simpler, more pliable
fragment that corresponds to their remit. Pupils, clients, patients, service users,
mentees, and so forth, have their own view on whom they want to work with and
whom they don't, whom they dislike and trust, whom they are glad to see the back
of and sorry to see go. It is implausible to expect all of these relationships to function in a mechanical way simply because the people involved have had some sort
of professional training.

For many organisations, however, it makes sense to try and drag the messy reality
of this type of work up to the high ground of manageable problems (Schön, 1987).
The reasons for this are twofold. First, from a technical-rational perspective, complexity is a source of volatile and potentially dangerous energies that must be contained
within successive layers of protection (Woods et al., 2010). The language of technical
rationality therefore emphasises certainty and solidity; plans must be robust, objectives measurable, positive outcomes 'ensured' (Hood, 2014). Second, the assumption
of a linear relationship between cause (intervention) and effect (outcome) allows for
a much greater degree of proceduralisation. Detailed procedures, protocols, and practice guidelines can be developed and fine-tuned in order to maximise the chance of
success but also minimise the risk of being blamed if things go wrong.

Procedures are undoubtedly helpful and reassuring for social workers, particularly early on in their careers (Fook et al., 2000), and essential for dealing with
emergencies where there is little time to think and act. Indeed, social workers dealing
with very volatile situations may well find themselves in a constant mode of crisis
response (Moynihan, 2009). Since volatility can be a manifestation of complexity,
however, constant fire-fighting may also indicate and disguise drift – for example,
because practitioners have been unable to address the underlying problems producing the volatile behaviour. Furthermore, while a procedural approach can facilitate
a prompt and effective response to crisis situations, it is of limited use for working
with complexity. There are various reasons for this:

• Standardisation and prescription of their work makes practitioners less able to
  innovate, be creative, and adapt their practice to new challenges
• The emphasis on 'doing things by the book' makes social workers reluctant to
  take risks, encourages defensive practice and can alienate service users
• Unwanted outcomes are analysed with the benefit of hindsight and assumed
  to be both predictable and preventable. This promotes blame culture (see
  Chapter 9) and leads to a proliferation of procedures, increasing the administrative burden on social workers and reducing the time available to work
  directly with people

In areas of practice characterised by a highly procedural approach, such as child protection, the cumulative effect of these issues leads to poor morale, high levels of stress and burnout, erosion in skills and knowledge, and difficulties in developing and retaining professional expertise in frontline roles (Ayre and Preston-Shoot, 2010). The procedural approach turns out to be counterproductive because it ignores complexity and therefore leaves practitioners ill-prepared for what they experience in their work.

Professional expertise and resilience

An alternative approach is to make sure that procedures augment rather than substitute for professional expertise and resilience. These are the hallmarks of a 'socio-technical' approach to practice, which is further discussed in Chapter 8. As the name suggests, a socio-technical approach is appropriate for situations in which technical knowledge and skills are acquired and wielded in the context of social relationships and interactions (Munro, 2010). Examples outside health and social care might include running a commercial airline flight, or operating a nuclear power station (Woods et al., 2010). In this type of situation, the variety of work is too high to be managed by standardised tools and procedures alone. Instead, expertise must be deployed at the sharp end of practice so that the response to problems is flexible and adaptable enough to cope with complexity. We will return to these issues in more detail in Chapter 8.

Expertise

Expertise refers to the development of attributes, skills, and knowledge necessary for 'superior performance within a specific domain or activity' (Gillingham and Humphreys, 2010: 77). Gaining such proficiency takes time because experience is necessary in order to apply the knowledge, develop the skills, and integrate all the attributes of an expert practitioner. According to Hood et al. (2016a: 494), expertise generally has the following characteristics:

- Progression over time from novice to expert (Baird and Wagner, 2000; Dreyfus and Dreyfus, 1986)
- Combination of formal/propositional knowledge and non-formal/tacit knowledge (Kinchin and Cabot, 2010; Eraut, 2000)
- Application to problems characterised by complexity and uncertainty, and which are not amenable to technical solutions (Fook, Ryan and Hawkins, 2000; Rittel and Webber, 1973)

The literature cited above suggests that expert practitioners are more likely to have an intuitive grasp of situations, adopt an holistic approach, perceive underlying issues, and find creative solutions to problems (Hood et al., 2017). In contrast, novice practitioners tend to be more reliant on rules and protocols, tend to consider only individual aspects of a complex situation, and are reluctant to use their discretion. One problem with highly procedural work environments is that practitioners with greater expertise may eventually become frustrated by the constraints on their practice and go elsewhere, leaving less experienced workers in their place. The result is something of a vicious circle, with procedural controls being seen as necessary to manage the continual influx of newly qualified workers (see Munro, 2011).

Readers who are at the beginning of their careers may wonder where this leaves them, since all practitioners have to start somewhere. In the UK, 'somewhere' often means statutory services such as child protection, where the high turnover of front-line staff creates vacancies for novice practitioners to 'cut their teeth' before moving on. The important thing here is to acknowledge the complexity of the work and find ways to develop expertise, even in very procedure-driven organisations. This is partly about formal knowledge, e.g. attending training and post-qualifying courses, or reading the literature relevant to specific assessments or interventions. It is also about adopting the mindset of a more experienced social worker, e.g. approaching your manager with a suggested course of action rather than just asking her what to do. Maintaining a commitment to expert practice also requires resilience, as discussed below.

Resilience

In general terms, resilience denotes the capacity to cope successfully with stress, adversity, and hardship. In developmental psychology, the term refers more specifically to the emergence of 'good outcomes in spite of serious threats to adaptation or development' (Masten, 2001: 227). It is not an innate trait so much as a phenomenon that is inferred from someone's circumstances and life history. When we say that people are resilient, we mean that they have been exposed to a developmental risk factor (e.g. poverty, abuse, or serious illness) and have also demonstrated successful coping, e.g. educational or vocational achievement. The concept of resilience has been used to explain why some children are able to 'bounce back' from adverse experiences in their early life (Glover, 2009), for example because they happen to have an easy temperament or a supportive grandparent.

Social workers need to be resilient because the job itself presents a risk to their health and wellbeing, as demonstrated by the evidence of stress-related illness, secondary trauma, and 'burnout' in many areas of social work (Lloyd et al., 2002). Successful coping, in this context, would be demonstrated by the capacity to do a difficult and demanding job to the best of one's ability over a sustained period. High levels of turnover in social work agencies, as well as the relatively short professional lifespan of social workers themselves, suggest that many people in fact find it hard to sustain a career in frontline practice. There are several possible reasons for this, some of which are probably common to many occupations, e.g. heavy workloads, pressure from deadlines, lack of recognition, limited career opportunities, lack of managerial and supervisory support. What is perhaps unique to social work is the toxic blame culture and institutional anxiety about risk, particularly in statutory settings, which exacerbates rather than relieves the emotional and psychological toll of the work (see Chapter 9).

So what makes social workers resilient? Kinman and Grant (2011) found that emotional intelligence, reflective ability, empathy, and social competence were predictive of stress resilience in social work trainees. They also argued that while qualifying and post-qualifying programmes should focus more on developing these qualities, the key thing was to improve working conditions. In other words, rather than seeing stress and burnout as an unavoidable consequence of a difficult job, it should be the joint responsibility of social workers, employers, and professional bodies to actively support and develop resilient practitioners. Some suggestions are listed in Table 2.1 below, and will also be covered in other chapters in the book.

Table 2.1 Building professional resilience

Individual	Organisational	Professional
• Ask for reflective as well as task-focused supervision • Make time for peer and group supervision • Risk assess all newly allocated cases, e.g. personal safety, 'trigger' issues • Don't do solo home visits to dangerous clients or areas • Make sure to de-brief with a colleague after a difficult encounter (and offer to do the same for them) • Tell your manager or supervisor if events in your personal life are affecting your work • Don't ignore tell-tale signs of burnout, e.g. crying in the morning before going to work • Have an annual schedule of training and stick to it • Request study leave for post-qualifying courses	• Team-based models of allocation and casework, e.g. social work units • Train managers to deliver reflective supervision • Streamline administrative procedures • Stagger complexity of work for newly qualified and inexperienced staff • Reward experience and commitment to frontline work • Encourage and support staff to attend training and CPD • If offices are open-plan, ensure that team members have a protected space • Provide counselling and therapeutic de-briefing for frontline staff • Reduced caseloads for senior practitioners taking on a student	• Regulators and professional bodies to recognise, e.g. with kitemark, agencies that develop and support resilient, expert practitioners • Regulators and professional bodies to speak out on behalf of social workers during public crises of confidence • Regulation to be less punitive, e.g. to focus on helping agencies to develop expertise rather than just monitoring compliance with standards

CONCLUSiON

In the previous chapter, complex needs were discussed in relation to non-linear dynamics, which make social work assessments susceptible to sudden or unexpected change. This chapter has considered the challenges of understanding and managing the process of change, often with a specific set of outcomes in mind. In this respect, complexity creates a characteristic set of uncertainties, e.g. lack of consensus about what to do and how to do it, limited agency and individual influence over events, and the unpredictable nature of emergent change. Practitioners working with such cases sometimes experience volatile patterns of change, which produce anxiety about risk and a sense of having to deal with successive crises rather than tackle their underlying causes. At other times, social workers may perceive 'drift', a frustrating sense that all their activity and intervention is not improving matters in any fundamental way. Both volatility and drift can be viewed as manifestations of the uncertainty produced by complex change. This uncertainty can be understood and managed in different ways. A procedural approach is to reduce complex issues to a set of technical problems that are amenable to standardised solutions. The alternative approach is to acknowledge and respond to complexity within an institutional framework that develops and supports professional expertise and resilience. It has been argued that the latter approach stands a better chance of addressing the stress, anxiety, and burnout that afflicts too many frontline social workers and contributes to the high turnover and vacancy rates in many parts of the profession.

Making Decisions and Judgements

3

CHAPTER SUMMARY

This chapter considers the challenges associated with making judgements and decisions in social work. The question of what constitutes a justifiable decision is discussed in terms of rationality, ethicality, and reasonableness. Analytic and intuitive approaches to decision-making are compared before exploring some of the cognitive biases that can unwittingly affect people's judgement, including confirmation bias, hindsight error, and the rule of optimism. The discussion then moves onto judgements about harm, which involve a probabilistic analysis based on predictive risk factors and draw on a combination of clinical, consensus-based and actuarial approaches to risk assessment. Finally, there is a discussion of bounded rationality, which suggests that heuristic models continue to be useful in complex situations where there is pressure to make decisions quickly and with limited information.

INTRODUCTION

Like all professionals, social workers are constantly making judgements and decisions. The terms are sometimes used interchangeably, but it is worth distinguishing between them here. According to Taylor (2010), judgement refers to the process of considering alternative explanations and courses of action, whereas decisions refer to the choices that are made at specific points in time (see also Dowie, 1993). Sometimes these processes are conscious and even formal in nature, drawing on institutional and organisational frameworks for making certain kinds of decisions. The latter are particularly prominent in legal and statutory contexts, while risk-sensitive areas of practice also tend towards a more procedural approach, as discussed in Chapter 2. In a broader sense, however, judgements and decisions are part and parcel of everyday social work; they emerge spontaneously from dialogue and interaction – 'in action' as Schön (1991) puts it – as practitioners evaluate problems and decide how to deal with them. In that sense, 'good judgement' could be seen as a virtue rather than an activity, a somewhat intangible quality that manifests itself in expert practice.

Of course, even expert judgements and decisions involve an element of risk. Making a choice inevitably involves 'opportunity cost' in terms of the alternatives forgone, while the preferred option may end up having an undesired outcome. As professionals, social workers are accountable for the work they do, which does not mean they should be infallible but that their decisions should be reasonable and justifiable at the time. Most social workers get anxious about being held responsible for outcomes that (with hindsight) could be attributed to poor judgement or a 'bad decision' on their part. Moreover, decisions in social work are usually made with others: service users, carers, managers, and other professionals. Decision-making should therefore be seen as a psycho-social process as much as an act of cognition; even explicitly rational decisions may be unconsciously affected by instincts, emotions, and biases, shaped by relationships and patterns of communication, or driven by dynamics of collaboration and conflict.

COMPLEX DECISIONS

Like other professionals, social workers are valued for their ability to weigh up complex situations within their remit of expertise, and give informed advice about the best course of action. It could be argued that all the situations encountered by social workers are complex in their own way. However, decisions and judgements that may be experienced as particularly complex include:

- **Contested decisions** – where social workers have divergent or conflicting opinions with those of service users, with other professionals, or with managers
- **Decisions about capacity and consent** – where social workers are required to judge an adult's capacity to make a decision that seems inimical to their own welfare, for example, or a child's right to make a decision that contravenes the wishes of one or both parents
- **Safeguarding decisions** – where social workers need to evaluate the presence and significance of various risk factors to determine the degree of harm to which an adult or child is being exposed
- **Threshold decisions** – also known as 'criterion-based' judgements, where social workers have to reduce a complex social context to a yes/no recommendation

in relation to a category of risk, such as significant harm in child protection, or a gatekeeping threshold, such as access to adult social care services

- **Benefit vs harm decisions** – where professionals have to 'take a risk' in the sense of weighing up the potential benefits of a decision against possible harms, e.g. a young disabled adult moving to independent living for the first time
- **Statutory decisions** – decisions such as whether a child needs a protection plan, or whether someone needs to be admitted to hospital for psychiatric assessment, have far-reaching consequences for service users and may well be contested
- **Legal decisions** – decisions that are part of a social worker's statutory role could eventually contribute to court proceedings and may have to be justified under cross-examination

JUSTifiable DECiSiONS

Decisions cannot be justified or condemned solely on the basis of what happens after they are made. Nonetheless, certain characteristics of the decision-making process arguably make a good outcome – or at least a 'good decision' – more likely. Research into decision-making points to the importance of three interlinked concepts: rationality, ethicality, and reasonableness.

Rationality

Rational judgements follow a logical process for evaluating the 'expected utility' of different options and deciding between them (Van de Luitgaarden, 2009). Utility here means the value of a particular outcome to the person or people concerned, once the pros and cons have been taken into account. For example, an elderly person with deteriorating health may have to consider whether they should remain at home or move to supported accommodation. To begin with, the utility value of remaining at home may be perceived as quite high, or at least higher than having to move. However, this ignores the availability of good enough support, care, and treatment, without which there might be a high risk of serious illness or injury. A rational decision must therefore consider 'the alternatives for action, the outcomes that might be the result of those actions, the likelihood of each outcome, and the subjective value that is attached to each event by the decision maker' (Van de Luitgaarden, 2009: 245). For social workers, this means gathering information about all the variables relevant to the decision, such as available networks of care and support, possible adjustments to the home, costs involved, and so on. However, possessing information by itself is not enough to make a decision – it needs to be structured in some way for analysis.

One method of weighing up the utility value of alternative options is to construct a decision tree (Munro, 2008). A tree is constructed by combining three types of nodes: a decision (represented by a square), a consequence (represented by a circle) and an outcome (represented by a triangle). Time goes from left to right and the tree can extended over several consequences and subsequent decision points. Munro (2008: 105) suggests the following series of questions as a framework for constructing a decision tree:

1. What decision is to be made?
2. What options are there?
3. What information is needed to help make the choice?
4. What are the likely/possible consequences of each option?
5. How probable is each consequence?
6. What are the pros and cons of each consequence (i.e. what is their expected utility value)?
7. What is the final decision?

CASE STUDY 3.1

Mr Olson

Mr Olson, 82, lives alone in a three-bedroom house in a village, 20 miles from the city where his two adult sons live. He has had increasing problems with memory loss and last week was found walking in the streets in a dressing gown on a very cold winter night. His neighbours say that he has been coming round to their house in a confused and sometimes panicked state of mind, and he has suffered a number of falls that luckily have not resulted in him being injured. After discussing the situation with Mr Olson and his children, the social worker is able to gain an idea of what support he might

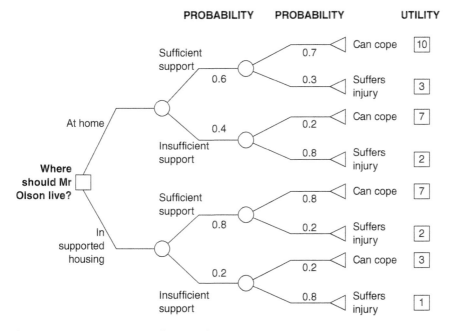

Figure 3.1   Decision-tree for Mr Olson

(Continued)

need in order to stay at home without suffering injury. The family is also able to inform the social worker how they could contribute to Mr Olson's care, what concerns they have, and what extra resources they feel are needed. On the basis of this discussion, the social worker constructs the decision tree above.

According to the decision tree, what is the final decision? (see below).

Making a decision tree is quite an involved process; even a relatively simple example, such as the one in Case Study 3.1, can be quite tricky to work out. In complex scenarios, the number of possible options and consequences can quickly expand into an overwhelming amount of information. For this reason, as discussed in Chapter 1, it is important that professionals are clear about the priorities and scope of their decision-making, so that they can focus the analytical process on elements that seem most crucial or problematic (Munro, 2008). As Taylor (2017) points out, an attribute of human cognition is simplifying the information needed to make a decision in complex scenarios. Most of the time this happens subconsciously, which can lead to various types of bias, as discussed below. However, people often take similar short-cuts when they use formal decision-making tools; for example, during the course of making a decision tree it might quickly become apparent which course of action is preferable or undesirable. The objectivity of such tools should therefore not be over-emphasised (Munro, 2008).

Rational approaches to decision-making are often linked to evidence-based practice (EBP), a set of principles for using empirical research findings to guide clinical judgements and interventions (Gambrill, 1999; McNeece and Thyer, 2004). In the example discussed above, knowledge of risk factors for serious injuries sustained from falls at home, or the factors contributing to positive transitions to supported accommodation, might help the social worker assign values to their decision model. The point here is that social workers should try whenever possible to use knowledge derived from empirical studies that have been conducted according to the principles of scientific method (see Chapter 7). The targeted use of research evidence also lies at the heart of actuarial models of risk assessment, which present social workers with a pre-formulated decision tree to which they match the information they have gathered about a case.

CASE STUDY 3.1

(Continued) The decision tree

Working out the decision tree goes in the opposite direction to its construction, i.e. from right to left. For each pathway on the right-hand side, the expected utility of an outcome is multiplied by its probability. Since each consequence node is followed by two pathways, the results for both pathways are added together to yield a new expected utility value for that node. For example, the total value for the pathway 'at home with sufficient support' is 7.9. The process is repeated for the next set of pathways to the left, which result in expected utility values for 'at home' and 'in supported housing' of 5.9 and 5.1 respectively. Since the overall expected utility of Mr Olson remaining at home is higher, this is the decision indicated by the tree. Of course, the result depends entirely on the assumptions and information underlying the values and probabilities that were initially assigned to the model. It is also important to acknowledge that the decision may prove to be the wrong one; the anticipated support may not materialise, for example, or Mr Olson's condition may deteriorate more quickly than expected. However, if the social worker has to justify their decision, they can show how information available at the time of the decision was weighted and taken into account.

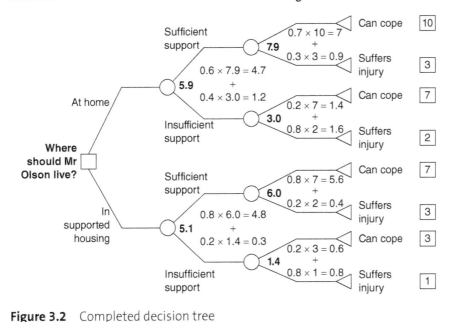

Figure 3.2 Completed decision tree

Ethicality

Decisions made by social workers are ethical in nature because they have consequences for others and must be 'both legal and acceptable to the larger community' (Jones, 1991: 367). Ethical decisions may be based on general principles, such as those set out in professional codes of practice (Banks, 2006). They may refer to generally accepted decisions in similar cases (see below). They may also derive from a person's deeply held beliefs about what constitutes meaningful or virtuous behaviour (Osmo and Landau, 2001). Jones (1991) argues that moral issues vary in their intensity depending on characteristics such as the magnitude of consequences, probability of effect, temporal immediacy, and the perceived proximity of those affected by the decision. Social workers often face moral dilemmas around rights, responsibilities and 'best interests', for example when contributing to the decision to deprive someone of their liberty, or to remove a child from the care of her parents. It is also possible that someone's professional judgement of a situation might differ in some respects from their ethical judgement, e.g. if the morally desirable solution is at odds with the available resources (Osmo and Landau, 2001).

Ethical decision-making essentially means taking a rational approach to navigating these issues. Social workers are encouraged to set out explicitly their reasons for adopting a particular course of action, which includes exploring limitations as well as supporting evidence for any statements made (Dolgoff et al., 2012; Reamer, 1983; Osmo and Landau, 2001; Toulmin, 1970). A frequently cited model is that of Toulmin (1958), who suggested that ethical arguments are structured using six types of statement (see also Taylor, 2010: 57; Osmo and Landau, 2001: 486):

1. A claim or conclusion, e.g. that a particular 15-year-old girl should be accommodated in a secure children's home
2. Data, evidence, or grounds for the claim, e.g. information indicating that this girl is associating with known gang members, is being sexually exploited, is beyond parental control, and has a history of absconding from extended family and foster placements
3. Warrant or justify the connection between the data and the claim by appealing to a rule of inference, e.g. empirical evidence of multiple risk factors for sexual exploitation and abuse, particularly in connection with gangs
4. Qualify a claim or conclusion by expressing degrees of confidence and likelihood, e.g. the likelihood that a period in secure care will help to address underlying issues around identity, self-esteem, and family relationships
5. Highlight any limitations or reservations about the claim, e.g. that any secure placement should be close enough for family members to be able to visit
6. Back up, justify, or otherwise support an inference warrant by appealing to further evidence, e.g. empirical data, common knowledge, professional practice, scientific theory

REFLECTIVE EXERCISE 3.1

Think about a complex decision you had to make in your life – either from your personal or working life.

1. What made the decision complex?
2. Did you write anything down to help you make the decision?
3. If you did a list of 'pros and cons', did you consider their relative importance or likelihood?
4. Was there a key factor or piece of information that 'clinched' the decision for you?
5. Did you have to justify your decision to anybody? If so, what kind of arguments did you use?

Reasonableness

In general terms, a reasonable decision may be described as one that may not be optimal but which 'gets the job done' (Brehmer, 1999). This links to ideas such as heuristic judgement and practical validity that are discussed later in the chapter. A more specific concept of reasonableness relates to the legal context of social work. In this respect, practitioners and their organisations need to know the specific duties and powers conferred by legislation in their area of practice, respect the purpose for which statutes are drawn up, and act in accordance with the principles of procedural propriety and proportionality. In relation to standards of care, UK case law offers a precedent called the 'Bolam Test', which suggests that a professional cannot be found guilty of negligence if she or he has acted in accordance with a practice accepted as proper by a responsible body of professionals skilled in that particular art.[1] However, as Taylor et al. (2015) point out, a more recent judgement in the case of Bolith v. City & Hackney Health Authority ([1998] House of Lords AC232) suggests that professionals should also be able to give a rationale for their decisions in terms of research evidence or an appropriate theoretical framework. The legal concept of reasonableness therefore aligns with the need to demonstrate a rational and ethical approach to decision-making.

ANalytic aNd iNtUitiVe aPPROaches

Clearly it is not feasible for social workers to do a decision-tree analysis or draft an ethical argument every time they have to decide something. Nor is it necessarily obvious which decisions – other than the formal recommendations of an assessment or report – are the important ones. For example, Hassett and Stevens (2014) analyse a serious case review to show how an ultimately tragic chain of events was triggered by the fact that a care home resident did not have an egg for breakfast. As we have seen, complexity theory shows that outcomes emerge from unpredictable dynamics of cause and effect, so that seemingly trivial actions and omissions can eventually turn out to have serious consequences. However, unpredictability does not invalidate the need for rational, ethical behaviour, and most social workers would probably accept that their decisions ought to involve some sort of logical thought process. What they might be tempted to argue is that a more 'realistic' view, i.e. reflecting what happens in practice rather than in textbooks, should acknowledge practice wisdom, 'gut feeling', and the need to think quickly and make decisions under pressure. This type of decision-making is sometimes referred to as implicit or 'intuitive', as opposed to the explicit or 'analytic' approaches described above.

The idea that people have two distinct modes of thinking and reasoning is based on psychological research (Evans, 2003). Stanovich and West (2000) describe these modes as System 1 and System 2, terms later popularised by Kahneman (2011) as

---

[1]The judgement in question relates to alleged negligence by a medical doctor, and was given by Mr Justice McNair in Bolam v Friern Hospital Management Committee 1957 2 All ER 118 [1957] 1 WLR 582.

'Thinking, Fast and Slow'. It is thought that System 1 (fast) thinking developed early on in our evolutionary history. It encompasses a range of cognitive processes that are rapid and automatic, often emotional and largely subconscious in nature – 'only their final product is posted in consciousness' (Evans, 2003: 454). System 2 (slow) thinking, on the other hand, is a relatively new development in evolutionary terms, and is possibly unique to human beings. It is deliberate and sequential, conscious and calculating, uses working memory, and makes use of abstract hypothetical ideas that are beyond System 1. This type of thinking takes a lot of effort and concentration, and can be easily hijacked by the automatic System 1 processes if we are distracted or in a hurry.

Importantly for practitioners, the distinction between intuitive and analytical thought does not amount to an 'either-or' way of making decisions. There is evidence that both systems are active in reasoning tasks. System 2 processes often serve to inhibit and override System 1 tendencies, such as placing too much weight on prior knowledge (Evans, 2003). This is why social workers are exhorted to 'test their hypotheses' (see Chapter 1) or to think about their initial assumptions and potential sources of bias, both examples of activating System 2 thinking. Equally, the discipline of assembling information for a structured assessment tool can improve intuitive judgements (see Kahneman, 2011: 231). It has been shown that emotions are not – as is often thought – a superfluous distraction to rational thinking, but are in some way essential to making decisions (Munro, 2008; Damasio, 2006). Research into clinical reasoning and expertise also suggests that practitioners learn to integrate formal and informal forms of knowledge into their professional judgements, rather than switching from one to the other (Higgs et al., 2008).

Nonetheless, it would be unwise for any social worker to rely on gut feeling to justify their decisions! Quite apart from the difficulties this might pose on cross-examination in court, the evidence from numerous studies is that intuitive reasoning on its own – including diagnosis by experienced clinicians – is inconsistent and often little better than guesswork. This is largely because human beings have developed a range of 'heuristics' (inferential short-cuts, or rules-of-thumb) for navigating the complexity of everyday life. Without these heuristics, we might be so paralysed by the task of analysis that we would struggle to make any decisions at all. However, compared to more objective and rational approaches, heuristics are prone to 'bias' in the sense of systematic flaws that skew our judgement.

Heuristics and Biases

There is an extensive body of research into cognitive heuristics and biases, which leaves little doubt as to the pitfalls of relying on intuition alone. Here there is space only to discuss a selection that seem particularly relevant to social workers.

Confirmation bias and 'anchoring'

Confirmation bias is our reluctance to change our initial opinion about something, so that we actively look for evidence that confirms that opinion while overlooking or 'explaining away' evidence that might contradict it. Munro and Fish (2015: 19) give the example of workers in an institution being 'slow to consider that a respected colleague was in fact grooming and abusing a child'. Confirmation bias is often linked to a phenomenon called 'anchoring', which Nurius and Gibson (1990: 18) define as 'excessive weighting of initial information derived about a client that subsequently serves as a template against which further information is judged'. Social workers therefore need to be mindful of being unduly influenced by their first impressions of someone's character or situation, or even by a particularly convincing report in the case file, and be careful to consider new information on its own merits.

Representativeness

The representativeness heuristic is our tendency to over-generalise from categories. This may refer to stereotypes and prejudices, such as a belief that people claiming welfare benefits are lazy or that people with disabilities cannot live independently, so that an individual belonging to those groups is assumed from the outset to share those qualities (Heath and Tindale, 2013). It may also have to do with assessing individuals on the basis of a personal standard or reference point, such as an idea of how a 'normally' developed child or an adult with severe depression would act and speak. This is not just something that affects novice practitioners; experienced social workers need to be mindful that their hard-won practice knowledge, along the lines of 'I've seen cases like this before', may mislead them on occasion.

Availability

The availability heuristic refers to our tendency to recall information that 'stands out' in some way. This might include particularly recent, frequent, or distinctive events, including what we experience personally or see/read in the media. Conversely, we are more likely to overlook information that is abstract, mundane, or without emotional resonance. Nurius and Gibson (1990: 22) give the example of professionals in multi-agency meetings looking out for 'case evidence with which they are most familiar or concerned', whether drug misuse, mental health symptoms, or domestic violence, rather than what is most relevant to the decision. Very dramatic and vivid incidents, even if they are statistically improbable, tend to unduly influence our predictions and can therefore skew risk assessments.

Rule of optimism

The 'rule of optimism' was coined by Dingwall et al. (1983) to describe the tendency of child protection social workers to adhere to a positive view of parents, which in some cases made them slow to recognise and act on indicators of abuse and neglect. This bias towards optimism was linked to the structural and cultural context in which practitioners operated, which encouraged practitioners to 'think the best' of the people they worked with. Of course, the opposite tendency – that of always suspecting the worst – can also lead professionals astray. Past inquiries into child sexual abuse scandals in Cleveland (Department of Health and Social Security, 1987) and Orkney (Department of Health, 1991) showed how an unduly negative view of families had a pervasive effect on assessment and intervention, so that allegations and clinical diagnoses of abuse were uncritically accepted rather than being investigated and challenged (Munro, 1996).

Hindsight bias

Hindsight bias is our tendency to consistently overestimate what could have been anticipated in foresight (Fischhoff, 1975). People tend to judge a process by its outcome and so 'decisions and actions followed by a negative outcome will be judged more harshly than if the same decisions had resulted in a neutral or positive outcome' (Woods et al., 2010: 33). Hindsight also tends to drastically simplify the complexity of the situation facing decision-makers at the time, so that all sorts of uncertainties, dilemmas, trade-offs, and attentional demands are overlooked or under-emphasised. As social workers are only too aware, hindsight error is particularly apparent in the reaction of the public and media to tragic deaths from child abuse (see Chapter 9). Once the public is made aware what has happened, evidence of the dangers and risks seems obvious and any professionals involved are inevitably criticised for failing to see 'what should have been obvious' and to take steps to protect the child (Munro and Fish, 2015). Unfortunately, as Woods et al. (2010) point out, this type of thinking tends to persist even if those reviewing the circumstances of a tragic outcome are warned about the potential for hindsight error.

PREDICTING HARM

The contrast between intuitive and analytic judgement is important when it comes to predicting the likelihood of harm, which is a central concern for social workers making safeguarding decisions. There seems to be a widespread belief among politicians and the media that such decisions should effectively prevent all occurrences of harm, so that if things go wrong, social workers (and possibly their managers) must be to blame. In fact, what practitioners are mostly doing is assessing and managing *risk*, i.e. the probability and severity of harmful outcomes. The uncertainties inherent in this activity mean that mistakes are unavoidable. Hindsight bias aside, social workers are not expected to be infallible; if asked, they should be able to justify their decisions based on what they knew at the time. In the context of safeguarding, this means matching the available relevant information to empirical knowledge of risk factors in a rational and systematic way.

Risk factors

According to Taylor (2010: 74), key areas of practice in which social workers are required to predict the likelihood of harm are: child protection (e.g. risk of abuse or neglect), mental health (e.g. risk of suicide or violence to others), and criminal justice (e.g. risk of re-offending). In these areas, researchers have tried to establish the characteristics of individuals and their environment, relationships, and life histories that show a statistical correlation with an undesired outcome, such as abuse, suicide, or reoffending. These characteristics are termed 'risk factors' because they are more prevalent among people who have suffered or committed harm than in the population as a whole. However, risk factors are only useful for *predicting* harm if there is a wide gap between general and specific prevalence. Munro (2008: 62) gives the example of poverty, which is a common feature of abusive families but may not be particularly useful as a predictor of abuse given that poverty is experienced by 21% of families in the country. On the other hand, multiple rib fractures are extremely rare in non-abused children and so are considered highly predictive of physical abuse (Kemp et al., 2008). The best evidence for risk factors comes from systematic reviews of the literature (for example, Hawton et al. 2013, on risk factors for suicide in individuals with depression), which evaluate the relevance and quality of studies as part of the criteria for inclusion. However, it is important to remember that while knowledge of risk factors helps professionals to assess the *risk* of harm in individual cases, it does *not* enable them to predict whether or not harm will occur.

Clinical, consensus-based and actuarial approaches

There are three main methods of using knowledge of risk factors to assess risk. The first is unstructured clinical judgement, which relies on the knowledge and experience of an individual expert to weigh up the information and arrive at a conclusion (van der Put et al., 2016). However, even if steps are taken to counteract the heuristics and biases discussed above, clinical judgements are still prone to inaccurate and inconsistent predictions (Grove and Meehl, 1996; Meehl, 1954). The second method is to use a 'consensus-based' assessment tool, which is based on the risk factors agreed by consensus among experts in the field. An example from the field of youth justice is the 'Asset' assessment tool used by youth offending teams in England and Wales to inform court reports and programmes of intervention for young people who come into contact with the criminal justice system (Youth Justice Board, 2005). Such tools aim to identify conditions that underlie and perpetuate unwanted behaviour, such as perpetrating abuse or committing a crime, as well as identifying strengths and protective factors that reduce the risk (Mendoza et al., 2016). They also help practitioners to present information and analysis in their assessments in a structured way.

The third method is 'actuarial' risk assessment, which uses empirical research into the risk factors for a clinical population to develop a formal, algorithmic procedure for reaching a decision in specific cases. This type of assessment usually follows the format of a structured questionnaire, in which practitioners are required to give each risk factor a rating or score based on the available information. The actuarial procedure then governs how overall scores are then calculated and interpreted, e.g. establishing whether the case meets the thresholds for different levels of concern or intervention. Such procedures are sometimes incorporated into 'structured decision making' (SDM) tools, which use actuarial analysis to guide practitioners towards defined decision points, e.g. whether an investigation is needed and, if so, how urgently it should be initiated. Case Study 3.2 below describes how researchers developed an actuarial assessment procedure for adult protection services in New Hampshire, USA.

Consensus-based and actuarial assessments both take a more analytical approach than that of unaided clinical judgement. Actuarial approaches have the advantage of being more objective than other methods, and tend to have better evidence of validity (accurately predicting harm), and reliability (consistent interpretation of similar situations) (Baird and Wagner, 2000; van der Put et al., 2016; Mendoza et al., 2016). On the other hand, consensus-based and clinical approaches are more flexible and comprehensive, offer greater scope to consider contextual information, and allow practitioners to contribute to assessment and care planning (Mendoza et al., 2016). It has therefore been argued that assessments should integrate both an actuarial assessment of risk (of future harm) and a contextual assessment of individual and family functioning (Shlonsky and Wagner, 2005). As well as accurately classifying the level of risk, such integrated assessment models should help professionals to decide which needs to prioritise for support and intervention (see Chapter 1), and which services might be most effective in doing so (see Chapter 7).

CASE STUDY 3.2

Developing an Actuarial Risk Assessment to Inform the Decisions Made by Adult Protective Service Workers (Johnson et al., 2010)

In this study from the USA, a team of researchers set out to develop an actuarial risk assessment for users of adult and elderly services in the state of New Hampshire, aiming to classify them by the likelihood of elder maltreatment and/or self-neglect. The study sample consisted of 763 individuals investigated for allegations of self-neglect or maltreatment within a seven-month period in 2009. Demographic data was collected on clients, carers, and perpetrators, along with psychosocial characteristics and health information, and whether services were arranged or refused. Outcomes data were collected six months after the initial report, using measures such as repeated reports of self-neglect or maltreatment or confirmed findings of maltreatment during the follow-up period. The researchers used statistical analysis to identify client characteristics with a significant relation to outcomes and to establish their predictive power relative to other variables.

The results were used to construct an assessment tool with two separate indices to estimate the likelihood of (1) future self-neglect, and (2) future abuse or neglect by another person. Practitioners using the tool were required to complete both indices and to give a rating to each item. For example, question 8 on the 'self-neglect' index reads as follows (Johnson et al., 2010: 40):

SN8. Number of inpatient hospital stays in past 12 months

a. None 0

b. One or two 1

c. Three or more 2

At the end of the assessment, all the items on each index are added together to give an overall score for likelihood of self-neglect, and an overall score for maltreatment by others. The highest of these two scores is used to classify the level of risk, as follows:

Self-neglect Score	Maltreatment Score	Scored Risk Level
_____ 0–2	_____ 0–2	_____ Low
_____ 3–5	_____ 3–5	_____ Moderate
_____ 6 +	_____ 6 +	_____ High

Finally, there are some criteria for overriding or adjusting the scored risk level in order to allow consideration of important contextual information, such as homelessness or loss of access to critical services. The practitioner then allocates a final risk level subject to managerial approval.

After developing the risk assessment tool, Johnson et al. (2010) tested its validity by following up the outcomes of cases across the three risk classifications. As expected, a higher proportion of cases that were classified as high risk were subsequently substantiated or re-investigated than those classified as medium risk, and the latter in turn were more likely to have negative outcomes than low risk cases. The authors conclude by recommending that such actuarial instruments be integrated into case management in order to assess families more accurately and prioritise services where they are most needed. They emphasise that such tools are meant to augment and not substitute for the judgement and skill of social workers.

'Satisficing' and Bounded Rationality

The literature examined above makes a convincing case for analytical decision-making but also indicates how easily it can be undermined! This is a significant issue for social workers, who are constantly faced with situations where there is insufficient time, information, or resources to follow every step of an explicit process. Moreover, as Taylor (2010) points out, many decisions are not 'one-off' major events but small and incremental; they contribute to an iterative process of assessment, intervention, and care planning that may take months or even years to complete. Emergencies and crises often require fast, practical action, or imperfect 'holding decisions' that allay the immediate crisis and buy time to gather more information and explore further options. Rather than being overwhelmed by the task, practitioners must try to make their decisions as rational as possible within the constraints and possibilities available.

Making decisions in complex situations, characterised by uncertainty, unpredictability, incomplete information, and time pressure, leads us to models of 'bounded rationality' (Gigerenzer and Grassmeier, 2011). Unlike completely rational models, which take time and assume that all the necessary information is to hand, bounded rationality enables practitioners to make quick and sensible decisions that are 'good enough' to address the immediate concerns. This approach is sometimes known as 'satisficing', and is closely related to the concept of heuristics, which was introduced earlier. Heuristics are usually associated with the largely unconscious cognitive processes that skew our judgement when making intuitive decisions (see above). However, heuristics can also be deployed in a more conscious way when a quick decision is called for, e.g. when responding to an initial referral or to an unexpected crisis. In these circumstances, professionals can apply their knowledge and practice wisdom in a deliberately limited way to make reasonable decisions.

Taylor (2017) describes this kind of heuristic model as 'small-range', or 'fast and frugal'; such models are suited to contexts where it would be impracticable to try and collect *all* the information that is possibly relevant to a decision. For example, professionals may adopt simple rules (see Introduction) around searching for information and when to stop searching. When dealing with a child protection referral, an initial contact worker might look out for a limited number of risk factors that are associated with serious injury to children, such as indicators of violent behaviour, rather than embarking straight away on a lengthy assessment of the full range of possible variables relating to child abuse with their appropriate statistical weighting (Taylor, 2017). The aim is to simplify information in order to manage complexity, which is a key attribute of human cognition. Of course, this is also a potential source of bias, as discussed above, and later assessments may require a more comprehensive analysis of risk factors. Nonetheless, social workers are more likely to encounter situations where there is a high level of uncertainty, and limited time and information to make a decision, than those where all the relevant risk factors are known and quantified. In this sense, heuristic models that have been developed specifically for such contexts may be entirely sensible – they display what Taylor (2017) calls 'psycho-social rationality', i.e. an understanding of 'how people act in a rational way in a complex world' (2017: 1047).

CONCLUSION

This chapter has explored some of the challenges associated with judgement and decision-making in social work. Differentiating between 'good', 'bad', and 'acceptable' decisions is subject to overlapping ethical, legal, and institutional concerns, and may be subject to hindsight bias when decisions are reviewed in the light of adverse outcomes. In this context, the distinction between analytic and intuitive judgement may also be more ambiguous than it first seems. On the face of it, there is plenty of evidence to show that clinical judgement on its own (along with gut instinct and professional 'hunches') is unreliable and almost always outperformed by systematic decision-making tools. Such tools are also valued for their ability to incorporate research evidence on risk factors. On the other hand, practitioners dealing with complex situations often require some sort of heuristic model in order to make decisions quickly in the context of limited information. In these contexts, 'fast and frugal' approaches may be considered to be an appropriate and rational response to the demands placed on the decision-maker.

BUILDING AND MAINTAINING RELATIONSHIPS

4

CHAPTER SUMMARY

The focus of this chapter is on the relationship between social workers and their clients. Initial considerations include the significance of relationships within the social work role and the skills required to build and maintain relationships with people in order to help them to achieve positive change. These ideas are integrated into an account of the 'helping relationship' drawing on the counselling theories of Rogers and Egan. The chapter then outlines some key psychodynamic concepts for understanding the underlying dynamics of practitioner–client interactions and behaviour, including transference and counter-transference, containment, and holding. There follows a discussion of complexity in relationship-based practice, which includes working with strong feelings, understanding and addressing resistance, and managing dilemmas and transitions in long-term work.

INTRODUCTION

It seems a truism to state that relationships have always been at the heart of social work. Yet it is also true to say that relationship-based perspectives have made something of a comeback in the social work literature over the past decade (Ruch, 2005; Ruch et al., 2010; Howe, 1998; Murphy et al., 2013; Trevithick, 2003). The contradiction arises because such perspectives have long been associated with the psychodynamic tradition in social work, which came under sustained attack from behaviourist and 'radical' perspectives during the 1970s (Howe, 1998). In subsequent decades, client–practitioner relationships were ascribed rather less importance in social work, which also had to adapt to institutional changes that gathered pace during the 1980s and 1990s. These changes included a growing emphasis on legalistic ways of working, reinforced by the managerial control and prescription of social work through guidelines, procedures, and assessment frameworks. In more recent years, it has become common to record and audit social work practice as 'workflows' on computer databases, one consequence of the shift from social to 'informational' knowledge described by Parton (2008). In summary, social workers – particularly in statutory settings – have become increasingly technocratic in their dealings with citizens: filling out assessment forms, deciding thresholds, allocating resources, and coordinating care packages. Most social workers' time is nowadays spent in the office (Jones et al., 2013), while higher workloads and ever tighter financial constraints have meant even less time to get to know people and understand their lives.

Despite – and indeed because of – these developments, there has been an effort in recent years to reclaim the importance of relationship-based practice. In part, this can be attributed to the increasingly complex and multifaceted nature of the problems encountered by social workers. As we have seen in previous chapters, complex problems do not lend themselves to simple, technocratic solutions. Instead, they require careful, sensitive understanding of the constellation of factors involved in each case, including the social complexity of human interactions and behaviour. As Trevithick (2003: 168) points out, 'a successful outcome may not be possible unless time is taken – and skills used – to establish some form of meaningful and constructive connection with the individuals in question'. This chapter will explore the nature of such connections, as well as the skills needed to build and sustain them, before moving on to the opportunities and pitfalls of building positive relationships in social work.

The Social Work Relationship

How should we characterise the professional relationship between social workers and the people they work with? Howe (1998) describes three broad positions. The first is to regard the relationship simply as 'a function of the social work role', whereas the second position acknowledges the need for social workers to acquire specific 'relationship skills' in order to work effectively with service users and help them achieve their goals. The third position, which is developed in the main part of Howe's paper, is to see the relationship as the fundamental basis for social work practice, the place where 'most of the important things happen, for good or for ill, whether social workers recognise it or not' (Howe, 1998: 45). The latter is congruent with the principles of psychodynamic casework referred to earlier, and subsumes the other two positions within an overarching framework of practice based on empathetic and authentic communication, reflection, the use of self, and the analysis of emotions. Nonetheless, it is important not to dismiss the importance of the social work role, or the skills needed to engage people and establish a connection with them, as these play a significant part in shaping the relationship itself.

The social work role

Social workers typically have a set of roles that are interconnected:

- They are registered members of a profession, bound by associated codes of ethics and practice
- They are employees of an agency or organisation, with a remit for carrying out tasks and activities with a defined group of people
- When working in a statutory context, they are agents of the state, operating under the duties and powers set out by legislation and statutory guidance
- They are part of a network of multi-agency provision, often with the role of coordinating a care plan involving other professionals
- They play an important role in the lives of individuals and families, especially at times when people need additional resources and expertise to address the issues that matter to them

Arguably the last role is the most important one, which all the others should be oriented around (see Chapter 8). In practice, social workers often find themselves trying to balance the competing priorities. As noted previously, this may mean negotiating dilemmas around care and control, risk and need, best interests and autonomy, protection and prevention, and how these dilemmas are resolved will affect the professional relationship. A key issue in this respect is power. Each of the role types outlined above is a potential source of power over others, e.g. the knowledge and competence attributed to professionals in their area of expertise, or the ability to recommend how scarce resources are allocated (French and Raven, 1968). Relationships between social workers and the people they work with may be equitable and harmonious. At other times, they may be prone to power dynamics, such as oppression, antagonism, collusion, compliance, and resistance, which undermine the purpose of providing a service. Learning to recognise and understand such dynamics is an essential part of a social worker's skillset, and is explored at various points in this chapter (and also in Chapters 5 and 6).

It is worth bearing in mind the impact that circumstances have on a practitioner's role, and therefore on her relationship with people. This can be seen in Case Study 4.1 below, where Anne's response to Karina's concerns may lead to fundamental shifts in their relationship.

CASE STUDY 4.1

Anne and Karina

Anne is a social worker who runs a parenting group at a children's centre. One of the mothers attending the group is Karina, who has two daughters aged two and four, and a 12-year-old son, Robert. In the fourth week, Karina stays behind after the group and tells Anne she is worried about Robert's behaviour. He has started leaving the house in the middle of the night, locks himself in the bathroom for long periods of time, and sometimes seems to be conversing with people who are not in the room. She asks Anne for advice about what she should do.

- How would you describe Anne's current role and her relationship with the family?
- How might that role and relationship be affected by the new information?

From a relationship-based perspective, it becomes apparent that people and their lives do not easily fit into what social workers might regard as their formal role. In Case Study 4.1, Anne's initial involvement with Karina stems from her role as parenting group facilitator. This role is presumably part of a broader remit around family support and early intervention focused on parents with young children. However, the issue presented by Karina relates to an older child, Robert, who is possibly experiencing mental health problems. The issue itself may fall outside Anne's formal remit, even though she is the one who has the relationship with the family. She may be able to adapt her role to some extent to encompass these new concerns, e.g. visiting the home to meet Robert and then liaising if necessary with mental health services. She could prove to be a valuable resource in helping the family to acknowledge and cope with the anxieties, fears, and prejudices associated with mental illness. Nonetheless, depending on what support is needed, it is likely that Robert and his mother will have to meet and manage multiple relationships with various other professionals.

Relationship skills: authenticity, empathy, and respect

Most social workers would probably agree that forming relationships with clients – however brief the relationship or reluctant the client – is an important part of their role. Like any aspect of social work it requires a variety of skills. Some of these skills may be acquired through formal training and gradually refined through practice experience, while others stem more intuitively from a practitioner's personality and 'natural' way of relating to people. A good starting point for considering relationships in social work is therefore to consider the meaning of authenticity in a professional context. In this respect, a simple but useful concept from the north European tradition of social pedagogy is the distinction between 'Three Ps': the professional, personal, and private self (Eichsteller and Holthoff, 2012).

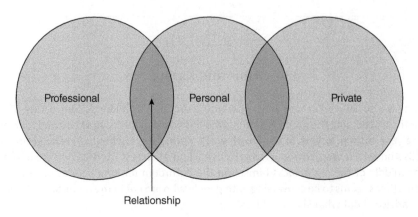

Figure 4.1   The 'Three Ps': professional, personal and private self

Figure 4.1 represents the 3Ps model and its implications for relationships in social work. The professional self, shown on the left, draws on various forms of knowledge, including evidence from research, laws and policies, as well as practice wisdom, in order to ensure that the relationship has a defined purpose and is acceptable in social, legal, and ethical terms. The personal self, in the centre, is able to engage with clients in an authentic and spontaneous way, express genuine feelings, and sometimes share life experiences. For example, in a study of palliative care social work, Beresford et al. (2008) found that service users valued 'reciprocity' in their relationships with social workers. However, as Turney (2010) points out, the unequal distribution of power and authority in social work relationships means that there is a distinction to be made between 'friendliness' and 'friendship', particularly in areas of social work where people do not necessarily have a choice about 'using' services. As a result, social workers need to place boundaries around areas of their life that they do not want to share and should remain outside of the relationship; this 'private self' (on the right-hand side of Figure 4.1) might include details of private family life, for example, or of personal difficulties that are still raw and unresolved. The relationship is therefore defined in the overlap between the professional and personal self; while the private informs the personal, it is kept separate from any interactions with clients. Understanding and negotiating these boundaries is not straightforward and requires social workers to notice and reflect on patterns of communication in particular cases (see also Chapter 5).

Closely linked to the idea of authenticity in social work is a set of skills associated with empathy and empathetic communication (Gerdes and Segal, 2011; Hepworth et al., 2006). Perhaps the best-known clinical application of empathy emerged in the work of Carl Rogers (1957), and has since exerted great influence on psychotherapy and counselling as well as 'person-centred' approaches to social work (Neukrug et al., 2013). Rogers saw empathy as a holistic set of skills that together formed the cornerstone of the therapeutic relationship:

To sense the client's private world as if it were your own, but without ever losing the 'as if' quality – this is empathy, and this seems essential to therapy. To sense the client's anger, fear, or confusion as if it were your own, yet without your own anger, fear, or confusion getting bound up in it, is the condition we are endeavoring to describe. (Rogers, 1957: 99)

Rogers' concept involves the therapist in an emotional but also rational and reflective process of attuning oneself to the inner world of another person and trying to understand it from their perspective. This is a skilled process because the therapist must listen attentively to what their client says and also demonstrate that they have understood correctly. What is more, it is possible to achieve a more advanced or 'additive' form of empathy that can reveal more about clients' feelings and experiences than they may be consciously aware of themselves (Neukrug et al., 2013). Similar ideas can be found in the techniques of 'active listening' that many social workers learn both formally and informally (Rogers and Welch, 2009), and which also convey the idea that practitioners can develop more advanced skills in empathetic communication through specialist training and experience.

The final cornerstone of relationships in social work, particularly in the humanistic, person-centred tradition, is respect for the person with whom one is working. Carl Rogers' term was 'unconditional positive regard', suggesting that 'growth and change are more likely to occur the more that the counselor is experiencing a warm, positive, acceptant attitude toward what *is* in the client' (Rogers, 1973: 180). Gerard Egan, whose work is discussed below, refers to respect as the 'foundation value' for any helping relationship (Egan, 2013: 46). In a similar vein, the 'strengths perspective' in social work (Goldstein, 2002) invokes the centrality of relationships based on 'respect for and affirmation of human dignity' (Gray, 2011: 7). Hepworth et al. (2006) also discuss the importance of respect or 'non-possessive warmth' as one of the core conditions of social work practice, which they link to the operationalising of ethical principles around client self-determination, professional boundaries, informed consent, and confidentiality.

The helPiNG RelatiONShiP

A defining feature of relationship-based approaches is the central importance of the relationship itself in the process of change. Building and maintaining relationships with people is seen as more than just an aspect of the professional role or as one set of skills among many. Although contemporary social work often seems to be geared around the written (or electronic) artefacts of assessments, reports, and care plans, relationships continue to be 'where the important things happen' (Howe, 1998) even if this does not always accord with bureaucratic and managerial priorities. Egan's notion of the 'skilled helper' embodies many of the principles of such an approach (Egan, 2013). What he calls 'helping relationships' are established on the basis of respectful, empathetic, and authentic communication. Helping relationships aim to achieve client-led outcomes via a three-stage process.

Explore the client's existing situation ('What is going on?')

The first stage of a helping relationship involves establishing rapport and trust, bearing in mind that clients may be reluctant or resistant to being 'helped' – particularly if they have had little choice about it. Having gained some sort of initial acceptance, the practitioner can go on to explore what matters to the individual or people involved, how they think about themselves and evaluate their lives. Egan calls this helping clients to 'tell their stories', although he goes on to distinguish between 'the real story' and 'the right story' from the client's point of view. The aim is to identify the most important problems but also the resources and opportunities that are available to people, and in doing so challenge negative or misleading thought processes, distinguish between 'wants' and 'needs', and clarify priorities for action.

Help the client establish aims and goals ('What do I want instead?')

The second stage aims to achieve some sort of change in perspective. As clients develop a more objective and informed understanding of their situation they should begin to see that better options exist for them. The practitioner's skill lies in finding ways to facilitate this shift in thinking, for example by demonstrating (even in a minor way) the possibility of proactively tackling problems with the right expertise and support (see also Davis, 2016). This approach acknowledges the importance of intrinsic motivation (Benabou and Tirole, 2003; Ryan and Deci, 2000), i.e. the individual's own desire to change their lives for the better. Social workers – particularly in statutory settings – often engage clients initially through some form of extrinsic motivation, i.e. contingent rewards and punishments, such as compliance with a court order or the prospect of their child 'coming off' a protection plan. However, longer-term change cannot rely on extrinsic motivation alone because people need to be both competent and confident enough to sustain any short-term improvements. The incremental achievement of mutually agreed-on goals can help build this sense of competence and self-efficacy (Bandura and Schunk, 1981). In the field of drug addiction, for example, a professional may undertake some form of 'consciousness-raising' with a client who is contemplating change, but it is the client's willingness to evaluate their own life that unlocks their capacity to take action (Prochaska and Diclemente, 1986).

Help the client design a way forward ('How do I get there?')

The third stage in Egan's model empowers clients to take action by considering possible paths towards their goals, choosing the strategy that makes the most sense for them, and then 'crafting a practical action plan' (Egan, 2013: 345). The action plan is designed to move individuals from their current situation, which they have found to be problematic for various reasons, towards a preferable one. However, such transitions are rarely smooth, and setbacks may leave people feeling vulnerable and exposed.

It is therefore important to consider interim or 'adaptive' goals that can be achieved within reasonable limits of time and energy, leading towards a single 'big' goal that might seem too daunting on its own. In this stage, practitioners can also help clients to predict and pre-empt potential problems and obstacles, and to reframe challenges as opportunities for personal growth and resilience. As people implement their plan of action, drawing on their own resources and building their networks of support, the need for the helping relationship will in many cases gradually fade.

As Davis (2016) points out, rather than just 'providing a service', the aim of such work is to build capability and responsibility – not just in individuals but also in communities. This is partly because the relationship between practitioner and citizen provides the essential medium though which an 'envisioned future' can be discussed and achieved. It is also because social work interventions generally try to improve people's relationships with those close to them; sustainable change often means developing the networks of intimacy and support that contribute to individual resilience. It is therefore important for social workers to realise that their relationships with clients are not exclusive but are shaped and defined by a constellation of other relationships. Indeed, the practitioner's ability to work effectively may well depend on other relationships about which she may have little knowledge or control.

REFLECTIVE EXERCISE 4.1

THE HELPING RELATIONSHIP

Think about an occasion when you helped someone, either in a professional or personal capacity. In the light of the section above on the helping relationship, consider the following questions:

1. What was the 'real story' behind the person's problematic situation? How did you help him/her to understand that story?
2. Was the initial motivation for change intrinsic or extrinsic? Did that change over time?
3. What was the main goal of change? Were any incremental goals needed in order to build confidence and move in the right direction?
4. What networks of support are around the person to help them sustain the change?

PSYChODYNAMIC APPROACHES

Psychodynamic approaches include a range of theoretical frameworks that have common roots in Freudian psychoanalysis (Brandell, 2013; Goldstein, 1995; Bower and Trowell, 1995). They are underpinned by the idea that early relationships and experiences are fundamental for our emotional and psychological development in later life. A distinction is made between conscious and unconscious mental processes, both of which drive human behaviour. As with the System 1 and System 2 processes discussed in Chapter 3 (from a completely different field of psychology) we are inclined to overestimate the influence of the conscious, rational part of our minds; much of our behaviour is driven by unconscious motivations and impulses that are not easily recognised. For this reason, strong emotions such as anger, distress, and anxiety may be important indicators of unconscious processes, and often play an important role in therapeutic or psychodynamic interventions. Other psychodynamic insights include the powerful role of anxiety in shaping our responses to stressful or overwhelming situations (Trowell, 1995), and the recognition that seemingly irrational or extreme behaviour may be rooted in traumatic or abusive experiences in early life.

Transference and counter-transference

Psychodynamic approaches reinforce the need to reflect on how we interact with others and how they respond to us, remaining alert for emotional cues that may signify important information or shifts in attitude. Ruch (2010b) refers to this process as 'making the invisible visible'. In social work, the concepts of transference and counter-transference are often used to delve beneath the surface of relationships – both the remarkably smooth as well as the overtly problematic. In simple terms, 'transference is the client's personally distorted way of relating to people; counter-transference is the worker's distorted way of viewing or relating to the client' (Wood, 1971, cited in Abbott, 2003: 37). Transference is generally linked to the unconscious influence of impulses and feelings originating in significant early relationships, particularly with parents. For example, a client who has unresolved feelings about being raised by a very authoritarian parent may be unconsciously inclined to view their social worker as a punitive authority figure rather than as a supportive, helpful person. Perceived similarities in terms of gender, age, or other characteristics may also play a role. This 'transfer' of feelings from the original object to a new one may then elicit an unconscious response on the part of the worker, i.e. 'counter-transference'. In the example above, the social worker may 'accept' the client's implicit invitation to behave in an uncharacteristically harsh or punitive way, without necessarily realising that her behaviour is being affected by these dynamics. Transference and counter-transference may occur to varying degrees in different cases, depending on the social worker's own personal history but also on their capacity to reflect on the nature and quality of their interactions with others (see Chapter 5).

Containment and holding

Given that practitioners often have to manage emotions that originate in the clients' own experiences, it follows that when those experiences have been traumatic or abusive, the associated emotions may well be negative, powerful, and even unbearable. This phenomenon affects many areas of social work, where secondary traumatic stress is viewed as 'an occupational hazard of providing direct services to traumatized populations' including the survivors of childhood abuse, domestic violence, violent crime, disasters, war and terrorism (Bride, 2007: 63). Although social workers are not usually perceived as therapists, their relationships with clients often have a therapeutic element. For example, social workers may help clients understand and cope with the psychological consequences of grief, loss, and trauma. This also applies to people who receive a service primarily because they are a source of risk to others but who are themselves survivors of violence or abuse, or where the involvement of services itself causes distress. For example, Ruch (2010a) describes the difficult balancing act performed by a social worker who gives evidence in court as part of care proceedings but is still viewed on some level as a source of support by the child's mother.

Bion's (1962) concept of 'containment' is often cited in relation to managing emotions that have the potential to be psychologically damaging. In Bion's sense, containment refers to the process through which an infant projects overpowering feelings onto the primary caregiver, who is then able to modify and return them in a way that is tolerable. In other words, the infant is 'contained' and the mother is the 'container'. Over time, the experience of containment allows inchoate feelings to be brought into the realm of conscious thought and language, where they become more manageable. These early interactions are fundamental to healthy emotional development and enable the child to understand and regulate their emotional responses in later life. Winnicott (1965) developed a similar concept called 'holding', which linked the infant's experience of being held (in his mother's arms) to the safe and nurturing 'holding environment' that promotes trust, efficacy, and self-regulation in the developing child. Such ideas are also central to attachment theory, in which an internal working model of relationships based on 'security' emerges from a consistent experience of attuned and responsive caregiving (Howe, 2005). If the child's experience of containment or holding is inadequate or truncated, on the other hand, there may be developmental consequences in terms of relational difficulties and 'a reduced capacity to manage emotions' (Steckley, 2010).

These ideas highlight the potential for social workers to provide a containing experience or a 'holding environment' through their relationships with vulnerable people. This may be the result of an explicitly psychodynamic approach to practice, which is apparent in most of the case studies discussed in Ruch et al. (2010). However, such skills are relevant to all types of social work intervention. For example, Ferguson (2010) describes an example of what he calls 'systemic casework', observing a social worker who 'developed and skilfully used the relationship with mother to "hold" and contain her emotionally and build up her internal resources as she struggled with drugs' (Ferguson, 2010: 33). Ferguson also makes the point that this social worker saw herself primarily as a 'case manager', a technocratic self-description that does not do justice to the expertise and support she is actually providing. In effect, the institutional context – in this case, of statutory child protection – discouraged the practitioner from acknowledging the emotional labour involved or even any practical and therapeutic benefits for the client. This could be seen as an example of 'de-professionalisation' (Ayre and Calder, 2010) and also matters because social workers themselves need to be held and contained due to the powerful emotions associated with their work. As noted already, failure to help social workers to understand and manage the impact of overwhelming feelings can impair their ability to engage clients effectively, while an inability – or self-protective reluctance – to understand the world from the client's point of view can affect judgements of need and risk. Such tendencies have often been observed in relation to child abuse (Cooper, 2004; Ferguson, 2005). As Ruch points out:

> the primitive feelings generated by complex, unpredictable situations can have the effect of disrupting cognition and fragmenting thought processes. Such experiences make it difficult for an individual or group to think coherently about a situation. (Ruch, 2007: 662).

Splitting and projection

Splitting is a concept associated with the work of the psychoanalyst Melanie Klein (Klein, 1946; Segal, 2012). It is connected to the psychological defence mechanisms identified by Freud, which include denial, repression, avoidance, and displacement (Trowell, 1995). These mechanisms are ways for the individual to deal with anxiety and other strong emotions that threaten to overwhelm the psyche (see Chapter 6 for their application to organisations and groups). In Klein's sense, splitting involves separating out the good from the bad aspects of an experience, in order to deal with the anxiety provoked by ambiguity and uncertainty – particularly in close or caregiving relationships. An example might be a young child who regards one of their parents as embodying all of the nurturing and satisfying elements of the parental relationship, while the other is seen as the source of frustration and angry feelings. Over time, the child learns to tolerate the ambiguity of relationships and the existence of contradictory feelings towards the same person. However, when a person's experience of care has been very inconsistent or abusive, it may be more difficult for them to integrate strong conflicting emotions. The tendency may then be to project the 'split-off' feelings – particularly the painful, unwanted ones – onto another 'object', i.e. someone else. As with transference and counter-transference, such dynamics can lead practitioners to experience and identify with the emotions being projected onto them, and may even cause communication difficulties and splits in professional networks around vulnerable or traumatised clients (see Conway, 2009).

CASE EXERCISE 4.1 APPLYING PSYCHODYNAMIC THEORY

Can you use some of the psychodynamic concepts outlined above to understand the following scenarios?

1. Daniel is a social worker in an adult social care team. He is working with a 70-year-old woman, Iris, whose son moved to Australia many years ago. Iris is always delighted when Daniel visits her and insists that he stay for another cup of tea when he gets up to go. Daniel realises he is spending more time on visits than he usually does and although he likes Iris this aspect of their relationship is starting to annoy him.

2. Selena is an experienced foster carer, who has just taken in two siblings, Ronnie (8) and Lara (5). Both children experienced neglect by their parents and were often left unsupervised in the family home. Ronnie is prone to nightmares and often wakes up screaming and shouting. Selena decides to 'swaddle' him at such times by tucking him up tightly in the sheets, stays up with him for a while reading a story, and leaves the light on when she leaves the room. After a few days the nightmares stop and Ronnie does not wake up as much, although he continues to want to have a nightlight on when he sleeps.

3. Sophia is a newly qualified social worker in a community mental health team. She is allocated as care coordinator to Josephine, who has a borderline personality disorder and often suffers from acute anxiety. Josephine seems very taken with Sophia and tells her that she has never had a social worker who is so responsive and understanding. Sophia feels a great boost in confidence as she had been warned by a colleague that Josephine was 'a nightmare to work with'. However, one day she phones Josephine to rearrange a planned appointment due to an emergency with one of her other clients. Josephine is furious with Sophia, accusing her of being unprofessional and stating her intention to lodge a complaint against her before hanging up. Sophia feels bewildered and deflated, and worries that she has done something wrong.

COMPLEX RELATIONSHIPS

In the above discussion, some readers may already have noted a thematic connection with Chapter 2, which was also concerned with the effects of volatile dynamics in complex cases. Psychodynamic theory explains the influence that such dynamics can have on individual behaviour and thought processes as well as those of groups and institutions (see Chapter 6). In other words, powerful and potentially disorientating emotions and unconscious impulses are causal factors; they are part and parcel of dealing with complex situations and should not simply be dismissed as aberrant, irrational, or unprofessional. However, such ideas sit uncomfortably with the technical-rational approach discussed in the Introduction and Chapter 2, with its emphasis on certainty and on determining and controlling linear patterns of cause-and-effect. From this perspective, unpredictability is associated with dangerous, uncontrollable energies that must be battened down beneath protective layers of procedures and protocols (Woods et al., 2010). Taken to the extreme, this type of approach can become divorced from the overall aims of care and intervention. For example, Steckley (2010) argues that the use of physical restraint in residential care settings must be understood in terms of the therapeutic context of containment and holding environments; if deployed primarily as a means of subduing aggressive and 'out-of-control' children, the chances of abusive and re-traumatising forms of restraint are likely to be higher.

More generally, the distinction between vulnerability and dangerousness is often a fine line in social work, particularly in statutory and forensic contexts where risk-to-others and risk-to-self may assume particular significance within a 'blaming system'

(Parton, 2011). When development is viewed in terms of dynamic systems (Thelen and Smith, 1994), deviation from normalised developmental pathways can become reconstituted as a bundle of risk factors that create the potential for a disruptive or even violent eruption of energies (Hood, 2015a). For Nybell (2001), this is linked to changing conceptions of the individual in late modern society, part of which involves conceptualising people in terms of complex systems that become dangerous when unstable. In Nybell's case example, a child whose aggressive and unstable behaviour has marked him out as being in a critical state is described by educators as being 'in meltdown' and is subject to 'wraparound' services composed of multiple interventions designed to 'erect physical and social boundaries around the child' (Nybell, 2001: 225). Unfortunately, these efforts to curb and contain system dynamics are doomed to periodic failure as critical instability builds up towards another burst of disruptive behaviour (see also Rocco-Briggs, 2008). As a result, professionals can begin to feel paralysed and powerless to change recurrent patterns of crisis. The challenge therefore is to understand and find a way of working with the underlying forces driving volatility and instability in complex cases, rather seeking to suppress their manifestation. Meeting this challenge will involve working with and through relationships, and understanding the role of emotions in driving relational dynamics in complex cases.

Working with strong negative feelings

Some of the contributors in Ruch et al. (2010) discuss the challenges faced by social workers who try to sustain relationships in the context of strong negative feelings such as anger and hostility, hopelessness, and despair. Most obviously, the threat or reality of being attacked by a client has serious ramifications for practitioners' welfare and secondarily for their ability to sustain a working relationship. In common with other health and care professions, violence against social workers is a widespread occupational hazard (Newhill, 1995; Ringstad, 2005; Smith, 2005) and although learning to manage aggressive behaviour has long been part of social work training (e.g. Laird, 2014), physical aggression is only one aspect of the range of hostility encountered by social workers. For example, Smith (2010) found that social workers were often more worried about complaints being made against them than they were about the threat of assault; this was also linked to the fear of being criticised in internal investigations and left 'hung out to dry' by their organisations. Unfortunately, having (or believing oneself to have) a positive relationship with a client does not preclude being assaulted by them, especially at times of crisis, which is one reason social workers should not ignore what Smith (2010) calls the 'gift of fear'. This might include warning signs that your client is 'not their usual self', heeding your gut instinct that something is wrong, or maintaining basic keep-safe precautions such as making sure someone in the office knows where you are. Smith also points out that counter-transference dynamics (see above) mean that social workers may sometimes experience strong feelings of animosity towards certain clients, which they may be understandably reluctant to bring up in formal supervision. This suggests a need for independent counselling or psychological de-briefing for frontline practitioners (Raphael and Wilson, 2000), which is still something of a rarity in social work organisations.

Parkinson (2010) discusses the impact of working with depression, which as the most common form of mental ill health is experienced by many users of social services. Building and sustaining a helping relationship based on warmth, empathy, and trust will therefore require practitioners to acknowledge and tolerate painful feelings of deep sadness and distress, as well as low self-worth, rejection, contempt, and suicidal impulses. Despite the difficulties in relating to others that come with depression, Parkinson (2010) argues that social workers can provide a 'therapeutic opportunity' by listening to a client's experiences in order to understand the context of their illness and the factors – including in their family history – which may have led to increased susceptibility. At the same time, there are pitfalls for the unwary – or unsupported – practitioner who may unconsciously seek to avoid dealing with the painful feelings involved in this type of work. An attempt at 'psychic retreat' (Steiner, 2003) may manifest itself in various ways, including the avoidance of contact, looking to transfer the case to a colleague, or minimising the indicators of escalating risk (Parkinson, 2010). Again, the pressure on casework supervision may require additional counselling and debriefing for practitioners experiencing such psychological stressors.

Attending to the positive relationship

Turney (2010) notes that while warm, empathetic, and authentic relationships are valued by social workers and clients alike, practitioners should nonetheless pay as much attention to them as to the relationships that seem to be less positive. This is partly because of the nature of the social work role and the inescapable power difference between professionals and their clients. Friendliness and 'professional closeness' (Kendrick and Smith, 2002) should enable practitioners to share their concerns and conduct difficult conversations in a respectful and open manner. For some practitioners, however, positive feelings may lead instead to the avoidance of conflict, e.g. through fear of 'losing' the good relationship (Hood, 2015a), unfounded optimism based on relatively minor changes (Dingwall et al., 1983), or an unrealistic belief that this relationship will work where previous ones have failed (Brandon, 2009). In some cases, such dynamics may lead to a form of collusion with clients where concerns are consistently minimised and risks downplayed. Turney (2010) draws on the Kleinian notion of splitting (see above) to remind practitioners to be careful when clients seem to compare them favourably to other professionals or previous social workers; being idealised as 'the good worker' may be initially flattering (or a welcome change!) but can contribute to interprofessional conflicts (Hood, 2015a) as well as masking or misrepresenting the combination of care and control that is characteristic of the social work role (Howe, 2014). Relationships that are superficially positive may also serve to inhibit effective intervention through the phenomenon of 'disguised compliance' (Turney, 2012), where clients maintain the appearance of cooperation but are not motivated to change their behaviour, or stage-manage visits and meetings in order to create a misleading impression of family life.

Working with resistance

Resistance to services is a very common feature of social work, particularly in statutory settings (Forrester et al., 2012; Ferguson, 2011; Barber, 1991). From a psychodynamic perspective, resistant behaviour including aggression can be linked to psychological defence mechanisms that are amplified in the interaction between practitioner and client, e.g. through transference and counter-transference responses (see above). Similarly some clients might be described as being 'hard-to-reach' (Kroll, 2010) because their earlier experiences of family or institutional life have predisposed them to be wary and distrustful of prospective carers or 'helpers'. As Forrester et al. (2012) point out, users of social services are often excluded and stigmatised because of their problems and behaviour, creating strong feelings of shame that can inhibit an open dialogue with professionals. Clients may be deeply ambivalent about the need for change, which could serve to entrench their resistance if efforts are made to persuade or coerce them (Forrester and Harwin, 2011). Finally, even when clients recognise the need for change, they may lack any kind of confidence in their ability to do so; in such circumstances, the prospect of draconian intervention (such as the removal of their child) might actually prove demotivating, with feelings of despair leading to an increase in problem behaviour such as substance misuse (Forrester et al., 2012; Forrester and Harwin, 2011).

Approaches that focus on individual factors – i.e. characteristics of the resistant or 'difficult' client – can underplay the significance of wider contextual factors. It is important for social workers to recognise the role that their interventions might play (or be perceived to play) in aggravating and perpetuating social equalities (Bywaters et al., 2016) and in the surveillance and control of marginalised communities (Bilson and Martin, 2016). In the tradition of radical social work (Bailey and Brake, 1975), resistance could even be seen as a justifiable response on the part of those communities. Nonetheless, it is important social workers and other professionals are not disempowered from recognising and responding to abuse and exploitation, for example because they are worried about appearing racist (Jay, 2014). In a minority of cases, resistance to services may in fact be a deliberate strategy of deceit and obfuscation (Laming, 2003).

Navigating such treacherous waters requires a confident, skilled, and stable workforce, as well as a supportive working environment in which organisational learning takes precedence over blaming people for mistakes (see Chapter 8). Unfortunately this is not always the case (Munro, 2010) and some social workers may well be inclined to take a 'tough line' on resistance. In a study of communication styles in child protection, Forrester et al. (2008) found that while most practitioners were able to clearly express their concerns about a child (to an actor playing the role of the parent), they adopted such a confrontational manner that the 'parent' became even less inclined to cooperate. As Forrester et al. (2012) point out, similar findings have emerged in studies of motivational interviewing (Miller and Rollnick, 2002); practitioners who are more confrontational create more resistance on the part of clients and this is also associated with poorer intervention outcomes. The ability to combine openness and clarity (in terms of concerns) with respect, authenticity, and empathy (in terms of communication style) is what enables practitioners to reduce resistance and build the motivation for change. On this basis, Forrester et al. (2012) make a case for the use of motivational interviewing techniques to work with families in child protection work, and more generally it will be apparent that the same skills were discussed earlier in connection with helping relationships.

Long-term relationships

McMahon (2010) notes that most social services are geared towards short-term or at least time-limited periods of intervention, owing to the laudable aim of empowering clients to lead their lives independently as well as the less laudable aim of saving money. However, some people will have a longer-term need for professional support, e.g. because of a severe disability or chronic health problems linked to old age. In such cases, the relationship with a particular social worker may last for several years and with the social work agency for even longer. McMahon (2010) points out that since people's needs change over time, organisations need to find ways to maintain a rounded picture of the individual even as workers come and go. This puts an onus on communication and partnership between social work agencies, carers, and family members. There can also be a tension between dependence and independence in long-term social work relationships; practitioners will need to find the right balance between caring for a person and developing the person's life skills and sense of self-competence. The pitfalls of excessive emotional involvement, such as social workers who want to 'rescue' clients or become overwhelmed at times of crisis, find their counterpart in the attitude of professionals who are too detached and uninvolved to really understand the other's needs. McMahon describes a stance that avoids both of these extreme positions, 'a place between "too close in" and "too far out"', which allows social workers to 'provide an emotional holding that helps someone in turn to manage their own feelings' (McMahon, 2010: 152). Long-term relationships also create additional challenges around endings, not only for clients but also for practitioners. In this respect, institutions have an important role in acknowledging and managing people's experience of bereavement and loss, most obviously in settings where end of life care is being provided but also where life transitions mark the end of a period of long-term involvement such as foster care or residential education.

CONCLUSiON

The introductory chapter to this book highlighted the importance of understanding how people interact, communicate, and perceive themselves, or what might be termed the 'social complexity' of any system involving human beings. This chapter has focused on one aspect of that complexity, namely the relationships between social workers and their clients, while the relationships that professionals have with each other are considered in Chapter 6. One of the key themes in both chapters is that people's thoughts and feelings – including the unconscious or apparently 'irrational' ones – have a causal influence on actions and behaviour. Relationships should not be considered as a vehicle for interventions, they *are* an intervention in themselves, and this is reflected in the continuing relevance of writers in the counselling tradition such as Rogers and Egan for the practice of humane and effective social work. Furthermore, the psychodynamic concepts explored here tell us that building and maintaining the 'helping relationship' is not just a matter of technical proficiency, or a linear outcome of the techniques of active listening and empathetic communication. Of course having these skills helps enormously but practitioners must bear in mind that relationships are mediated by many factors beyond their control: events, memories, family histories, similarities and contrasts, lucky as well as unlucky coincidences. Most of all, relationships are influenced by other relationships. Complexity is the result: in such circumstances relationships will be unpredictable, unstable, and sometimes volatile. The expert practitioner will be aware of this but will understand and work with uncertainty. Key to such resilience is the capacity and opportunity to practise reflectively, and this is the subject of the next chapter.

ReflecTiNG ON PRactice

5

CHAPTER SUMMARY

The chapter examines the role of reflection in helping social workers to understand and manage complexity. It begins with some overarching theories and concepts from the work of John Dewey and Donald Schön before exploring what is meant by reflective practice and critical reflection in social work. There follows an account of key areas for reflection, such as emotions, ethical dilemmas, and power dynamics, with common applications and tools designed to help practitioners think about these issues. The chapter concludes by putting the reflective process in a wider institutional context, outlining the concept of the learning organisation and the importance of supervision for reflective practice.

iNTRODUCtiON

Reflection means different things to different people, and its prominent place in social work training and education has been questioned by some (Ixer, 1999). Nonetheless, the literature on reflection in professional practice is closely linked to many of the concerns explored in this book. A central idea is that social workers benefit from structured ways of thinking about messy, uncertain, and unpredictable situations, about relationships and social dynamics, impulses and emotions, the use of power and authority, and the role of ethics and values. There are no technical fixes to such issues, no toolkit for the perfect intervention strategy. Instead there is the equally messy and uncertain business of developing professional expertise, so that social workers gradually acquire the knowledge and skills to undertake such complex, demanding work without being overwhelmed or paralysed. As we shall see, it is the conscious, purposeful nature of reflection that distinguishes it from just 'thinking'; even seemingly intuitive adjustments, the 'thinking-while-doing' that professionals exhibit when dealing with complex problems, evolve over time through specialist training and experience. Reflection is therefore a way for social workers to learn about themselves, to understand their practice through an in-depth exploration of what they do and why they do it. Another theme of this chapter is that while reflection is often presented as an individual activity – as thinking and learning often are – it is fundamentally social in nature. In the literature it is often presented as a dialogue – with the situation, with the citizen, with a supervisor, with a colleague, or in a group of professionals. As such, reflection must be placed in its social context, which means considering not only how organisations facilitate the learning of practitioners but also how organisations themselves learn from their collective forms of practice. However, before exploring these ideas further, it is necessary to define the concept of reflection and explain its relevance to working with complexity in social work.

Theories of Reflection

Wilson et al. (2011: 13) consider reflection to be 'holistic thinking, which embraces facts and feelings, artistic and scientific understanding, and subjective and objective perspectives'. In a professional context, reflection is linked to processes of learning and the development of expertise; the 'ongoing process of reflection allows for practitioners to develop their theory from their own experience' (Fook, 2002: 40). It requires close attention to the way knowledge is situated in real-world contexts and challenges the notion that practitioners just need to learn and apply foundational knowledge, i.e. supposedly universal theories about human behaviour and how to change it. Instead, professionals have to adapt and adjust their approach to individual people and situations as their use of formal knowledge is refracted through the complexity of personal interactions and relationships. This is not to say that reflection is 'unscientific'; on the contrary, it has been described as a 'systematic, rigorous, disciplined way of thinking with its roots in scientific inquiry' (Rodgers, 2002: 845). However, reflection is as much about constructing meaning *from* experience as it is about applying knowledge *to* experience; it is a learning process that requires interaction with others and is embedded in a social context.

Dewey's model of reflection

John Dewey wrote extensively about reflection, which he saw as a mode of thinking that was oriented towards experience and practical problem-solving. In his book *How We Think*, first published in 1910, Dewey outlined a five-stage model of reflection (Dewey, 1997: 72–8):

1. Identify a 'felt difficulty', e.g. an event or situation that is experienced as perplexing, problematic or troubling in some way
2. Locate and define the specific character of the problem, which may involve carrying out some further observations
3. Develop a hypothesis, or preferably 'a variety of alternative suggestions', about what has caused the problem and how it can be solved
4. Subject the hypothesis to a process of reasoning in order to gauge its implications and assess how plausible it is
5. Test the hypothesis in practice to see 'if the results theoretically indicated by the idea actually occur'

Many models of reflection have adopted a similar approach to Dewey, albeit with variations in terms of what is being observed and hypothesised about. A common idea is that of a 'reflective learning cycle', in which there is a constant dialogue between knowledge and experience, and between subjective and objective theories of practice. A well-known example is Kolb's experiential learning cycle (Kolb, 1984), which is based on four steps. First practitioners think about a specific situation or experience; second, they draw out what was significant about it, third, make the link to relevant theoretical ideas, and finally apply what has been learned to a new situation. Borton (1970) narrows the cycle down to three questions (what, so what, and now what?) while Gibbs (1988) and Johns (2000) extend it in order to highlight the need to think about our emotional responses as well as our habitual assumptions and beliefs. Due to its focus on in-depth learning, reflection is often couched in terms of its potential for personal development (Thompson and Thompson, 2008) and even transformation (Mezirow, 1991). This connects it not only to psychodynamic ideas about the 'use of self' (Ruch, 2005), but also to the 'critical' analysis of power dynamics and the underlying political dimension of common knowledge and everyday aspects of life (Fook et al., 2006; Fook and Askeland, 2006). Some of these different perspectives on reflection are discussed below.

Schön's 'reflection-in-action'

The work of Donald Schön (1991, 1987) has greatly influenced ideas about reflection in professional contexts. Schön based his concept of 'the reflective practitioner' on a critique of technical rationality, which he saw as an approach to professional knowledge and skill emphasising objectivity and control:

> According to the model of Technical Rationality, there is an objectively knowable world, independent of the practitioner's values and views. In order to gain technical knowledge of it, the practitioner must maintain a clear boundary between himself and his object of inquiry. In order to exert technical control over it, he must observe it and keep his distance from it... His stance toward inquiry is that of the spectator/manipulator. (Schön, 1991: 163)

According to Schön, such an approach was doomed to failure because professionals deal with complex and ill-defined situations that are characterised by uncertainty and unpredictability. This recalls Rittel and Webber's concept of 'wicked problems', which was discussed in the Introduction. Schön was not disputing the value of technical knowledge and skills; his point was that they are necessary but not sufficient to resolve messy problems in the real world. For example, building a new road across a stretch of countryside requires a lot of technical know-how but also throws up a unique set of financial, economic, environmental, and political issues, all of which could potentially affect the success of the project. In dealing with such issues, professionals are neither passive spectators nor remote manipulators of events, but are actively involved in constructing the social world of their interventions. In *The Reflective Practitioner*, Schön discusses several closely observed vignettes of professional activity, which illustrate the intuitive skill and artistry that he considered to be the hallmark of an expert at work.

> In a practitioner's reflective conversation with a situation that he treats as unique and uncertain, he functions as an agent/experient. Through his transaction with the situation, he shapes it and makes himself a part of it. Hence, the

sense he makes of the situation must include his own contribution to it. Yet he recognises that the situation, having a life of its own distinct from his intentions, may foil his projects and reveal new meanings. (Schön, 1991: 163)

What Schön here describes as a 'reflective conversation with a situation' is key to his concept of reflection-in-action, which happens while the professional is still engaged in the activity that is being reflected on. This is linked to the idea of 'thinking on one's feet' and reacting quickly to an unforeseen turn of events – something that most social workers have to do on a regular basis! However, Schön argues that such thought processes are actually intrinsic to expertise, whether or not the practitioner is responding to a crisis. Indeed, if they do not reflect on what they are doing while they are doing it, professionals may be adopting a routine, procedural approach to their work – what Thompson and Thompson (2008) call BOB, or 'Bypassing Our Brain' – which is unlikely to be appreciated by service users and in some cases could lead to vital information being missed or misunderstood. Instead, Schön's concept of reflection-in-action emphasises the creativity and spontaneous skill of professional work, and the value of knowledge that is co-produced *with* people in the situation rather than knowledge that is applied *by* experts to the situation.

Schön contrasted reflection-in-action with the activity of thinking about a situation that has occurred in the past, which he called reflection-on-action. He associated the latter with less experienced practitioners, who were still developing the ability to integrate theory with practice in a way that would allow them to reflect-while-doing rather than after the event. In social work, both reflection-on-action and in-action are deemed to promote good practice at all levels of experience and expertise. Thompson and Thompson (2008) go further and propose a third type, reflection-for-action, which concerns the forethought and planning that are necessary for effective intervention but which allows for flexibility rather than rigid adherence to a fixed way of working. Social work students will be familiar with this 'before-during-after' model of reflection, which is embedded into the direct observations of practice that are completed on placements (University of York, 2000).

Reflective practice

Knott and Scragg (2016) suggest that reflection becomes reflective practice when it results in some sort of action, i.e. thinking that is explicitly linked to doing. The reflective learning cycles mentioned above also make this link, although their focus tends to be more on individual development than on the social context in which the suggested action takes place. Ruch (2005) makes a connection between reflective practice and relationship-based practice, arguing that the former is necessary for the latter (see Chapter 4) and that both present a challenge to 'reductionist understandings of human behaviour and narrowly conceived bureaucratic responses to complex problems' (Ruch, 2005: 111). The argument is reminiscent of Schön (1991), who thought that technical rationality had brought about a 'crisis of confidence' in the professions because its claims to certainty and control were unachievable. Ruch goes on to distinguish between 'technical' and 'holistic' reflective practice. In her study of child care social workers, practitioners with a 'technically reflective orientation' tended to be focused on practical aspects of improving their performance, i.e. 'how to do it better next time', rather than exploring the reasons why things happened the way they did. In contrast, 'holistically reflective' practitioners were interested in the complex dynamics that gave rise to a given situation or outcome, to 'engage with practice from a position of each encounter being unique, unpredictable and requiring negotiation through the professional relationship' (Ruch, 2005: 117).

CASE STUDY 5.1

Bel, Jasmine, and Graham

Bel is a student social worker on her final placement in an inner-city community mental health team. As part of her induction, she accompanies an experienced social worker, Jasmine, on a home visit. They are meeting with Graham, who has a long-term mental health condition managed under a community treatment order (CTO). When they knock on his door, they hear footsteps and a man's voice tells them to go away. Jasmine crouches to introduce herself through the letter box. Graham seems agitated and tells her loudly to go away. Jasmine keeps talking in a calm and friendly tone, reminding Graham that they had spoken on the phone in the morning. She suggests that they speak with the door ajar and Graham eventually opens the door a little. Jasmine then introduces Bel and asks Graham if he remembers her previous social work student. They carry on the conversation for a while, keeping the topics neutral so that no confidential information is discussed. As Graham appears to relax and become more communicative, Jasmine asks him whether they might be able to speak somewhere more privately, and he invites them inside.

On the way back from the visit, Bel asks Jasmine about the way she managed the situation at the door. Jasmine initially refers to the intuitive knowledge gained through years of experience – 'you just learn what to do'. However, when questioned more closely she acknowledges the complex domains of knowledge and skill that underlie her actions. One of these is the practice and policy context of CTOs, Graham's history of treatment, relapse, and recall, and his recent attendance at outpatient appointments for medical treatment. Another is Jasmine's relationship-based approach to her practice, through which she finds ways to engage citizens who are resistant to involvement with social workers without confronting or antagonising them. Another is Jasmine's knowledge of signs and indicators of mental illness as well as other forms of psychological and social distress, which enabled her to make a 'fast and frugal' assessment of Graham's health and wellbeing (see Chapter 3). Another is Jasmine's sense of professional responsibility for her own and her student's safety and welfare, which meant that she undertook a quick risk assessment at the front door before going inside Graham's house.

Critical reflection

Thompson and Thompson (2008) argue that reflective practice requires a critical perspective, which they define in terms of 'depth and breadth' in the use of knowledge:

- Critical depth comes from not accepting things at face value but instead 'looking beneath the surface to see what assumptions and forms of reasoning are influencing the circumstances' (Thompson and Thompson, 2008: 26)
- Critical breadth comes from placing people's individual situation, and their relationships with others, in a wider social context and considering how economic, social and political conditions on the 'macro-level' affect people's lives

It is not entirely clear whether and how we should distinguish between reflective practice and critical reflection (Thompson and Thompson, 2008; White et al., 2006). In the context of social research, Hammersley has expressed scepticism about adopting the 'honorific title' of being critical as a way of adopting explicit political positions; in his view this obscures the essential task of critique, which is to assess the merits of competing knowledge claims (Hammersley, 2005). From this standpoint, the notion of 'critical depth' outlined above is unproblematic, since it concerns the kind of critical thinking skills that have long been promoted in social work as well as other professions (Rutter and Brown, 2015; Bandman and Bandman, 1995; McPeck, 2016). Broadly speaking, critical thinking is about evaluating the rationality of statements, beliefs, and arguments – both our own and those of others. It is a constructive form of scepticism that aims to define problems clearly, formulate premises based on sound evidence, and reach conclusions that are logical and justifiable. In this sense of the term, it would be difficult to imagine reflection that was 'uncritical'.

The other sense of criticality, which Thompson and Thompson describe as 'critical breadth', concerns the 'wider socio-political aspects of the situation' (Thompson and Thompson, 2008: 28). This seems particularly important in social work, which is perhaps unique among professions in having a commitment to social justice as part of its raison d'être (IFSW, 2014). Critical reflection therefore involves an analysis of power at all levels of social organisation, from one's personal influence on the immediate environment to the broad socio-political context of social life. It includes the institutional role of social workers, who may be perceived by their citizens as agents of state surveillance and control, but also the unequal distribution of economic, political, and cultural resources in society, which makes some people more likely to need or 'use' social work interventions than others. Such considerations go beyond the 'micro' focus on the individual and their circumstances underlying reflective models based on Dewey or Schön, which place little emphasis on broader social issues such as deprivation, discrimination, and inequality. Taking a position on these issues is an explicitly political act, which aims to transform the practice of social work in order to emancipate people from discrimination, stigma, and poverty. For this reason, Fook and Askeland (2006) make a case for a distinct form of critical reflection that is expressly focused on 'challenging and changing dominant power relations' so that 'changes in the immediate context may build into changes at broader levels' (Fook and Askeland, 2006: 47). In other words, critical reflection aims to help social workers achieve social change. It is this political dimension to which Hammersley (2005) objects in connection with 'critical research', but which may be considered to be fundamental in social work, particularly for proponents of its more radical tradition. By extension, of course, social workers have a choice as to how they intend to be critical and what they mean by it.

Reflexivity

Reflection is often linked with a similar-sounding term: 'reflexivity' (D'Cruz et al., 2007). Simply put, reflexivity is about 'factoring ourselves as players into the situations we practice in' (Fook and Askeland, 2006: 45). Reflexivity is an important concept in sociology, where it is associated with the work of Giddens (1990) and Beck (1992). Their analysis of 'reflexive modernisation' (Beck et al., 1994) is that self-awareness has become a defining feature of contemporary Western society, characterised by rapid social change, preoccupation with risk, a highly individualistic culture, and fluid forms of identity that are no longer anchored in social norms. Ferguson (2001) has argued that social workers need to adapt their practice to the contemporary 'post-traditional' society. In this view, social problems and inequality are best confronted by intervening with 'individual lives, as embedded in interdependent relationships in families, institutions and communities, rather than through

Table 5.1 Reflection and related concepts

Reflection	A structured way of thinking and learning that is oriented towards experience and practical problem-solving
Reflexivity	The principle that as social beings we affect the things we seek to observe and make judgements about; professionals therefore have to factor themselves into their work with citizens – a key aspect of reflection in social work
Reflective practice	Reflecting in a way that is geared towards action; the purposeful use of reflection to inform your professional practice
Reflection-in-action	Reflecting on an activity that is still going on; this type of reflection enables you to adapt and improve your work while you do it
Reflection-on-action	Reflecting on an incident or piece of work that has already happened; this type of reflection helps you to think about how to do things differently in future
Reflection-for-action	Reflecting on an activity that has not yet happened; this type of reflection helps you to plan and prepare your work
Critical reflection	Reflecting in a way that considers power dynamics and wider structures of inequality and oppression; this type of reflection allows for the possibility of social transformation in professional practice

objectified structures' (Ferguson, 2003: 704). Ferguson's concept of 'life politics' has attracted criticism from commentators such as Garrett (2003), who are concerned that over-emphasising individual volition and agency downplays the role of structural factors in restricting choice and opportunity. In some respects, the debate on reflexivity echoes the distinction between 'critical reflection', with its emancipatory political agenda, and other forms of reflection that are oriented more towards individual casework and personal and professional development.

To assist with the terminological confusion, Table 5.1 offers a summary of commonly used terms.

PR∂CtiSiNG ReFLeCtiON

Having established a broad theoretical basis for reflection, this section will explore some of the most common focal points for reflective practice in social work. It does not opt for one particular approach, but will consider a range of methods and concerns that are often found within social work practice.

Planning and preparing work

Reflective practitioners think carefully about what they do and why they are doing it. This includes what Thompson and Thompson (2008) call 'reflection-for-action': preparing for activities, meetings, and encounters, anticipating potential difficulties, and having a contingency plan. Preparatory work may involve practising communication and interviewing skills through some kind of verbal or written role play, either on one's own or with a colleague, friend, or family member. Self-recording and self-videoing can be a useful way of increasing awareness of body language, e.g. distracting gestures such as clicking a pen, a tendency to interrupt, or an off-putting 'default facial expression' (Henderson and Matthew-Byrne, 2016: 18). Before engaging with service users, social workers need to be clear about the legislative framework and legal remit for their work as well as other 'governing variables' including ethical codes of practice, regulatory standards, and organisational constraints and priorities (Knott and Scragg, 2016: 75). Before starting work, it is often helpful to think about whether the aims and objectives of an intervention are congruent with the envisaged methods, and how outcomes will be evaluated. Thompson and Thompson (2008) suggest some tools to do this, including a model of 'systematic practice' based around three reflective questions:

- What are you trying to achieve?
- How are you going to achieve it?
- How will you know when you have achieved it?

Social work assessments – whether or not they involve completing a form – entail a great deal of preparation. Assessments tend to follow a cyclical rather than linear progression, so that practitioners are constantly having to integrate knowledge and method in response to new information and events. Nonetheless, before meeting anyone for the first time, social workers should have read any available background information and be able to explain to the person (in jargon-free language) the purpose of the assessment. They should consider whether and how the assessment fits into an overall model of practice, e.g. psychodynamic, task-centred, or solution-focused (Milner and O'Byrne, 2015) and look for research evidence that is pertinent to the information that will be collected and how it is analysed (Hood, 2016a). Equally important is to reflect on some of the areas considered below such as ethics and values, cultural difference, conflict, and power.

Reflecting on emotions

Knott and Scragg (2016: 41) define emotions as 'strong feelings arising from an altered state of mind'. They can be distinguished from moods, which are less intense and longer lasting and tend not to have an immediate cause or object. In contrast, emotions are usually linked to a situation or person that is perceived as having triggered the emotional response. Emotions affect cognitive processes in the brain and so have traditionally been viewed as a hindrance to rational thought. Yet the dualistic opposition of emotion vs reason is not supported by research evidence, which shows that emotional responses actually play an important part in making judgements and decisions (Damasio, 2006). One problem is that 'affective' judgements (i.e. those made on an emotional basis) occur faster and more intuitively than the 'slow' thinking associated with rational deliberation (see Chapter 3). Judgements that are supposedly objective may therefore be influenced by cognitive bias stemming from an early intuition or 'hunch': the emotional tail may end up wagging the rational dog, as Haidt (2001) puts it. Of course, many social workers rightly pay attention to their 'gut feeling', which can be a crucial indicator that something is amiss. Emotions are a source of information about ourselves as well as others and may alert us to assumptions or values that we would prefer not to acknowledge. We might feel disgust when entering a cluttered or dirty home, for example, or relief when a knock on the front door goes unanswered (Ferguson, 2010), or indeed warmth towards someone we happen to get along with (Turney, 2010). It is important to acknowledge such emotional responses and consider how they might influence our thoughts and actions.

The importance of attending to feelings in relationship-based work has already been discussed in Chapter 4. From a psychodynamic perspective, strong emotions that seem unexpected or uncharacteristic may be linked to unconscious processes such as transference and countertransference. Secondary trauma, emotional 'burnout', and psychological defence mechanisms all have the potential to inhibit social workers' ability to recognise and respond appropriately to situations where people are at risk of abuse, oppression, and violence (Cooper, 2004; Reder and Duncan, 2004). This process is sometimes referred to as 'professional dangerousness' (Reder and Duncan, 1999), although it is a term that arguably underplays the importance of institutional context in creating a containing and reflective environment for social workers (see below). While most models of reflective learning (e.g. Kolb, Gibbs) encourage practitioners to consider their emotional response to particular situations, one of the advantages of thinking about social work as based on relationships is that reflection on emotions is seen as a core part of practice, rather than as a supplementary tool to be used now and again.

Reflecting on ethics and values

Akhtar (2016: 43) defines values as 'a standard of behaviour or a fundamental belief about what constitutes right action'. Our efforts to apply values systematically to the world are the basis for ethical or moral codes, some of which may be personal and unspoken while others are formal, written down, and to some extent prescriptive. Personal values influence the way professionals carry out their work; for example, a practitioner who believes in the value of honesty will make an effort to be open and transparent in their dealings with service users. More formally, professional codes of practice set out explicit standards of 'good' conduct, and many social workers draw on ethical frameworks of anti-oppressive or anti-discriminatory practice (Thompson, 2016). Legislation, statutory guidance, and local policies and procedures also impose duties and constraints on social workers' actions.

Given this complex legal and ethical terrain, it is unsurprising that social workers sometimes experience dissonance – their actions do not correspond in some way to their values – or dilemmas – a push and pull between different kinds of values. An approved mental health practitioner who believes strongly in treating people with respect, for example, may recommend that a citizen experiencing a relapse into mental illness be admitted to hospital for psychiatric treatment, knowing that the process of admission is likely to be distressing and perhaps even demeaning for that person. A social worker for elderly adults may believe that their organisation's eligibility criteria for social care services are too strict in principle, but still tries to apply those criteria fairly and consistently in their everyday work.

Thompson and Thompson (2008) consider values to be one of the main dimensions of reflective practice. They argue that practitioners should be able to identify their own personal values, relate them to their professional code of practice and the values of their organisation, identify any differences or conflicts and consider how they might be reconciled. As Hood (2016a) points out, many social work agencies separate needs assessment from decisions about resources, which creates potential for a split between *deontological* (principle-based) and *utilitarian* (consequence-based) ethical stances (Banks, 2006), e.g. frontline practitioners advocating for 'their' citizens to receive services that will help them, while managers try to allocate a finite budget in a reasonable way. Also influential in social work is the 'ethic of care' approach developed by Gilligan (1993) and Tronto (1993), which emphasises the moral value of human relationships and of giving and receiving care. Applying these theories helps social workers to analyse how their own values and moral codes influence how they interpret a given situation, and to understand the interpretations of others.

Ideas about sameness and difference often contribute to reflecting on values. As discussed in the previous chapter, the empathetic ability to relate to others – and to be seen as relatable by others – is an important part of relationship-based practice. Social workers will rarely be perceived as an 'insider' in the citizen's context – not least because of the power and authority they wield. Nor do citizens necessarily want a social worker who is 'like them' in some way, although similarities in background can help with building rapport (Yan, 2008). Nonetheless, the reality of difference is that social workers will often have to wrestle with their prejudices and assumptions about particular problems, client groups, or communities. An obvious example is the salience of personal values and life experience when working with perpetrators of crime, abuse, and violence; on some occasions, practitioners may find it hard to respect a particular citizen as someone 'worth doing business with' (Turnell and Edwards, 1999: 25). Conversely, as discussed in the previous chapter, social workers who identify strongly with the person they are working with may find it harder to challenge them, or accept that they see the world differently. Assumptions and prejudices about certain groups and communities can affect organisational cultures in various ways. Disabled citizens may be perceived as helpless and vulnerable, for example, which could inhibit efforts on their part to become more autonomous and self-sufficient. Broader structural forms of discrimination, experienced by citizens in their everyday life because of some aspect of their identity, may intersect and overlap to varying degrees with the experience of practitioners. Ryde (2009), for example, discusses the experience of being a white practitioner in the 'helping professions', including the feelings of guilt and shame that awareness of white privilege can engender. In her inquiry into child sexual exploitation in Rotherham, Jay (2014) noted that some professionals as well as councillors were nervous about identifying the ethnic origins of perpetrators 'for fear of being thought racist' (2014: 2). As with all complex issues, there is no technical solution; theoretical frameworks such as 'anti-oppressive practice' and 'cultural competence' encourage practitioners to work thoughtfully and reflectively, and to consider how their work could promote equality and social justice, but do not make the differences between people somehow 'not matter' (see Abrams and Moio, 2009).

REFLECTIVE EXERCISE 5.2

CRITICAL INCIDENT ANALYSIS

(Adapted from Fook, 1999; Fook and Askeland, 2006; Fook and Gardner, 2007)

Think of a situation or piece of work that you consider to have had a significant effect upon your learning or practice as a social worker. This 'critical incident' should be brief and specific, but comprehensive enough for you to observe and analyse what went on and why. Examples of critical incidents include:

- a piece of work that went particularly well
- a piece of work that that you found particularly difficult or demanding
- a piece of work where you made a mistake and where you recognised your mistake
- a situation that challenged your understanding of social work practice
- a situation in which you experienced conflict, hostility, or aggression

Having thought of a critical incident, use the following questions to write down a structured analysis of the incident:

1. Describe the context (e.g. the agency you work for, your role and how long you have had this role)
2. Describe the incident in detail, including the time of day and the physical environment in which it took place
3. Why was the incident critical to you?
4. What were your aims and objectives at the time?
5. Was anything particularly difficult or demanding about the situation?
6. What were you thinking and feeling as it was taking place; and afterwards?
7. What did you learn about yourself, in relation to:

    i.   Being a social work professional, e.g. in relation to ethics and values
    ii. Being a practitioner, e.g. your skills and competences?

8. What were some of your theoretical assumptions, e.g. about approaches to assessment and intervention, theories of human motivation and behaviour, which were reflected in this incident?
9. How has your learning from this incident changed your thinking and your practice?

Exploring power dynamics

Social workers have various forms of power at their disposal, both personal and professional (Smith, 2008). They may assess eligibility for resources and services (reward power), for example, or monitor compliance with a protection plan or court order (coercive power). They have authority vested in them through their statutory duties to assess and investigate (legitimate power) or through the knowledge and skills associated with their professional status (expert power). Some people are deferred to by others because of personal qualities, such as trustworthiness, which have nothing to do with their job (referent power). It is therefore important that social workers acknowledge their power and use it in the right way. Working with 'involuntary clients', citizens who have little or no choice in dealing with social workers, puts a particular onus on what Ferguson (2009: 477) calls the 'skilful use of good authority'. Barber (1991) sets out three practice options for such work (cited in Ferguson, 2011: 172–3):

*   *Casework by concession* – social workers who are uneasy about using their authority may avoid conflict and confrontation, placing a premium on having a 'positive relationship' at all costs. This could lead to 'professional dangerousness' (see above) and make it hard to identify and address underlying issues.

- *Casework by oppression* – some social workers may embrace their authority to such an extent that they concentrate on the use of coercive power to ensure that citizens comply with plans and address the 'concerns' of professionals. As was seen in Forrester et al.'s (2008) study, this approach is likely to elicit an antagonistic response. An emphasis on extrinsic motivators is also unlikely to lead to sustainable change.
- *Casework by negotiation* – social workers accept that there is potential for conflict in their relationships with citizens but remain open to dialogue and negotiation. Of course, there will always be some things that are non-negotiable, particularly in statutory contexts. Nonetheless, if social workers make an effort to listen to citizens and find out what matters to them, they will be in a better position to understand 'resistance' and build on strengths rather than overly focus on deficits (Ferguson, 2011; Turney, 2012).

It is important to understand power as a dynamic process rather than as a playing out of fixed structures, e.g. the powerful social worker and the powerless client. Terms such as 'refusal to engage' put the problem firmly at the citizen's door, but non-engagement can go both ways (Horwath, 2007). Feeling relieved because a 'difficult client' was not at home for an arranged meeting is a normal reaction; you still have to steel yourself for the early morning follow-up! It is also true that citizens have coercive power of their own; they can intimidate social workers through verbal abuse, threats of assault, or even letting their dogs do the intimidation (Ferguson, 2011). Again, because these are *dynamics* of power, social workers need to be alert to how their reactions and responses may be initiating or perpetuating unhelpful patterns of interaction. Being able to acknowledge and manage conflict is therefore an important skill for social workers. Practitioners may find it helpful to reflect on their preferred conflict style, e.g. whether their normal tendency is to avoid confrontation, to seek control and dominate the argument, or to try and find solutions (Rahim, 1983). Rosenberg (2015) discusses communication strategies to defuse conflict by encouraging people to acknowledge and articulate the feelings and needs that underlie their aggressive, confrontational behaviour. In a similar vein, Thompson and Thompson (2008: 92) advocate 'reframing', a reflective activity that aims to mitigate some of the counterproductive thought patterns that sustain strong negative feelings such as hopelessness and anger.

Evaluating practice

Social workers can use reflective methods to evaluate their own practice, either in supervision or training, or as part of their routine case recording and analysis. Reflective questions derived from adult learning cycles (e.g. Gibbs, 1988; Kolb, 1984) can be used as a form of 'reflection-on-action', for example to look back on a particular visit or meeting and consider whether anything should be done differently in future. Learning cycles encourage practitioners to link their analysis of the situation to broader theoretical considerations, e.g. theories about how to engage the perpetrators of domestic abuse or how to conduct assessments in a solution-focused way.

Doing this regularly not only enables practitioners to explore their hypotheses about the people they work with, and to consider different options for care planning and intervention, but also creates a structured pathway for developing expertise through practice experience.

For some people, the use of reflection to evaluate practice may suggest a link to quality assurance and performance management. This is a thorny issue in social work, where learning from one's successes is often seen as a luxury and learning from one's mistakes equated with being in trouble; the 'learning' undertaken by serious case reviews and public inquiries, for instance, often seems to boil down to a castigation of individual workers' failings and 'bad practice'. Not coincidentally, Yip (2006) suggests that in an oppressive working environment, self-reflection may actually prove counterproductive and even harmful to social workers' emotional and psychological wellbeing. Evaluating practice in supervision and in peer-to-peer contexts would therefore seem linked to issues around organisational learning that are explored further below.

Personal and professional development

The benefits of reflection should go beyond the discharge of duties associated with particular jobs and roles. In one sense, this is an obvious corollary of the connection between personal and professional domains of identity (see Chapter 4). Learning how to use non-violent communication strategies in conflict situations, for example, may well prove useful outside of work. In turn, there is an argument for using reflection in the workplace to enhance self-knowledge and promote personal development in a more general sense, rather than just focusing on individual clients or pieces of work. As Hawkins and Shohet (2012) point out, reflection is an important part of sustaining resilience in a demanding job, and can be used to identify some of the early warning signs of chronic stress. The Johari Window model (Luft, 1970), which explores how we perceive, disclose, and conceal information about ourselves, can be used to reflect on our motivations and behaviour in interpersonal relations. Honey and Mumford's (2000) model of learning styles, which is often used in social work training, can indicate our preferred way to learn about our practice; some people are inclined to start with a practical activity that they relate to theory afterwards, while others prefer to start with a theory that they then adapt and apply to a concrete situation.

The reflective space

The reflective space refers to the environment in which we do a reflective activity. This is partly about location, e.g. whether we are in a small, quiet room or in a large, open-plan office with lots of people talking on the phone. It is also about people, e.g. whether we are alone, in a team room with colleagues, one-to-one with our manager, or with a group of peers sitting in a circle. More broadly, it is also about the institutional context in which this space must be carved out, which includes the organisational culture as well as the demands and expectations placed on workers. The quality of the reflective space is important for various reasons. From a psychodynamic perspective, practitioners benefit from a 'holding' or 'containing' environment in order to help them to understand and regulate the strong emotions associated with their work (see Chapter 4). Conversely, it will not help social workers to be reflective if they are in what Yip (2006: 783) calls an 'oppressive psycho-social environment', which may be caused by factors such as 'a highly critical supervisor, apathetic colleagues, a working team full of oppressive politics and dynamics, or insecurity and uncertainty in the social worker's employment'. For social workers struggling with a heavy workload and the concomitant stream of emergencies, conflicts, and emotionally draining encounters with citizens, the requirement to be reflective may simply be perceived as an additional burden. These issues are sometimes downplayed in the literature; Thompson and Thompson (2008: 56), for example, argue that 'if we do not manage to be reflective, then we will have difficulty in managing our work pressures', which is true up to a point but also seems to put the onus on individual practitioners to think their way out of problems caused by the institution they work for. Others make an explicit link between reflection and the organisational and supervisory context in which it happens (Hawkins and Shohet, 2012; Gould and Baldwin, 2016).

In this context, it is worth noting that social work agencies do not have to adhere to an individual case-holder model of allocating work, i.e. the convention that citizens are 'cases' and social workers should have a 'caseload' of people for whom they are individually responsible. This model – and the associated terminology – tends to underlie conventional types of process reflection, in which social workers reflect on *their* work with *their* cases, either by themselves or with their supervisors. New ways of doing social work may create new kinds of reflective space. Contemporary examples include social work units (Goodman and Trowler, 2012), Family Recovery Projects (Local Government Leadership and City of Westminster, 2010) and the Frontline training programme (Maxwell et al., 2016). In different ways, these approaches put systems thinking, joint working, and reflective discussion at the heart of everyday practice. Such approaches form part of a growing awareness that individual reflection and learning is bound up with how organisations themselves seek to improve, innovate, and transform.

LeaRNiNG ORGaNiSatiONS

Learning organisations not only promote the kind of individual learning processes that much of this chapter has focused on but also develop strategies for collective learning. Senge (1990, 2006) proposed that learning organisations tend to develop expertise in five domains: systems thinking, personal mastery, mental models, shared visions, and team learning. These characteristics give organisations a strategic advantage because they generate capacity for responding and adapting to an unpredictable environment. Reflective practice, in various guises, is integral to the concept of the learning organisation. For example, Gould (2004) notes the connection between Senge's ideas and Revans' (1980) action learning theory, as well as Argyris and Schön's work on organisational learning (Argyris and Schön, 1978; 1974). Senge (2006) also acknowledges his debt to the management theorist W. Edwards Deming, whose work is discussed in Chapter 8. Much of this literature is concerned with the idea of organisations as systems.

Recalling the distinction between 'complex' and 'complicated' made in the Introduction, a starting point is to observe that organisations are not like machines, in which people perform narrowly defined roles and functions that can be standardised and perfected until they precisely serve organisational goals. Rather, organisations achieve their aims through networks of people, who think, act, and interact in ways that cannot entirely (or even at all) be predicted or controlled. In other words, organisations are like complex adaptive systems, although there are problems with this analogy (see Stacey, 2007). The systems perspective is particularly relevant to human service organisations, which operate very differently from the factory production-lines on which traditional 'Taylorist' management theory was based (see Chapter 8). It also has implications for how we conceptualise learning in an organisational context. The conventional model of professional bureaucracy assumes that practitioners complete their vocational education before assuming their posts, and are then required to 'top-up' their knowledge at regular intervals, e.g. by going on training courses. Arguably this is still the dominant model in most social work agencies, although it is widely recognised that practitioners learn in many other ways, e.g. through the experience of working with citizens, various forms of supervision, in communities of practice (Wenger, 1998), and by collaborating with other professionals in multi-disciplinary teams. It follows that organisations should not only support these forms of generating knowledge, and create structures for its dissemination and absorption, but should also consider how the collective activity of learning shapes and alters the organisation itself.

Double-loop learning

Argyris and Schön (1974) distinguish between single-loop and double-loop learning in organisations. Single-loop learning takes place when organisations do not question their fundamental assumptions, e.g. about why they do what they do, or whether they are doing the right thing; instead they focus on improving processes and performance within their existing models and frameworks. In contrast, double-loop learning requires the organisation to subject its basic principles and rules to critical scrutiny. Munro (2010) gives an example of the distinction in her analysis of the UK child protection system, where a dependence on procedures to regulate practice was perceived to have eroded social workers' professional skills (Ayre and Calder, 2010). This in turn affected the quality of service, e.g. insufficient analysis in social work assessments, or a lack of confidence in undertaking direct work with children. Using single-loop learning, statutory agencies would then try and raise standards by tightening compliance with existing procedures, e.g. auditing social work files to identify unsatisfactory practice, or by implementing new procedures, e.g. requiring every assessment to document the direct work undertaken with the child. The problem with this approach is that relying on procedural fixes actually exacerbates the conditions that produce a de-skilled workforce in the first place. Double-loop learning, on the other hand, would try to identify the organisational practices that result in such vicious circles, i.e. highlight the misplaced logic of using procedures to address the unintended consequences of overusing procedures. Munro's (2011) final report, which advocated for a 'child-centred system', drew on this kind of analysis in order to argue for significant changes to policy and practice.

Supervision

Supervision continues to play a fundamental role in the 'helping professions' (Hawkins and Shohet, 2012). However its role has arguably changed over the years to allow an accommodation of organisational objectives, professional discretion, and public accountability (Jones, 2004). According to Kadushin's well-known framework, supervision has three functions: administrative, educational, and supportive (Kadushin and Harkness, 2014). However, the responsibility for line management and quality assurance frequently found in supervisory roles can often reduce the time available for activities geared towards professional reflection, learning, and development (Jones, 2004; Hughes and Pengelly, 1997). In turn, professionally oriented, reflective supervision has been highlighted as a cornerstone of good practice in areas such as child protection (Munro, 2010; Laming, 2009). Many social work agencies promote initiatives to encourage reflective supervision outside of the line management function, including clinical supervision and group supervision (Carpenter et al., 2012; Bogo and McKnight, 2006). A potential problem is that separation from the line management function could make such initiatives vulnerable to budget constraints or the departure of a key facilitator (Jones, 2004), i.e. they may not form part of the organisation's 'core business'. As noted earlier, models of social work that emphasise joint working rather than sole case-holding might lead to innovative forms of reflective practice as part of the adjustment to supervisory practice.

CONCLUSiON

The previous chapter explored the importance of relationships in social work and also pointed to the close connection between reflective and relationship-based approaches. This chapter has examined the theory and practice of reflection in greater depth, arguing that social workers need time and space to think systematically about their work. The purpose of doing so is to maintain high standards of work but also to maintain professional resilience and the ability to be flexible and creative in complex situations. Reflective exercises go beyond the evidence-based sphere of 'what works?', considering instead questions like 'why did I think that might work?'. In striving to make sense of complex social dynamics, emotional responses and ethical dilemmas, social workers engage in 'double-loop learning' of their own; sticking to procedures or a tried-and-trusted set of techniques provides short-term certainty but at the cost of ignoring the unpredictable terrain of relationships and interactions, which is where the real risks and solutions are to be found. Yet the thoughtful, criti-cal analysis of work cannot just be left to practitioners' discretion or confined to one-to-one meetings with a line manager. It has to be embedded in organisational culture; demanding that social workers 'do more reflection' will not compensate for an oppressive work environment or obviate the need for manageable workloads. There is also a caveat to the idea of reflective practice presented in this chapter, which has largely focused on practitioners in their own professional and organisational context. Even an exemplary reflective practitioner in the most progressive of agencies does a lot of their work in collaboration with other professionals and other agencies. It is to this important facet of complexity, namely interprofessional working, to which we turn in the next chapter.

WORKING INTERPROFESSIONALLY

6

CHAPTER SUMMARY

This chapter examines interprofessional working as a response to complex needs. It starts by outlining the policy context to specialisation and professionalisation in the welfare state, and the move towards greater managerial control of professional work along with efforts to foster partnership and integration across agency boundaries. Theories of collaboration are then explored, including interprofessional education, continuum and gestalt models, ecological and organisational perspectives, and teamwork. Approaches to interprofessional ethics are followed by a discussion of conflict and consensus in collaborative contexts. Psychodynamic concepts are then applied to the role of anxiety in shaping patterns of communication and collaboration in institutional contexts. The chapter concludes by exploring some key areas of interprofessional expertise for social workers, including knowledge, communication, negotiation, and reflective practice.

INTRODUCTION

Contemporary social work almost always involves some form of interprofessional working. In some cases, social workers may act as brokers and gatekeepers, mediating between the citizen and the services they want or need. In other cases, social workers may coordinate the work of practitioners from a range of agencies in relation to an individual care plan. Social workers may liaise with other organisations in order to obtain information or advocate for citizens, for example in relation to housing or unemployment benefits. The nature of social workers' interactions with other professionals also varies according to their organisational setting. The most common setting for social workers, particularly in local authorities, continues to be what might be termed 'uni-professional', i.e. social workers occupy an office building or floor where they are surrounded by other social workers, managers, and administrators. Interactions with other professionals occur primarily through formal casework, e.g. meetings, consultations, or joint visits. Elsewhere, social workers may be part of a multi-agency service, where they work directly alongside other professionals, e.g. with police officers in Multi Agency Safeguarding Hubs, or with psychiatric nurses and psychologists in Community Mental Health Teams. In such settings, social workers will often be co-located (i.e. share their workspace) with other professionals, allowing a greater degree of informal or spontaneous interaction. However, members of 'multiprofessional teams' (Anning et al., 2006) will not necessarily be managed or supervised by the same person and may be seconded (temporarily assigned) from their 'home' agency. All these factors have been shown to affect the nature and quality of collaboration, as will be discussed further below.

Interprofessional working is connected to the issue of complexity in a number of ways. As discussed in Chapter 1, the term 'complex needs' in social work often refers to multiple, intersecting problems that straddle various professional domains. This means that people who are assessed as having complex needs tend to be referred to lots of different professionals, each with their own area of expertise. There are several potential drawbacks to this approach, as will be discussed later. However, perhaps the most obvious is that bringing professionals together creates additional complexity, due partly to the unpredictable social dynamics that result when human beings interact and relate to one another. These dynamics are shaped by institutional and organisational factors, including people's adherence to and identification with the values, roles, and practices associated with 'their' profession. Accordingly, when professionals work together to resolve complexity in the lives of citizens they must also be prepared to resolve complexity in their own collaborative activity. It is with this thorny problem that much of the chapter is concerned. First, however, we shall briefly consider the position of social work as one profession among many in the socio-political context of the welfare state.

The Policy Context

Professionalisation and the welfare state

Development of the welfare state in the UK, as well as in other countries, has been characterised by professionalisation (Molander, 2016). Occupational groups such as social workers, nurses, and teachers have become central to the provision of publicly funded services, and in the process have acquired many features of the 'classic' professions of medicine and law. In this sense, members of professions exercise 'jurisdictional claims' over particular areas of work, on the basis of specialist knowledge and expertise as well as a formal qualification route (Abbott, 1988). The state can choose to legitimise these claims in various ways, e.g. the title of 'social worker' is controlled and regulated in the UK by a statutory body (currently the Health and Care Professions Council) that enforces standards of conduct and competence. Professionalisation can be seen as a double-edged sword when it comes to service provision. On the one hand, service recipients are reassured that qualified and experienced professionals will behave ethically and 'know what they are doing'; on the other hand, professionals may resist forms of provision that are perceived to impinge on their occupational monopolies. Too much specialisation may therefore lead to fragmented services – a particular concern in cases of complex need, as will be discussed below. Citizens, as well as policymakers, may also be ambivalent about professional discretion, i.e. the freedom to make a judgement when applying specialist knowledge to a specific problem or task. Professionals have been called 'street-level bureaucrats' (Lipsky, 1980), whose everyday decisions and judgements – e.g. about eligibility or risk – determine how policies are implemented by agencies and experienced by citizens. Successive governments have therefore been concerned with reinforcing professional accountability in public services – both to taxpayers and elected officials.

REFLECTIVE EXERCISE 6.1.

Think about your own profession, or the profession you are training for, and consider the following questions:

1.   What is your 'jurisdictional claim', i.e. what is it that your profession does that no-one else can do?
2.   Do you know any professionals whose jobs you think you could do without too much difficulty?
3.   Do you think that social work is largely a matter of common sense? If so, what is the point of a social work qualification?

Modernisation and managerialism

Over recent decades, modernisation of public services has meant importing and adapting some of the managerial practices that are perceived to drive successful businesses (Cochrane, 2000). What has been called the 'new public management' approach (Levy, 2010) is centred around ideas of efficiency and cost-effectiveness and justified by the principles of user-centred care and public accountability. Instead of being clients of professional bureaucracies, recipients of services are seen as consumers, who should have a choice about which services they use. The idea is that market mechanisms will oblige agencies to deliver satisfactory and cost-effective services; rather than providing all taxpayer-funded services directly, local authorities should instead commission and manage a mixed economy of care. Modernisation has also led to an influx of managers in order to organise and monitor the work of professionals. Managerial goals are pursued through 'the application of management methods such as strategic planning, quality assurance, performance management and risk management' (Chard and Ayre, 2010: 95). According to Clarke et al. (2000: 9) managerialism represents a 'concerted effort to displace or subordinate the claims of professionalism', i.e. the approach where professionals largely control and manage their own activities.

Unsurprisingly, modernisation and managerialism have proved unpopular among the professions (Owens and Petch, 1995; Dominelli and Hoogvelt, 1996; Freidson, 2001). In health and social care services, for example, the effect of reforms was argued to 'dismantle traditional professional hierarchies and radically to change accepted patterns of care' (Owens and Petch, 1995: 37). However, these changes need to be seen in the context of what Schön (1991) called the 'crisis of confidence in professional knowledge' – the failure of technical rationality to predict and solve complex social and economic problems, contributing to public scepticism about the legitimacy and vested interests of professional groups.[1] Public outrage about poor practice or decision-making by social workers, e.g. following media-led scandals about deaths from child abuse, can be viewed in the same context; increased monitoring and prescription of social work practice is often recommended as a result of such scandals, leading to further managerial controls over professional work. However, one problem with managerialism is that it can reinforce technical-rational assumptions about professional knowledge and expertise, and therefore exacerbate the crisis of confidence that it was designed to solve (see Chapter 9). This problem is fundamental to the question of how professionals should collaborate, as will be seen below.

Fragmentation and integration

Professionalisation of the welfare state meant that different specialisms were able to carve out a separate remit and scope of expertise within a broad range of provision. Modernisation has arguably complicated matters further, particularly reforms designed to create a quasi-market by increasing the diversity of providers and splitting purchaser and provider functions within statutory bodies (Crawford, 2012; Carnwell and Buchanan, 2005). Fragmentation has in turn led to a greater onus on coordination, collaboration, and partnership between agencies, notably in health

---

[1]Some UK readers may be reminded of a widely reported comment by Conservative politician Michael Gove during the 2016 EU Referendum campaign. When asked during a television interview to name any economists who backed British withdrawal from the EU, Mr Gove declined to do so, saying that 'people in this country have had enough of experts'. Mr Gove was Secretary of State for Education from 2010–14.

and social care (Glendinning, 2002) and in children's services (Hallett and Birchall, 1995). Integrated services offering a 'seamless' and 'holistic' approach have been widely advocated (Danvers et al., 2003; Dawson, 2007; Audit Commission, 2002), although the evidence of success for such endeavours has been mixed (Brown and White, 2006; Cameron and Lart, 2003). Following the financial crisis of 2007/08 and the resulting politics of austerity, the trend of UK government policy has been to emphasise early intervention and the need to target services, rather than necessarily to integrate them (Lord et al., 2011; Allen, 2012).

Terms and Definitions

Collaboration in human services, particularly in health and social care, is notorious for its confusing terminology, with various terms (e.g. professional, disciplinary) and prefixes (e.g. inter-, multi-, trans-) being combined and used interchangeably. This chapter follows the usage recommended by the *Journal of Interprofessional Care*,[2] which disseminates research on interprofessional education and practice across a range of fields (see also Barr et al., 2005; Reeves et al., 2011). Professionals are considered to be occupational groups who provide services to others, and this includes occupations that are not part of established professions such as teaching, nursing, or social work. Professions are distinguished from disciplines, which are broad academic fields such as psychology or sociology. The main focus in this chapter is on *inter*professional working, which is when members of two or more professions interact and collaborate. This generally happens either as a team or as a network (see Anning et al., 2006; Ovretveit, 1997 for further typologies). Members of a team have a clear and defined organisational identity, are often co-located and may share some aspects of line management. Interprofessional networks, on the other hand, are more loosely organised groups that only meet periodically or form on an ad-hoc basis around specific pieces of work. The distinction is worth noting because groups of professionals are sometimes called 'teams' when in fact they are much more like networks. We shall return to this issue later in relation to the 'team around the child' in the English child safeguarding context.

Theories of Collaboration

Drawing on Barr (2013), a distinction can be made between theories about interprofessional *processes* and theories about the *context* in which interprofessional working takes place. Examples of the former might include theories of reflective practice (Schön, 1991), communities of practice (Wenger, 1998), intergroup contact (Allport, 1954), social identity (Brown and Williams, 1984), and psychodynamic theory (Woodhouse and Pengelly, 1991). Examples of the latter include the sociology of the professions (Abbott, 1988), general systems theory (Loxley, 1997),

---

[2]For a full list of terms and definitions see the 'Instructions for Authors' on the *Journal of Interprofessional Care* website: www.tandfonline.com/toc/ijic20/current

complex systems theory, activity theory (Engeström, 1999), and organisational theory (Argyris, 1992). Some of these perspectives have already been discussed in earlier chapters, while others will be explored below.

Interprofessional education (IPE)

Collaboration can be seen as a learning process, in which practitioners embark – perhaps reluctantly – on a journey to new forms of identity. As Barr (2013) notes, social identity theory suggests that we derive our sense of self through belonging to social groups, and so are inclined to evaluate members of the 'in-group' more positively than those outside the group (Brown and Williams, 1984). Some IPE programmes have therefore drawn on intergroup contact theory in order to generate the right conditions for practitioners to learn about and from each other in 'simulated' practice settings (Mohaupt et al., 2012). Such conditions include equality between the different groups involved, shared goals, a cooperative rather than hierarchical approach, positive expectations, appreciation of differences as well as similarities, and a perception that other practitioners are 'typical' rather than 'exceptional' of their group (Mohaupt et al., 2012: 2). Some of these conditions are similar to the findings on 'mechanisms' of interprofessional teamwork (see below).

Continuum models

Continuum models seek to explore and classify the degree to which professionals and their agencies work together in practice. Armitage's (1983) 'taxonomy of collaboration', which describes the transitional stages from lesser to greater degrees of collaboration, has been widely utilised and adapted (e.g. Gregson et al., 1992; Hallett and Birchall, 1995; Bond et al., 1987; Farmakopoulou, 2002). In such typologies, agencies range from operating in isolation to embarking on a full organisational merger (Frost, 2005), while professionals range from barely communicating or encountering each other to working together in multi-disciplinary settings (Ovretveit, 1996). A different schema is presented by Webb (1991), who distinguishes between 'routinised coordination', emphasising procedural cooperation, and 'radical coordination', which is more innovative and far-reaching but presents a 'disturbance of the existing order' (Webb, 1991: 231). Robinson et al. (2008) undertook a meta-analysis categorising models of integrated working within four main dimensions: the extent of integration, integration of structures, integration of processes, and the reach of integration. Each dimension was associated with different challenges, enablers, and impacts, with overarching themes that largely coincide with the findings of other reviews (Brown and White, 2006; Sloper, 2004). Leathard (2003) distinguishes between models dealing with professionals working together and organisations working together, with integration representing a kind of 'culmination' of both. The problem with continuum models is that they do not really explain why 'more' collaboration is better than less, nor the circumstances in which it is likely to succeed or fail.

Gestalt models

In their study of integrated children's services, O'Brien et al. (2009) define a gestalt model of practice as 'the belief that statutory and voluntary agencies working together with a common goal can achieve more than the sum of the individual parts' (2009: 9, citing Glass, 1999). Although she does not use the term gestalt, a similar concept is discussed by Leathard (2003) in relation to collaboration in health and social care. She draws on Rawson's (1994) distinction between 'additive' and 'multiplicative' effects of interprofessional work. Under the additive model, professionals continue to work on their separate areas of expertise but are aware of each other's perspective and contribution. The overall effect of collaboration is therefore the sum of their individual contributions. Under the multiplicative model, professionals working together generate new ideas, knowledge, and potential for solutions that would otherwise not have existed. According to Leathard (2003: 94) 'professionals thus working together can produce a magic between groups'.

a. Additive or disaggregated model

Complex needs are disaggregated into individual needs (N), interventions (I) and outcomes (O).

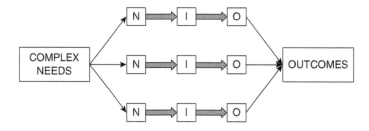

b. Gestalt or holistic model

Complex needs are considered holistically and interprofessional behaviour is part of multiple interventions that together influence outcomes.

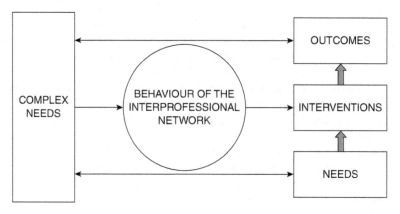

Figure 6.1   Interprofessional working and complex needs (adapted from Hood (2012)

The distinction between additive and gestalt models of interprofessional working can be applied to the problem of complex needs, which was discussed in Chapter 1. As Hood (2012) points out, one way of dealing with complex needs is to disaggregate them into separate needs, which are then targeted by specific interventions delivered by the appropriate professionals. Each of these interventions proceeds in parallel, with some degree of coordination, communication, and review of progress, until the requisite outcomes are achieved. This approach, illustrated in Figure 6.1a, is reminiscent of Schön's technical rationality (see Chapter 5) because 'it assumes a series of closed systems in which individual needs are directly susceptible to treatment by professional intervention' (Hood, 2012: 8). However, this is arguably a misunderstanding of how complex causality works in open systems (see Chapter 7). A more holistic – or 'gestalt' – approach to the situation is needed in order to identify the main priorities for action, deal with unpredictable events and respond to unintended consequences. This approach, illustrated in Figure 6.1b, acknowledges the social complexity of interprofessional behaviour and tries to understand the interconnections and dynamics that underpin complex needs and drive global outcomes.

Ecological and organisational models

Ecological models of interprofessional and interagency collaboration show the individual citizen to be at the centre of nested layers of support and provision. The innermost layers often constitute carers or close family members, followed by the agencies and services whose activities need to be coordinated if they are to 'wrap around' the user in a reassuring manner. Sometimes these arrangements are referred to as 'systems of care' (Anderson et al., 2005; Pumariega, 1997) or as a 'user-centred model' of care or help (Hornby and Atkins, 2000). Hood (2016b: 54) gives the example of an 'onion' model of children's services from statutory guidance (DCSF, 2010), which shows outcomes for children and families to be nested within concentric rings of integrated provision. This preventative system of care conveys a 'dual emphasis on containment and control', since it serves to promote children's welfare but also to protect them from harm. Ecological models are useful because they situate the work of collaborating professionals within the broader context of organisational and institutional arrangements, while revealing some of the assumptions underlying those arrangements.

The organisational context of interprofessional work is very important. Many health and social care professionals work within statutory organisations such as local authorities and the NHS. Not only does this mean that much of their activity is circumscribed and monitored by managerial bureaucracies, it also means that the conditions for *interprofessional* collaboration are often determined by *interagency* protocols and agreements (Hudson, 2007). Organisational theory offers rival explanations for why services should collaborate. The exchange perspective (Levine and White, 1961; Cook, 1977) sees collaboration as a rational, voluntary act based on negotiating to achieve goals and objectives. Alternatively, a power and dependency perspective sees organisations as seeking primarily to reduce uncertainty in a complex environment and establish control over scarce resources (Aldrich, 1972, 1976). In public services, particularly those in which social workers are employed, the role of legal frameworks and regulation is key in mandating particular forms of collaboration.

Teamwork

There is an extensive literature on teamwork in health and social care (e.g. Payne, 2000; Hewitt et al., 2014; Reeves and Harris, 2016; Reeves et al., 2011). From a continuum perspective (see above), teamwork tends to be characterised by a high level of integration, interdependence, and shared responsibility, which distinguish teams from 'looser' collaborative arrangements. Reeves and Harris (2016) give the example of a patient being admitted to hospital for an operation, which is carried out by a team of clinicians interacting in a focused and tightly organised way. Recovery and rehabilitation following discharge from hospital may still involve a number of professionals but their activity will be coordinated in a less intensive manner. According to Reeves and Harris (2016), teamwork is required when the tasks to be undertaken are urgent, unpredictable, and complex, whereas more routine, predictable tasks do not need such an intensive approach. This distinction can be linked to the 'tiered' approach to services in that multiprofessional teams are often to be found in the higher, more specialist tiers (see Chapter 8).

Over the years, researchers have endeavoured to identify the factors that facilitate and hinder effective teamwork. These include the constituent roles of team players (Belbin, 1981; Parker, 1990) as well as individual competencies for collaborating in teams (Engels, 1994; Suter et al., 2009). Some of the skills needed for interprofessional working – not just in teams but in other collaborative contexts – are discussed further below. Of course, from a complexity (and 'gestalt') perspective, teams are more than just the sum of their human components. Teams are complex because the decisions, actions, and interactions of team members, each with their own social and institutional context, all shape the behaviour of the group. In a realist synthesis of the evidence on interprofessional teamwork, Hewitt et al. (2014) outline 13 underlying processes, or 'mechanisms', which have been found to affect how teams function in health and social care. These mechanisms are summarised below in Table 6.1.

Of course, not all of these processes are apparent in all teams at all times. Indeed, not all of them are desirable (e.g. 'tactical communication') and some are complementary and potentially oppositional (e.g. role clarity and role blurring). Hewitt et al. (2014: 501) point out that collaborative teamwork should be seen as a 'complex social intervention', since the team's impact on the care given to a person will depend on how individual professionals respond to being part of a team. Their synthesis of the literature therefore seeks not only to identify the general nature of these responses, constituting the mechanisms listed in Table 6.1, but also the contexts that lead to specific mechanisms being 'triggered' and the outcomes that emerge in those circumstances. For example, Hewitt et al. (2014) discuss the variations in contexts that meant that 'support and value' (as defined above) was present in some teams but not others. When this mechanism was triggered, studies found that mutual support and valuing each other fostered motivation and commitment to the team and its

Table 6.1 Mechanisms of interprofessional teamwork in health and social care

Mechanism	Definition (Hewitt et al., 2014, Hewitt et al., 2015, Sims et al., 2015a, Sims et al., 2015b)
Support and value	Team members support one another, respect each other's skills and abilities and value each other's contributions
Collaboration and coordination	Team members have clear knowledge of each other's roles and responsibilities
Pooling of resources	Team members share their knowledge, skills, experience, resources, and networks in the interests of service users and their needs
Individual learning	There are opportunities for team members to learn from each other, which fosters mutual respect and improves problem-solving
Role blurring	Although professional roles are clearly defined, a shared body of knowledge and skill means that that team members can cover each other if needed and foster each other's professional development
Efficient, open, and equitable communication	Team members freely offer their opinion, constructively challenge one another, and mutually resolve disagreements, regardless of perceived professional status
Tactical communication	Team members try to control the amount or type of information they share with others, either for their own advantage or what they perceive to be their patient's advantage
Shared responsibility and influence	All team members can influence team decisions and share responsibility for those decisions and their outcomes
Team behavioural norms	Team members share behavioural 'norms' or rules which govern how they are expected to communicate and work together
Shared responsibility and influence	Teams have an explicit and shared understanding of their objectives, values, and vision that is mutually developed and/or agreed by team members
Critically reviewing performance and decisions	Teams offer an opportunity for group reflection and evaluation, giving team members space to reflect upon and critically review their performance, actions, and decisions, and give/receive feedback
Generating and implementing new ideas	Teams offer an opportunity for collective learning and development, the sharing of ideas, the discussion of innovative solutions to problems, and the identification and implementation of new ways of working
Leadership	The team has a clearly identified leader who sets the tone or culture of the team, engages and motivates team members, ensures that communication is open and equitable, and that all members are able to participate and feel supported

goals, and improved staff relationships. Hewitt and her colleagues go on to explore the contexts and outcomes of other mechanisms in a series of companion papers (see Table 6.1.). This method of systematic review is taken from Pawson et al. (2005), whose work is discussed in Chapter 7.

iNteRPROfeSSiONaL ethiCS

Hammick et al. (2009) define 'being interprofessional' almost as a state of mind, an internalised attitude that enables practitioners to understand, respect, and communicate with colleagues from different backgrounds. Professionalism on its own, they suggest, is no longer enough in a world of complex problems that make working together not just preferable, but essential. Whereas professionalism creates boundaries between competences, remits and roles, interprofessionalism is about crossing them. Studies have also developed the idea that interprofessionalism is underpinned by a shared value base. Professional ethics, usually formalised as standards of practice, often focus on the relationship between service providers and service users, aiming to mitigate power imbalances, manage expectations, and create trust (Hall, 2003). Differences between professional cultures result in different value-perspectives, for example about confidentiality or informed consent when it comes to information sharing (Reeves and Freeth, 2003), or about resource management and access to care (Leathard and Mclaren, 2002). The shift towards interprofessional collaboration in health and social care has therefore led to an emerging field of interprofessional ethics (Clark et al., 2007). Efforts have been made to establish a common ethical framework based on the 'primacy of the client's needs and interests' (Irvine et al., 2002: 208), and to design interdisciplinary courses accordingly (Stone et al., 2004). However, as Hall (2003) points out, it is not always feasible to distil different professional codes of practice into a single 'pan-professional' code. It is likely that professionals will need a more pluralist model of ethics in which openness and a willingness to negotiate are preferred to rigid compliance with one particular framework of practice. Practical examples include issues around confidentiality and information sharing, as discussed below.

CONfLiCt aNo CONSeNSUS

Interprofessional working is a complex social phenomenon, and is therefore unpredictable and in certain circumstances even volatile. Much of the literature on professional collaboration concerns itself with the tensions and conflicts that may arise from differences in cultures, identities, boundaries, language, remits, and status. Such conflicts are usually seen as 'barriers' to effective collaboration (Brown and White, 2006; Sloper, 2004). In team settings, practitioners may want to hold on to their specialist areas of expertise and therefore be reluctant to share knowledge and skills with colleagues from other professional backgrounds (Rose, 2011). Jones et al. (2013) refer to multi-professional teams as being like a 'salad' or 'soup'; in the former, the contributions and characteristics of individual team members are distinct and identifiable, whereas in the latter, team members are hybrid professionals with largely overlapping skills and expertise. Resistance to role-blurring and hybridisation, often linked to questions of power, status, and remuneration, can prove problematic for building a team culture based on open communication and the exchange of knowledge and skills (Anning et al., 2006).

Information sharing can be a source of difficulty and frustration, particularly in 'looser' interprofessional networks, where concerns about confidentiality may inhibit communication. It has been found, for example, that social workers often become frustrated when it comes to obtaining information from health professionals (Barnes, 2016), while teachers have reported similar frustrations with respect to social workers (Hood et al., 2017). Statutory guidance can inform professionals when the duty to share information overrides normal expectations around privacy and confidentiality (e.g. Department for Education, 2015). However, negotiations around information sharing – and about people's availability and responsiveness – are exposed to unpredictable dynamics around power, status, and institutional anxiety about risk (see below). It is therefore difficult completely to 'protocolise' information sharing, or indeed any other element of interprofessional working, in order to ensure consensus. Furthermore, it is open to question whether consensus is necessarily desirable, particularly when complex decisions with far-reaching consequences are being made (Janis, 1982).

Warmington et al. (2004) argue that instead of seeing conflict as a 'barrier' to be overcome, professionals, should recognise that instability and contradiction are the driving forces of change. Furthermore, services are often provided through emergent networks of agencies, professionals, and clients, rather than through monolithic organisational or team structures. Drawing on the activity theory of Yrjö Engestrom (1999, 2001) Warmington and colleagues argue that expertise is increasingly distributed across these networks and collaboration is largely improvised in focused, time-limited bursts of activity around particular cases. The inevitable tension between multiple perspectives and practices should not be seen as detrimental to collaboration, but should be harnessed as a creative force centred on the 'object' of the activity system, i.e. what professionals are working on together. However, harnessing disagreement constructively requires professionals to acknowledge its existence and recognise its underlying causes. As discussed in the next section, there are reasons why this may be more difficult in some cases than others.

ANXiety aND 'FaULt-LiNes' iN COLLaBORatiON

As discussed in previous chapters, stress and anxiety can have a significant impact on practitioners and will therefore also affect how they work with each other (Morrison, 1996). Apparent consensus in interprofessional networks can sometimes conceal underlying anxieties about status or accountability (Skjorshammer, 2001; Stevenson, 1994), while several studies have used a psychodynamic perspective to explore how defensive coping mechanisms affect not just individuals but also groups of professionals and entire institutions (Conway, 2009; Menzies Lyth, 1988; Woodhouse and Pengelly, 1991; Granville and Langton, 2002). A seminal paper by Isabel Menzies (1960) called 'A case study in the functioning of the social systems as a defence against anxiety' concerned nursing students in a teaching hospital. She found that they had developed an array of ritual tasks and routines in their work, which functioned as a defence against negative emotions aroused by their proximity to the death and suffering of patients as well as the latter's ambivalence about the nursing care provided to them. Over time, these tasks became so rigid and formalised that nurses started to feel alienated from the caring, relationship-based vocation that they had originally envisaged. Although her focus was on nurses, Menzies' findings may strike a chord with social workers' experience of lengthy, bureaucratic assessment procedures, which keep practitioners in the office and away from the people they are meant to be working with (Jones et al., 2013).

Woodhouse and Pengelly (1991) applied Menzies' insights in their study of inter-professional collaboration in marriage guidance, finding that social workers (along with other professionals) were caught up in institutionalised defences that impaired their capacity to work with others. Similarly, Cooper et al. (1995) comment on the 'fortress atmosphere' conveyed by the reception areas of English social work offices. Anxiety on an institutional level is often associated with attitudes to risk; for example, protocols and procedures stipulating a 'correct' way to deal with a case can serve a rather perverse function of insulating practitioners and their agencies from 'institutional risk' (Rothstein, 2006). As Hood (2015b) points out, when professionals communicate about risk in complex situations they may be perceived as trying to allocate or share accountability for outcomes. For example, if a practitioner rings a social worker to say 'I am concerned about X', they may mean (or be understood as meaning) 'I am worried about X', but also 'something must be done about X', or 'I've now told you about X', and even 'it's now your job to sort out X', and so on (Hood, 2015b: 11).

Problems in interprofessional communication have been a consistent feature of reports and inquiries into deaths from child abuse in the UK, going back at least to the death of Dennis O'Neill in 1945 (Munro, 2004; Reder and Duncan, 2004). Yet despite well-intentioned policies designed to ensure effective multi-agency provision, splits and fault-lines in collaboration between professionals continue to be endemic in the provision of services for vulnerable children and families. Conway (2009) suggests that the recommendations usually made to improve multi-agency working, such as developing a common language and joint training for children's professionals, overlook the importance of emotions and psychological processes in the system of care around a looked after child. She draws on the psychodynamic concepts of splitting and projection, which were discussed in Chapter 4, to suggest how volatile dynamics emerge in the system:

> in the system around the child there are two powerful dynamics at play: splitting, which divides the world and the people in it into separate, often hostile groups or states of mind; and projection, which fills people up with very powerful communications and feelings that can feel unbearable. In addition, there is a complex system around each looked after child that adds to the risk of these dynamics taking over, and can make working together feel like walking through an emotional minefield. It is a system with a multitude of what I call 'fault lines'. (Conway, 2009: 23)

Conway illustrates her argument by showing a pie chart divided into 30 segments, each corresponding to a different person – most of them professionals or managers – involved in the care of a looked after child. In her interpretation, the demarcations between all these people create a huge number of potential fault-lines along which powerful, often counterproductive, and sometimes destructive patterns of communication and interaction take shape. An example of such patterns is shown in Case Study 6.1 below, which describes how a multi-agency meeting becomes subject to disagreement and conflicts. Of course, the professionals taking part in the meeting might be unlikely to attribute their disagreements to unconscious processes of projection and splitting. Nonetheless, it is worth drawing attention – as the teacher does in the case study – to the adversarial quality of interactions in order to question their cause and purpose. A key issue here is the question of leadership, not only in terms of reaching a collective or mediated consensus but also on translating it into action. While Steven's social worker may be the lead professional, and therefore responsible for coordinating the care plan, her role comes with little authority over other professionals. Indeed, during meetings she may be subordinated to the independent reviewing officer's (IRO's) decisions. The IRO, on the other hand, has a degree of statutory authority but little involvement in day-to-day case management. Key professionals, such as doctors and police officers, may not be able to attend meetings and so may be even harder to draw into a cohesive network.

CASE STUDY 6.1

Steven

Read the following case study and consider the questions below.
Steven is a 12-year-old boy of dual heritage, White British and Black British Caribbean. He was taken into care two years ago, having experienced chronic neglect and emotional abuse, and has been living with his current foster family for eight months. He has weekly contact with his mother but rarely sees his father. Steven struggles to control his temper and can be angry and aggressive towards other children and adults. He is at risk of exclusion from school and his foster parents are wondering if they can cope with his behaviour at home. He has had frequent changes of social worker, and made a complaint about his last social worker with the support of his foster mother. Steven is currently being seen by a child psychiatrist following referral to child and adolescent mental health services (CAMHS). He is diagnosed with attention deficit hyperactivity disorder (ADHD) for which he has been prescribed medication. As part of his care plan, he has also been allocated a mentor to involve him in positive activities after school, and an independent advocate to help him express his wishes and feelings to the people responsible for his care. Steven's last looked after child (LAC) review was attended by 15 people, not including Steven himself who refused to be present and asked his advocate to represent him. During the meeting a number of disagreements

(Continued)

were aired. The independent advocate said that Steven had asked many times to see his father and wanted to know why the social worker had not arranged this. Steven's mother said that the school was acting unfairly to exclude Steven and that teachers these days seemed to care more about their exam results than children's welfare. Steven's social worker said that he did not agree with the CAMHS doctor's recommendation that the ADHD medication dose be increased, and was immediately challenged on his lack of medical expertise by the foster carer. Steven's mentor said that Steven found it hard to talk about his feelings and seemed to 'keep a lot of things bottled up'. The Independent Reviewing Officer, who chaired the meeting, sought to update the care plan by outlining some tasks to be carried out by the social worker. Steven's teacher observed that everyone seemed to be focused on getting annoyed with each other, when they were supposed to be working together to help Steven.

- On the basis of the limited information given above, what is your sense of what Steven's needs are and what should be done to support him?
- How do you think the interprofessional network is functioning at the moment?
- What might have been done differently in the LAC review meeting?

Hood et al. (2017) point out the significance of a different kind of fault-line, namely the threshold between statutory and non-statutory services. For teachers who took part in this study, the decision about whether to make a child protection referral was fraught with potential repercussions for their relationship with the parents. This was mainly because of the stigma of involvement with child protection services but also because teachers saw themselves as having an ongoing, everyday relationship with parents, which they would need to continue after any CP investigations or interventions had concluded. Accordingly, teachers expected social workers to take the lead in terms of explaining to parents what the concerns were, allowing them as far as possible to 'keep' a positive relationship with the parent. From the social worker's perspective, this was perceived as unhelpful in terms of giving consistent messages to parents and being set up as an 'authority figure' within the network of professionals (see also Hood, 2015a).

iNteRPROFeSSiONaL eXPeRtiSe

Since proficiency in a given field does not always bring with it the ability to work effectively with others, Hood et al. (2016a) argue that collaboration requires an additional set of knowledge and skills. They use the term interprofessional expertise in order to encompass formal knowledge and trained competences, as well as the tacit knowledge and skills that come from experience of working with others. Such expertise is 'domain-specific', in that it is developed and applied in a certain area of practice, e.g. child safeguarding or adult mental health, and for each practitioner 'is shaped by their role as well as the jurisdiction in which they have trained and worked' (Hood et al., 2016a: 494). Acquiring this type of expertise enables practitioners to tailor their collaborative practice to the uncertainty and complexity of specific conditions. Much has to be learned 'on the job' since professional training programmes tend to lack opportunities for practitioners to learn 'with and from and about each other' (Hood et al., 2016a). Along with the evidence on teamwork discussed earlier, the literature on interprofessional education also provides some strong indicators of what it takes for professionals to work together effectively. The key areas considered here are:

- Knowledge and awareness
- Communication
- Negotiation
- Reflective practice

Knowledge and awareness

Professional socialisation, through its formative influence on the construction of personal and group identity, can sometimes make it difficult for people from different professional backgrounds to collaborate. This could be attributed to mutual stereotyping, perceived changes in status, 'tribal' instincts, reluctance to do generic rather than specialist work, or ambivalence about developing a new professional identity. Even experienced practitioners may simply expect other professionals to think like them – 'it's *obvious* that the problem is X, I don't know how they can't see it....' An obvious way of counteracting these tendencies is to promote knowledge and awareness of other professions, the roles and remits they typically discharge, and the legal and institutional contexts that shape their practice. Interprofessional education and training is an obvious way of promoting contact and joint learning. Co-locating professionals in multi-professional teams has also been found to foster contact and mutual trust, e.g. through the increased scope for informal discussions and interactions (Cameron and Lart, 2003; Canavan et al., 2009; Sloper, 2004). In more distributed settings, it could be argued that practitioners are responsible for finding out themselves about the professions with whom they spend time working.

Communication

Professional communication encompasses a range of skills, many of which have been explored in earlier chapters. Communicating with professionals arguably requires the same skills as engaging any other citizen: active listening, empathy, respect for the person (even if disagreeing with their views), an openness to other perspectives, and a willingness to negotiate while being honest about what matters from one's own perspective. There are various reasons why social workers may find it harder to apply these principles to communicating with professionals than in dealing with 'service users'. Social workers may feel less powerful than other professionals, for example when requesting resources or information, and – somewhat ironically – become frustrated with delays caused by other agencies' bureaucratic procedures. When working with healthcare professionals, social workers may find themselves uncomfortable with discussions of individual pathology, diagnosis, and treatment. Perceived differences in power and influence may exacerbate these cultural differences, with social workers perhaps mindful (or sometimes reminded) of their relatively low status in the hierarchy of professions (Etzioni, 1969). Furthermore, counterproductive patterns of communication may be the result of group processes or unconscious defence mechanisms, as explored earlier. Interprofessional communication therefore requires close attention to the dynamics of relationships and interactions, and an ability to negotiate and manage conflict.

Negotiation

The ability to negotiate is vital to interprofessional social work (Barnes, 2016), and overlaps with the communication skills outlined above. The starting point is to be able to present one's own perspective clearly and concisely, making a case for any decisions or judgements that matter. However, it is equally important to understand the other person's perspective, and the reasons underlying their views. It is worth remembering that disagreement between professionals is not necessarily a bad thing, and can prove useful for clarifying the available evidence and avoiding confirmation bias. Where negotiations are necessary, or likely, professionals should consider how and in what context to carry them out; for example, holding a professionals' meeting before any joint discussion with citizens may be a useful way to formulate a consistent message, e.g. about what professionals are worried about and what they think needs to happen (Hood, 2015a). Negotiation may contain elements of conflict in that it involves similar trade-offs between assertiveness and cooperation (Shell, 2001). The 'dual concerns' model of conflict identifies five main conflict handling styles: avoidant, accommodating, competing, compromising, and collaborating (Ruble and Thomas, 1976); which style people adopt depends on the degree to which they give precedence to satisfying their own concerns as opposed to the concerns of others. Lewicki et al. (1992) review the literature on conflict, negotiation, mediation, and arbitration, noting the different theoretical frameworks associated with each form of activity. These are useful distinctions for social workers, who may well find themselves mediating between others as well as negotiating in their own right. As with most other things in social work, such tasks are challenging and can give rise to strong emotions that are difficult to manage in the heat of the moment (Smethurst and Long, 2013). Acknowledging and addressing such issues requires a reflective mindset.

Reflective practice

While social workers are familiar with reflective practice from their education and training, this is not always the case in other professions (Mann et al., 2009).

Nor may it be immediately obvious to practitioners that they should reflect on their dealings with each other, rather than focusing on their ostensible task of providing a service to people. Group reflection and critical feedback is arguably more likely to occur in tightly knit teams (Sims et al., 2015a) than in more dispersed networks, whose meetings will tend to focus more on reviewing outcomes and allocating tasks – what Webb (1991) calls 'routine coordination'. Nonetheless, reflective practice is intrinsic to many models of interprofessional collaboration (Hudson, 2007; Canavan et al., 2009), in which a shift towards interdependent decision-making and collective responsibility is argued to promote creative and innovative solutions to problems, i.e. what Webb (1991) calls 'radical coordination'. Hood (2013) found that core professionals in child protection networks would assume 'some of the characteristics of more formally organised teams' as they adapted to particularly complex cases, including a 'reflexive awareness' of their own activity and behaviour as a group (Hood, 2013: 234). However, it was also found that as these groups 'developed a sense of common identity and purpose, based on identifying the children's needs and arriving at a common understanding of the problem', they also needed a consistent and committed lead professional as a focal point, i.e. 'a professional with the necessary expertise and authority to articulate that understanding and coordinate a joint response' (Hood, 2013: 233). The implication for social workers coordinating multi-agency care plans is that while complexity may well stimulate an increase in the group's reflective capacity, this will only happen if there is an assumption of leadership. Since social workers generally have little or no authority over other professionals – even if they are coordinating their activity on a particular piece of work – they will often need all of their communication and negotiation skills to discharge their lead professional role.

CONCLUSION

This chapter has examined interprofessional working as a response to complexity. Social workers may be part of multi-professional teams, contribute to multi-agency care plans or coordinate a range of services to support service users with complex needs. In cases of complex need, networks of professionals tend to come together on an ad-hoc basis and continue to be managed in their respective agencies. These networks are not really teams (even though they may be called teams), and this dispersal of expertise may create difficulties when there is a need to think reflectively as a group, undertake tricky negotiations, and manage disagreement and conflict. A key problem is that while complexity of need tends to increase the number of professionals involved, this serves in turn to increase the social complexity of collaboration, for example by multiplying the potential fault-lines across which misunderstandings and defensive responses can proliferate. The literature shows that protocols to promote (and indeed mandate) collaboration can only accomplish so much; there is no way of designing out complexity. For professionals caught up in counterproductive patterns of communication and interaction, it may be difficult to 'step back' and take stock of the underlying reasons for discord or paralysis. Moreover, social workers are often in the position of having (or perceiving they have) accountability for outcomes but without the commensurate authority to direct the activity of professionals with quite separate lines of management. In many cases, social workers and their colleagues in other professions are impelled to go beyond the normal course of duty in their dedication to the health, safety, and welfare of others. For example, Hood et al. (2017) report a social worker's account of repeatedly visiting a deprived housing estate alone, at some considerable risk to her safety, and summoning a community midwife to successfully deliver a baby on a tower-block stairwell. In this context of everyday, unheralded, and often heroic dedication, it seems unfair to constantly make individual practitioners the scapegoats for negative outcomes in complex situations. Instead, it is managers, policymakers, and researchers on whom the spotlight falls in the next part of this book.

PART 2

ENGAGING WITH COMPLEX SYSTEMS

ADDRESSING COMPLEXITY IN RESEARCH AND EVALUATION

7

CHAPTER SUMMARY

This chapter considers the challenges faced by researchers and evaluators in producing scientifically robust explanations of complex social phenomena. Social work is described as an applied field of practice and research, which draws eclectically from a range of academic disciplines and approaches to the pursuit of knowledge. This leads to a consideration of research paradigms, of which scientific realism is argued to be the one that engages most comprehensively with the problem of complexity. The main principles of realist research are outlined and linked to a critique of the dominant positivist paradigm, before proceeding to discuss some of the methods commonly employed in realist designs. Particular attention is given to realist evaluation and realist synthesis, which provide an alternative to experimental field trials and meta-analysis as the standard approach to 'what works' in social work and related fields. The chapter concludes by examining some limitations of the realist approach and alternative ways of researching complexity.

iNtRODUCtiON

> What can be uttered in a word but contemplated forever? What do fools
> ignore and pragmatists suffer? What is evaluation's greatest challenge? These
> questions present no riddle, no mystery and no conundrum. The answers are
> complexity, complexity and complexity. (Pawson, 2013: 29)

Complexity provides researchers – including evaluators – with many of the same
challenges that it does practitioners, e.g. volatile relationships, uncertainty about
cause-and-effect, unintended consequences, and emergent properties. Complexity
puts context and contingency in the foreground of the search for scientific knowledge. What holds true in one situation may not apply elsewhere, making it harder
to obtain generalisable 'truth' about the social world. For example, social workers might be interested in the question of how services should help someone
with a learning disability to live with dignity, contribute to society, and achieve
'self-actualisation' (see Chapter 1). What this means in practice will depend on a
multitude of factors that can hardly be addressed by a 'one size fits all' model of
support or provision. With such questions, there is always an element of doubt
about regular patterns, such as correlations between one variable, e.g. 'access to
public transport', and another, e.g. 'participation in further education and employment' (Wolf-Branigin, 2013). Observations that appear to show a 'steady state',
where changes in one part of the system lead to proportionate changes elsewhere,
may no longer apply if the system becomes volatile and unstable (e.g. 'austerity
policies'). In such cases, the 'proven' hypothesis may no longer hold true. After
all, decisions, attitudes, and relationships lie at the heart of social systems. This
includes unconscious and emotional influences on people's behaviour, as well as
the effects of reflexive processes, e.g. awareness of research findings. Complexity
also invokes the 'gestalt' principle whereby group characteristics are more than just
an accumulation of individual characteristics, and the fluid, dynamic quality of the
social world. These tendencies make it untenable to view people purely as rational
agents pursing rational objectives, and cast doubt on our ability to know societies
in the same way we claim to know the natural world, i.e. as a set of structures and
relationships that remain constant over time. That is not to say that complexity
makes it impossible to conduct research in the field of social work; however, certain methods and approaches seem more suited to acknowledging and addressing
complexity than others.

These issues matter to social workers for various reasons. Most obviously, scientific research is the foundation for the formal or 'academic' knowledge that
practitioners learn as part of their training and education. Much of this knowledge
stems from other disciplines, such as developmental psychology or critical sociology,
and is then applied in social work settings. For example, education or 'treatment'
programmes for (usually male) perpetrators of domestic abuse draw on psychological theories of motivation and cognitive-behavioural intervention but also on
feminist theories about gendered dynamics of control and oppression in family life
(Pence and Paymar, 1993). In turn, the evaluation of such interventions forms part of
the literature or 'evidence-base' for engaging abusive men (Babcock et al., 2004) as

well as responding to domestic abuse as a child protection issue (Hester, 2011; Scott and Crooks, 2007). As we shall see below, studying whether and how such interventions 'work' means understanding the contextual factors that affect mechanisms of change, including the contribution of professional expertise and the relationships between practitioners and citizens. Social workers therefore need not only to 'know the evidence' but also how to use it. They need to know what evidence is relevant for whom in what circumstances and how it could inform their practice with individual people, families, and communities. In turn, researchers aim to provide practitioners with the knowledge they need to help them disentangle and address the complex problems they encounter on a daily basis.

Applied Research and Evidence

Most social work research falls into the category of 'applied research', being concerned with the practical application of theoretical ideas in social settings. For example, a well-known type of applied research is programme evaluation, which examines the impact of a social work intervention in order to find out whether it achieves its aims and objectives. Evaluations have become very prevalent in the public sector, where there is a concern to find out 'what works' and justify the use of public money and resources. Proponents of 'evidence-based' social work argue that social workers have a professional obligation to use intervention strategies that are known to be effective, and that the most convincing evidence of effectiveness comes from rigorously conducted scientific studies rather than practice wisdom or agency convention (Chaffin and Friedrich, 2004; Forrester, 2010; Gambrill, 1999; McNeece and Thyer, 2004). Critics of the evidence-based perspective, on the other hand, have argued that it produces a too narrow view of what constitutes evidence and ignores the complexity of problems in social work (Webb, 2001; Sanderson, 2006). In order to understand how the debate about evidence concerns complexity, it is worth outlining the difference between different research paradigms.

REFLECTIVE EXERCISE 7.1

Think of a time when you searched for a piece of research on a practice issue.

1. What question were you looking to answer? (e.g. Did you want to know what it is like to live with a particular health condition, or what type of intervention is known to help with a particular problem, or what causes people to behave in a particular way?)
2. How did you select the research to answer your question?
3. What type of research was it?
4. Did you look at a range of empirical studies, or a literature review on the subject?

Research Paradigms

Research paradigms emerge from the different assumptions, or 'cluster of beliefs' (Bryman, 1988: 4), which researchers have about the nature of reality (ontology) and what constitutes knowledge (epistemology). These assumptions affect the way knowledge claims are made and verified, i.e. research design and methodology. Positivism is generally held to be the dominant paradigm in social research, and indeed in science generally (Morris, 2006). Positivist research presupposes the existence of social facts and laws, which can be investigated using the same empirical methods employed in the natural sciences (see Guba and Lincoln, 2005: 193–6). This often means designing experiments to test hypotheses, measuring variables across a large number of cases or subjects, and obtaining quantitative data that is amenable to statistical analysis. Non-positivist studies fall into various different camps, e.g. constructivist/interpretivist, realist, and critical approaches.

- *Interpretivist* research examines the ways in which human beings understand and experience their social world. Social reality and meaning are seen as being constructed through language and interaction rather than governed by universal laws. Interpretivist research is usually ideographic, seeking to obtain rich, detailed accounts of people and their subjective viewpoints, and analysing these in the form of textual data (Abbott, 2001; Harvey, 2009). It is generally associated with qualitative methods of data collection and analysis.
- *Realist* researchers are interested in the causal mechanisms that generate events and behaviour in the social world. They share with positivists the belief that an external reality exists independently of our own subjective construction of the world. However, realist assumptions about causality differ in important ways from positivism, so that while it is necessary to go beyond the ideographic it is impossible to establish universal social laws. A mixture of qualitative and quantitative methods may be used in order to establish how particular configurations of cause and effect emerge in specific contexts or 'cases'.
- *Critical* social researchers are interested in power, inequality, exclusion, and emancipation. There is a focus on social structures that lie beneath the surface of everyday language and institutions, and on the collective action needed to change those structures. Rather than seeking social laws or an understanding of people in their environment, the aim of critical research is to improve people's lives. Often this means researchers working in partnership with particular groups of citizens in order to produce knowledge that is relevant to them and then act on it.

Social work research can fall into any (or more than one) of these categories. However, research in the positivist paradigm tends to have more credibility with academics, practitioners, and policymakers. This is partly because positivist studies claim close allegiance to the methodologies of natural science and seek to find generalisable facts about society; it may also be because their findings make for succinct and attractive summaries, e.g. 'it works' or 'it's true' (see Chapter 9). Notably, experimental and quasi-experimental designs are considered the most robust form of evidence when it comes to evaluating services and interventions. Small-scale qualitative studies in the interpretivist paradigm, or action research projects in the critical tradition, are much lower down in the 'hierarchy of evidence' because their treatment of social life is more subjective and context-specific. Realist research occupies something of a middle ground because while it is concerned with causal processes that apply beyond a specific situation or experience, it emphasises the fundamental role of contextual and temporal factors in triggering those processes and generating outcomes. The emphasis on contingent causality means that realist research is often explicitly concerned with complexity, which is less common for studies in the positivist, interpretivist, or critical traditions. Indeed, there is a 'complex realist' strand of research that formally integrates complexity principles into the realist paradigm (Byrne, 2009b). In what follows, the main principles of scientific realism are outlined and compared with the dominant positivist paradigm.

Realist Research

Realist research is based on the scientific philosophy of Harré (1970) and Bhaskar (1978) and exponents of their ideas in the social sciences (e.g. Archer, 1998; Sayer, 2010). Its key principles are oriented around the distinction between ontology (what exists) and epistemology (how we know things). While it is assumed that the world exists independently of our knowledge of it, we can never be sure that our knowledge provides a true picture of reality. Knowledge is fallible and 'theory-laden' (Sayer, 2010) but is not impervious to empirical feedback, i.e. some explanations are more successful and useful than others. Bhaskar (1978) refers to the difference between 'transitive' and 'intransitive' objects of science – our fallible theories are neither equivalent to the world nor independent of it. Like any other human activity, the scientific pursuit of knowledge is a social practice, mediated through language and intimately connected to the production and interpretation of texts. Evaluating knowledge therefore means being aware of these social and linguistic practices and their wider institutional, economic, and political context.

Scientific realism is distinguished by its generative model of causation, which is also its main link to complexity theory. It is assumed that objects have 'causal powers', or ways of acting that have an effect on the world around them. However, these effects are non-linear, since causal mechanisms interact and interfere with each other in unpredictable ways. This means that reality is 'stratified', since causal powers, or 'mechanisms', are still present even if their effects are not empirically observable. For example, the force of gravity is still present when an aeroplane takes off – in this case gravity's downward pull is being counteracted by aerodynamic forces acting on the wings. The human capacity for thought, feeling, and action also gives rise to causal mechanisms that may be evident or latent in particular situations. For example, a professional athlete's speed and stamina, acquired over years of training and competition, are clearly manifested when she is running a race and are still present, although not evident, when she is sitting down to dinner. Nonetheless, causal mechanisms in the social world are more concept-dependent than in the natural world. They rest on interpretation, or more precisely on the interpretation of other people's interpretations – what Danermark et al. (2002) call the 'double hermeneutic' of social inquiry. As a result there are differences as well as similarities in the methods used in the social and natural sciences.

The realist theory of causation

The realist theory of causation is generative and therefore distinguishes between observable events and the causal mechanisms that produce them. Bhaskar (1978) differentiates between three levels of reality: the empirical, the actual, and the real. The empirical is what we experience through our senses; the actual is all events, regardless of whether they are observed or experienced; the real consists of the causal mechanisms that generate actual (and therefore empirical) events (Hood, 2012). As causal mechanisms interact and influence each other in open systems, their empirical effects are irregular and unpredictable: mechanisms produce only 'tendencies' that can be counteracted by others (see Figure 7.1). In the social world, causal powers can be attributed to human intention and volition but also arise from social structures, e.g. customs, laws, fashions. Unlike the objects of natural science, people actively transform their own social world, just as their actions and perceptions are shaped by forces operating within societies and over time. For example, it has been found that people who experience sustained economic hardship are generally more likely to experience physical and mental illness (Everson et al., 2002). A potential mechanism for this relationship might be increased exposure to chronic stress and its physiological and psychological effects (Wilkinson, 2005). Contextual conditions and other mechanisms might include levels of social inequality and resilience factors such as coping strategies and social support networks (Eastwood et al., 2016).

The realist theory of causation contrasts with the positivist approach, which is not concerned with mechanisms but with the observation of law-like regularities. This method owes much to the eighteenth-century Scottish philosopher, David Hume, who argued that cause and effect was an assumption that people made when

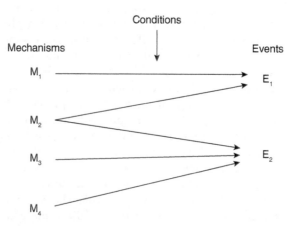

Figure 7.1   Causal mechanisms (adapted from Danermark et al., 2002 and Sayer, 2010)

they repeatedly saw one thing followed by another in time. As long as this law-like sequence continued to be observed then a causal explanation could be advanced. By implication, as Popper (2005) pointed out, scientists can never really prove a theory but only seek to refute it; a 'good' theory is one that has withstood multiple attempts at falsification.[1] Positivist science is therefore oriented around creating the conditions for these law-like regularities to occur as theoretically predicted. This means recreating as far as possible the ideal scientific experiment where a given change in one variable reliably leads to a proportionate change in another variable.[2] Contextual factors must be carefully manipulated so that the required conditions are produced. Since social experiments are difficult to engineer, much ingenuity goes into turning social phenomena – such as poverty, crime, or exclusion – into sets of variables that can be treated abstractly from the specific circumstances in which they arise (see Case Study 7.1 below). Once these variables are operationalised, i.e. can be reliably measured, numeric data are collected from a representative sample of the population of interest and various methods of statistical analysis are used to test hypotheses and create predictive models (Grant and Hood, 2017). Since an association between variables does not in itself indicate a causal relationship, as many contextual factors as possible must be turned into variables so that their potential influence on the hypothesised relationship can be analysed. Only in the absence of any confounding or mediating effects can a causal explanation be suggested.

CASE STUDY 7.1

Comparison of Service Effectiveness for Youth with Depressed Versus Non-depressed Caregivers (McCarthy et al., 2017)

This US study, published in the journal *Research on Social Work Practice*, illustrates the positivist approach to causation. The researchers aimed to test two hypotheses. The first hypothesis was that that young people with depressed caregivers would experience more severe depressive symptoms themselves, more behavioural issues, and fewer strengths compared to young people with non-depressed caregivers. The second hypothesis was that a community-based programme for reducing problematic behaviours and bolstering strengths would be equally effective for youth with depressed versus non-depressed caregivers. The study employed a 'post hoc comparison group design' with data collected from young people and caregivers at two time points: at the time of their enrolment in the programme and again six months later.

(Continued)

---

[1] Popper famously illustrated his argument by noting that no number of observations of white swans could ever prove the universal validity of the statement 'all swans are white', whereas only one observation of a black swan was needed to disprove it.

[2] Similar to the billiards table analogy in the Introduction.

A range of questionnaires were used to measure the variables of interest: signs of caregiver depression (in the six-month period before enrolment), caregiving strain, caregiver-reported youth strengths and behavioural problems, youth-reported depressive symptoms, and access to services. Statistical analysis was undertaken in the form of paired t-tests in order to test for significant changes in each outcome measure between enrolment on the programme and six months later, for each respective group, i.e. depressed vs non-depressed carers. The results showed that young people with depressed caregivers were generally reported (and to some extent self-reported) as having more problem behaviours, thus showing some support for the authors' first hypothesis. However, the programme itself actually seemed to work better for young people with depressed caregivers, who showed significant improvements over the six-month period whereas those with non-depressed caregivers did not. The results therefore ran entirely contrary to the study's second hypothesis. In the discussion, the authors speculate on the reasons for this unexpected finding, suggesting that 'depressed caregivers may be more open to discussing their own issues with FAST-TRAC staff rather than focusing exclusively on their children's issues'. However, they acknowledge that no data were collected to support this inference.

From a realist perspective, all this effort to remove contextual factors from the equation is a case of throwing the baby out with the bathwater. This is because statistical associations, however rigorously obtained, do not identify causal mechanisms, i.e. they do not actually explain anything (Danermark et al., 2002). For example, in the McCarthy et al. (2017) study described above, the researchers were unable to do more than speculate on *why* their second hypothesis had been proved wrong. This was not because of any gaps in their data but because the study was not designed to explain the reasons for unexpected patterns of behaviour. An exclusive emphasis on finding regularities in empirical data is also misconceived because these associations are at best what Lawson (1997) called 'demi-regularities', evident in some contexts and not others; social scientists should be just as (if not more) interested in those situations where they do not occur as those in which they do. Only by examining configurations of influence and effect in particular settings can researchers explore the mechanisms of change that are the object of realist scientific study. In this respect, readers may find it instructive to compare Case Study 7.1 with Case Studies 7.2 and 7.3 later on in the chapter.

CRITICAL REALISM

Realist research sometimes goes by the name of 'critical realism' (Danermark et al., 2002; Archer, 1998; Collier, 1994); indeed, some readers may already have come across this term in the social work literature (e.g. Houston, 2010). Broadly speaking there are two strands of realist research, one that eschews the label 'critical' and one that embraces it. The distinction is similar to that discussed in relation to reflective practice in Chapter 5, i.e. whether 'critique' requires an explicit engagement with issues of power and the potential for transformative action, or is concerned in a less ideological fashion with adjudicating knowledge claims through a robust application of scientific principles. Critical realism takes a normative turn in that certain explanations of society (particularly, it seems, Marxist ones) are preferred on an a-priori basis; research therefore becomes an opportunity to do something about unjust social practices, i.e. to change society as well as understanding and explaining it. This makes it attractive in many respects for social work, with its emphasis on social justice and ethical frameworks of action. However, the problem with ideological critique is that it effectively positions the critic – or the researcher – as arbiter of true and false consciousness and therefore undermines the basis for scientific scepticism: if you question the methods or findings of my study, you may be labouring under false beliefs! In this chapter, a distinction has therefore been made between realist and critical research paradigms (see above). Nonetheless, realist assumptions are generally compatible with studies with an explicit critical focus, including those with a long history in social work such as action research and participatory evaluation (Smith and Bryan, 2005). Conversely, some studies with a 'critical realist' label may actually be more straightforwardly realist when you examine them closely, e.g. Sword et al.'s (2012) research into post-partum depression (see Case Study 7.2).

Realist Social Research

Whatever the researcher's approach to social critique, the central concern of a realist study is developing theory in the form of causal mechanisms, along with the conditions that lead to their triggering or suppression. Realists aim to delve into complexity in order to decipher the underlying processes that generate events. Following Maxwell (2012), the following considerations are fundamental:

- Meanings and intentions, as well as observed behaviour, have causal significance
- Understanding a phenomenon requires knowledge of the context in which it occurs
- There is explanatory value in particular situations as well as in general patterns of events
- Theoretical explanations must address the processes through which a situation unfolds
- Our understanding of reality is interpretive but not constructivist, theory-informed but not dependent on theory

While there are many strategies for addressing these issues, realist social studies tend to share some common elements, some of which are discussed below.

Methodological pluralism

Methodological pluralism in realist research means that a combination of qualitative and quantitative methods is involved in theory building and causal explanation.

Mixed methods are also a feature of positivist research but often with a clear demarcation between them, e.g. qualitative data to describe processes and add ideographic detail, while explanatory models are developed via statistical analysis. In contrast, realist approaches tend to be more integrative; instead of the quantitative vs qualitative divide, there are 'intensive' and 'extensive' ways of investigating a topic (Sayer, 2010; Danermark et al., 2002). Intensive procedures look at interactions and behaviour between agents in a particular case (or small set of cases), aiming to find out how change happens and why people do what they do. Extensive procedures look at the properties of large populations, aiming to find regularities and patterns in selected variables. Intensive methods are mostly, but not exclusively, qualitative and produce causal explanations of non-representative cases. Extensive methods are mostly quantitative and produce representative generalisations that are non-explanatory. The statistical models that constitute causal explanation in positivist research may therefore contribute to theory in realist research but are not the basis for it.

Complex realism and case-based research

Byrne and Ragin (2009) present a compendium of case-based methods based on what they call a 'complex realist' approach to research, which develops the conceptual links between scientific realism and complexity theory into an integrative framework (Byrne, 1998; Harvey and Reed, 1996; Reed and Harvey, 1992). In complex realism, the principles outlined already in relation to generative causality are formally linked to the dynamics of complex social systems, and it is asserted that such dynamics can be studied and explored via the study of cases. According to Byrne, 'case studies of different kinds, and in particular multiple case studies founded on systematic comparison, are the foundations of useful theoretical descriptions of the social world' Byrne (2009a: 3). To this end, a broad range of methodological procedures – both quantitative and qualitative – are discussed with the aim of facilitating in-depth analysis and cross-case comparison.

Cases may be generally defined as a unit of social scientific inquiry that can be delimited in some way, e.g. by time, place, or people (Ragin and Becker, 1992). An everyday example is the concept of a 'household'. The 2011 UK Census employs a particular definition of the term: 'one person living alone, or a group of people (not necessarily related) living at the same address who share cooking facilities and share a living room or sitting room or dining area' (ONS, 2014: 21). For positivist researchers, households are an empirical source of information that can be abstracted in the form of variables, e.g. number of people, how many are employed or married, and so on. For realist researchers, households are a site of complex causal dynamics that are assumed to share some common features; the scope for comparative investigation and inquiry is shaped by the research process itself – what Ragin (1992) calls 'casing'. According to Danermark et al. (2002), there are four types of case that are of particular interest to realist researchers:

- *Odd or 'pathological' cases* – this type of case represents an unusual example of the phenomenon in question and therefore may provide more relevant information than an 'average' or representative case. For example, a recent UK study found that rates of child protection interventions were notably lower in Northern Ireland than in the other UK countries, given the level of deprivation (Bywaters, 2017). Exploring the reasons for this discrepancy might help to shed light on some of the complex factors shaping the link between poverty and intervention rates.
- *Extremely varied cases* – this comparative approach deliberately selects cases that are very different from each other in terms of the key dimensions important to the study. As with the extreme cases, the idea is that variation allows a study of how mechanisms operate and are triggered (or not) in different contexts. An example might be an evaluation of an intervention in two different localities where outcomes appear to have been successful in one and not in the other.
- *Critical cases* – this might be a case where a particular indicator has appeared where it was not expected to do so, or the opposite. An example might be a social work agency where there are historically low caseloads but rising levels of turnover and stress-related absence. Research into resilience has also made use of critical examples of children who have been able to 'bounce back' from conditions of adversity and hardship.
- *Normal cases* – this is perhaps the most obvious example, although clarifying what constitutes a normal case will often require some initial theoretical work, as in the household example discussed above.

Middle-range theory

In some respects, realist social research has an affinity with the concept of 'middle range theory' (MRT) espoused by Robert Merton, a well-known mid-twentieth-century sociologist. Merton (1968) criticised the tendency to seek all-encompassing theories of society, in the tradition of Marxism or functionalism. Instead, he thought social scientists should seek a middle ground between these universal theories (or 'grand narratives') and the everyday social worlds revealed by empirical data. A given MRT would therefore be more useful in some contexts than others; it is not limited to the specific situation but makes no claim to explain everything about society. An example from Merton's own work (1968) is the theory of reference group behaviour, which arises when people evaluate their circumstances, values, and actions with reference to the perceived standards of another social group. People's attitudes towards their reference groups differ in certain ways. They may aspire to membership ('I want to be like them') or be indifferent or antagonistic to the prospect; at the same time, they may feel welcomed or excluded from the group in question ('they'll never accept me'). Pawson (2013) shows the relevance of this theory to a variety of social interventions that target people who are marginalised or 'outsiders' in some way, e.g. young people not in education, training, or employment.

Examples might include skills training, mentoring and peer support, and public disclosure of criminal or antisocial behaviour. How people engage with such interventions, and whether their behaviour changes in a way that conforms with expectations, will depend to some extent on their orientation towards mainstream ('in-group') norms and attitudes. In realist terms, reference group theory points to a number of causal mechanisms that may be at play in such scenarios, and which are transferable in a range of different interventions and contexts.

Inference to the best explanation

Realist procedures for analysing data and building theory differ in important respects from positivist and interpretivist social research. The differences are linked to the mode of explanatory reasoning they commonly use. Experiments rely on deductive reasoning: more specifically a 'hypothetico-deductive' approach in which studies are designed to test predictive statements (hypotheses). Alternatively, explanatory reasoning in the social sciences, notably in grounded theory (Glaser and Strauss, 1967), is often inductive, i.e. theory is built cumulatively based on what is discovered first-hand in empirical data. As we have seen, complexity limits the feasibility of social experiments because contextual conditions cannot reliably be controlled or replicated. However, it also limits the explanatory power of inductively built theory because causal mechanisms may not be manifested in empirical events. For this reason, realist research employs another form of explanatory reasoning called 'abduction', or inference to the best explanation.

Although the terminology seems forbidding, abduction is actually an everyday form of reasoning. For example, imagine a friend told you last week that she and her partner are currently not on speaking terms after a row. However, today you happen to see them deep in conversation in a coffee shop. Your immediate assumption would probably be that they have made up (or are in the process of doing so). This is an 'inference to the best explanation' in that it is the simplest and most plausible theory that fits the observed facts. There are other possibilities of course (e.g. they might also be business associates who are having to put aside their personal difficulties). You have not based your conclusion on some sort of statistical correlation, e.g. between têtes-à-têtes in Starbucks and amicable relationships; nor have you conducted an experiment to test the proposition that caffeine stimulates dispute resolution. The connection between data and theory is based neither on first premises nor on probabilistic association. Instead, it goes beyond what can logically be attributed to the facts alone in order to justify a particular explanation. In realist terms, this type of 'informed guesswork' is what researchers should be doing. However, researchers (and practitioners) have to do more than just make inferences; they have to justify their explanation. A comprehensive example of this process can be found in Eastwood et al. (2016); they draw on a plethora of research findings to construct a realist explanation of neighbourhood context and post-natal depression, with a view to informing the provision of perinatal services (see also Case Study 7.2).

CASE STUDY 7.2

The complexity of post-partum mental health and illness (Sword et al., 2012)

Sword et al. (2012) describe a critical realist study aiming to identify the main mechanisms and factors associated with the presence or absence of post-partum depression (PPD) in women with a history of depression, and the presence of PPD in women without a history. They observe that PPD outcomes are neither chaotic nor entirely predictable but display 'demi-regularities'; for example, PPD is more likely to occur in women with prior depression, but not always, pointing to the 'counter-ing or moderating effects of other mechanisms'. For the study, quantitative and qualitative methods were combined in a pluralist design. Participants, who were between 32 and 36 weeks pregnant, were recruited from medical clinics and other healthcare settings from Hamilton, a city in Ontario, Canada, after being assessed for major depressive episodes or other psychiatric illness. Women with no psychiat-ric morbidity completed questionnaires (n=83) in relation to mood, anxiety, stress, social support, and prior depression. Respondents were then contacted by tele-phone six to eight weeks after giving birth and again completed surveys (n=73) in relation to stress, anxiety, and depression to determine if any changes had occurred. At this stage, women were invited to take part in a face-to-face qualita-tive interview (n=20) in order to explore their perceptions of factors promoting or inhibiting the development of PPD. Results from post-partum survey responses indicated that 22% of women had a history of depression but none had developed PPD, while 70% had no previous history but 4% of this group did develop PPD. Survey data as well as transcripts from qualitative interviews were analysed for evidence of causal mechanisms that appeared to influence post-partum mental health and illness. The findings highlighted personal factors such as physical recov-ery from labour and delivery, thought processes and expectations, personal insecurity, and implementation of goal-oriented actions. Contextual factors included social support (instrumental and emotional) and infant temperament. The interplay between these factors was seen as crucial and the authors proceed to discuss findings in relation to previous studies into PPD.

Realist evaluation

Realist evaluation is a theoretical and methodological framework for evaluating social programmes (Pawson, 2013, 2006; Pawson and Tilley, 1997). It draws on the principles of realisy social research outlined above, and is also based on a critique of the positivist approach to evaluation, particularly the renowned experimental design known as the randomised control trial (RCT). Initially geared towards the conduct of empirical studies, Pawson's later work has extended his realist approach into a form of systematic review called realist synthesis (Pawson, 2006). As the method's scope has broadened, a concern with complexity has assumed central importance – Pawson's (2013) 'Realist Manifesto' essentially deals with the challenges of evaluating complex interventions, as suggested by the epigraph to this chapter. Nonetheless, before considering the merits of realist evaluation (and synthesis) for addressing complexity, it should not be overlooked that experimental or quasi-experimental designs, with the RCT at their apex, continue to be considered the 'gold standard' of evaluation – including in social work. It is therefore worth recapping how these types of evaluation work and why realists think they are not as useful as is commonly thought.

Evaluation and the RCT

Experimental evaluations are something of a mythical beast in social work. Most social workers know (or vaguely remember from their studies) that they are the only real way to find out whether a given intervention 'works' or not. The reasons for this have already been explored – experiments seek to isolate the causal agent from contextual interference so that any changes can be attributed to the former. However, there are very few examples of true experimental studies in social work – hence the 'mythical' tag – and the ones that do exist tend to be linked to clinical interventions (e.g. Barrowclough et al., 2001; Chamberlain et al., 2007). This is unsurprising, since the ideal experimental evaluation, the randomised control trial (RCT), was developed for the testing of new medicines and medical treatments. Forrester (2012: 442) describes the methodology for RCTs as 'one of the greatest intellectual achievements of the 20th century', to which many of the marvels of modern medicine can be attributed.

So what is an RCT? Essentially the design of an RCT involves comparing pre-defined outcome measures between a programme cohort and a matched control group. In randomised designs, participants are allocated to these two groups on a random basis to avoid self-selection or other forms of potential bias. Sample sizes have to be large enough to allow for statistical significance and generalisation. The design seeks to ensure that any significant difference in outcomes between the programme group and control group is attributable only to the programme, rather than to other mediating or confounding factors. More sophisticated variants of the medical RCT include the 'three arm trial', featuring an additional group whose members are treated with a placebo, and the 'augmented trial', in which elements of process evaluation are added to the core RCT component. The latter is interesting for the current discussion since it was specifically developed for 'complex interventions' (Craig et al., 2008).

In whatever guise it appears, there are grounds for considering the RCT to be a flawed model for evaluating social interventions (Featherstone et al., 2014). As we have seen already, experimental designs test programme outcomes but not programme theory. This is not so much of an issue for medicines, which only proceed to clinical trial after an extensive period of theoretical and practical work has been done (Pawson, 2006). In contrast, there is often a lack of programme theory about social interventions, particularly when they are being piloted. Effectively this turns the intervention into a 'black box' whose exact workings remain a mystery to the evaluator. There will always be factors affecting outcomes that are not known or taken into account by the would-be experimenter; this applies as much to the 'control' group as to the experimental group:

> [I]f researchers ignore the labyrinthine processes whereby an intervention has been introduced in the field, or the equally labyrinthine processes that occur in its absence, they will remain in the dark about the precise combination of mechanisms and contexts that generate any subsequent differences. (Pawson, 2006: 52)

The other key problem with RCT designs is that they assume that the intervention is the causal agent. This may be justified for the trial of medications with a known biological effect on the human organism, although the well-known 'placebo effect' shows that social and psychological mechanisms are also significant for clinical treatments. In social work there is no doubt about it: people are the causal agents, and it is their choices and decisions that make or break the intervention. For the same reason, it is difficult to ascribe an equivalent to 'dosage' in respect of interventions that are made up of myriads of everyday actions and interactions – the rather hopeful concept of 'programme fidelity' is difficult to validate given the complexity involved (Mowbray et al., 2003). Inevitably, interventions work better for some people than they do for others, just as they work better in some areas than in others (Shaw et al., 2009). The result is what Rossi (1987) calls the 'iron law' of evaluation – eventually, given enough trials in enough areas, the net effect of any social programme will be shown to be zero! And for that result, RCTs are extremely expensive to run. Small wonder that they are rarely conducted in social work.

The realist alternative

As an alternative to the RCT or quasi-experimental approach, the realist approach puts programme theory at the heart of evaluation. The principles are similar to those outlined already – the search for causal mechanisms, a commitment to methodological pluralism, the building of middle-range theory, and a focus on complexity. Realist evaluation even has its own slogan, being concerned not merely with 'what works' but with 'what works for whom, in what circumstances … and why?' (Pawson, 2013). Answering these questions requires evaluators to construct testable propositions about the theory of change underlying the intervention. Pawson and Tilley (1997) suggest that such propositions should be expressed in the form of a context-mechanism-outcome (CMO) configuration, in which the context might be the potential participant, the mechanism how the intervention is presumed to act on their choices and decisions, and the outcome an expected change in their behaviour. Since interventions are likely to encompass several such propositions, evaluators should compile a list of CMO configurations, preferably in close consultation with key stakeholders in the intervention, and design the study to examine as many of them as is feasible. Since this is 'inference to the best explanation', rather than a hypothetico-deductive form of testing, evaluators are able to discard, add, and alter their propositions in line with the accumulating evidence about how the intervention is working. By the end of the evaluation, a revised programme theory should be able to inform future trials and implementations. An example of a realist study from Pawson and Tilley (1997), including CMO configurations, is outlined below in Case Study 7.3.

CASE STUDY 7.3

Prisoner education (Pawson and Tilley, 1997)

Pawson and Tilley (1997: 103–14) describe a realist study of a large-scale prisoner education programme in British Columbia. Its aim was to penetrate the 'black box' of the programme, i.e. to identify the contextual conditions and causal mechanisms leading to differentiated outcomes (reconviction rates) for prisoners graduating from the programme. The study was designed in three phases employing mixed methods. The first phase was a literature review focusing on practitioners' 'folk theories' on why such programmes work for some prisoners and not for others. Having developed some hypotheses about contexts and mechanisms, the second phase tested this theory by conducting a quantitative analysis of outcomes relating to two sub-groups of participants (see CMO configuration table below). The third phase was a qualitative study of prisoners' own reasoning on why their behaviour might have changed following participation. The findings from Phase 1 identified two types of prisoner who were predicted to benefit in different ways from the programme. First there were people with little or no previous education, representing a 'disadvantaged background'. For this group, the key mechanism of change was thought to be 'self-realisation and the experience of social acceptability'. Second there were people serving long sentences in maximum security prisons, representing a 'criminal background', for whom the key mechanism was a change in their 'powers of self-reflection and reasoning'. In Phase 2, improvement in reconviction rates for these two groups was compared to what would be expected, on average, from prisoners with equivalent characteristics, i.e. success was defined in terms of whether actual rates were lower than predicted rates. The findings showed that the first group needed only modest levels of engagement and success with the programme in order to achieve an improvement; for the second group, the maximum security inmates, rehabilitation was only possible if they committed wholeheartedly to the programme. The interviews conducted as part of Phase 3 pointed to prisoners' own views on the effects of education, e.g. that it was a 'civilising process' and prompted them to develop 'an interest inside you'. These findings were crucial as they prompted a turn in the programme theory towards the importance of 'cognitive change' as a key mechanism for rehabilitation.

Table 7.1   Context-mechanism-outcome (CMO) configuration table (adapted from Pawson and Tilley, 1997: 113)

Context	Mechanism	Outcome
Group 1. Prisoners from 'disadvantaged background'	Modest levels of engagement and success with the programme lead to experience of self-realisation and social acceptability	Reconviction rates significantly lower than predicted for equivalent group
Group 2. Prisoners from 'criminal background'	High levels of engagement and success with the programme lead to increased powers of self-reflection and reasoning	Reconviction rates significantly lower than predicted for equivalent group

Unlike experimental trials there is no 'recipe' or step-by-step template for conducting a realist evaluation. This has advantages and disadvantages. As Case Studies 7.2 and 7.3 suggest, there is no need to reinvent the wheel methodologically; the tried and tested techniques of social scientific inquiry, from surveys to semi-structured interviews, are perfectly adequate for realist designs. The main difficulty is conceptual, i.e. how these methods should be combined to uncover causal mechanisms without reducing them to their empirical traces. As Pawson and Manzano-Santaella (2012) note in their 'diagnostic workshop' of evaluations adopting the realist label, there are pitfalls for the unwary researcher, such as omitting to explain how contextual factors contribute to a range of differentiated outcomes, or concentrating so much on aspects of process and engagement that it is hard to know who the 'winners' and 'losers' are among the participants. Without a well-constructed programme theory it can also be difficult to distinguish between contexts, mechanisms, and outcomes, leading researchers to compile lists of interchangeable factors as CMO tables. Another problem often encountered by evaluators, whether realist or not, is the implicit assumption on the part of commissioners that their intervention is completely unique and unheard of, rather than a combination of various things that have been tried elsewhere at different times with different sorts of people. Addressing this issue requires evaluators to examine not just the family of programmes to which their subject belongs, but also the family of *programme theories* underlying its theory of change. Realist synthesis was developed with this undertaking in mind.

Realist synthesis

Realist synthesis (Pawson 2006, 2013) is a form of systematic review designed to assess the overall weight of evidence for a social programme or intervention. Readers may remember an example of realist synthesis in Chapter 6, in the form of Hewitt et al.'s (2014) study of the mechanisms of interprofessional teamwork.

As with realist evaluation in general, the focus is on programme theory rather than experimental outcomes. This distinguishes realist synthesis from the dominant form of systematic review, often termed 'meta-analysis', which like the RCT was developed initially in the field of evidence-based medicine and has since transferred to the applied social sciences. The purpose of meta-analysis is to evaluate and aggregate the results of experimental trials, using strict criteria for inclusion and an a-priori preference for RCT-type designs. The main outcome is a statistical measure of change, or 'effect size', which can be attributed to the intervention across the entire sample included in the analysis. Pawson argues that meta-analysis is flawed for a number of reasons, mostly stemming from the drawbacks of RCTs that were discussed earlier. Aggregating the outcomes from experimental trials accentuates their propensity to smooth over contextual disparities including differentiated outcome patterns associated with participant sub-groups (see Case Study 7.3). There is little scope for exploring explanatory hypotheses and a very restricted body of research due to the inclusion criteria for the review. The latter problem is particularly acute if more sophisticated – and therefore more expensive – multi-variate designs are preferred, where it is even harder to ensure the compatibility of methods and findings.

As always, the realist alternative is to focus on theory-building and casual mechanisms rather than on effect sizes and experimental rigour. Pawson's (2006) method for realist synthesis envisages six stages:

1. *Identifying the review question* – mapping key programme theories, prioritising those for investigation and formulating the hypotheses to be tested
2. *Searching for primary studies* – finding empirical studies that test particular elements of the programme theory, including after the theory has been revised in the light of evidence
3. *Quality appraisal* – assessing the relevance and rigour of empirical studies in relation to that part of the theory they are meant to test
4. *Extracting the data* – collation of materials and notes from selected primary sources
5. *Synthesising the data* – consolidating and adjudicating between different sources and materials to refine the different elements of the programme theory
6. *Disseminating the findings* – following negotiation and consultation with key stakeholders, summarising the theory in order to inform future implementation

As with most research projects, these steps do not occur as a strictly linear sequence but are iterative in nature, e.g. revisions to programme theory may impel a search for more primary research, and so on. Indeed, Pawson (2006) acknowledges that realist synthesis is just as time consuming as meta-analysis, and in some respects is even more labour-intensive due to the conceptual work needed to synthesise the findings. In his last book on the subject, Pawson (2013) emphasises that programme theory should encompass as many aspects of complexity as possible, shaping the course and outcomes of any intervention. These not only include the choices that people have to make if the intervention is to achieve its aims, but also the implementation chains that bring together practitioners, managers and participants, the social, institutional and organisational contexts in which implementation occurs, and the longitudinal development of the intervention over time, including its track record of success and failure and how it is adapted for particular settings. Evidence for the review should also include the definition and measurement of outcomes, how these link to the purpose of the intervention as understood by different stakeholders, and how other policies and interventions may contribute to the intentions and behaviour of the people who are being studied.

Limitations of Realist Research

Scientific realism has been called a 'philosophy in search of a method' (Yeung, 1997) and to some extent that remains true, although the studies cited in this chapter show the emergence of some methodological principles and frameworks. The flexible, pluralistic approach to method espoused by realist research may seem pragmatic but is actually driven by some fairly programmatic assumptions about how knowledge corresponds to reality: mechanisms, necessary relations, CMO configurations, and so on. Since academics tend to learn and ply their trade in traditional positivist environs, aided by statistical 'cookbooks' and the like (Grant and Hood, 2017), there can be something rather highbrow about the realist insistence on philosophical and conceptual difficulty. This is accentuated by the reliance on abduction for theory-building (see earlier), which may leave researchers open to the charge of privileging their own stance under the guise of explanatory goodness (Thagard, 1978). This would seem particularly relevant to self-avowedly 'critical' research, where the methodological basis for generating findings from data is not always explicit, and knowledge claims may be assessed as much for their political implications as their scientific validity (Hammersley, 2005; Widdowson, 1995). Another limitation, which is particularly apparent in the 'complex realist' strand, is the assumption that society is a system, or a multitude of interconnected systems. Stewart (2001) criticises this assumption for its functionalist overtones, while Stacey (2007) argues that equating social phenomena with systems is misleading because it leads us to posit a boundary outside which such systems can be studied and manipulated. In realist science, such boundaries are also inherent in the distinction between the transitive and intransitive objects of science, i.e. between the 'knower' and the object that is known. For Stacey, this dualistic notion of the individual vis-à-vis the system, which he associates with Kantian philosophy, fails to represent the complexity of social behaviour, which is emergent and transformative. Stacey's alternative approach, which he calls 'responsive processes', is described below (and in Chapter 8).

Non-Realist Approaches to Complexity

While much of this chapter has been devoted to realist approaches, it is important to recognise that complexity may also be researched using other research paradigms. One example is the guidance produced by the Medical Research Council on evaluating complex interventions (Craig et al., 2008), which presents various modifications to the RCT format that remains the basis for evaluations and field trials. Yin's (2009) method of comparative case study research has many elements of the 'configurational approach' advocated by Byrne and Ragin (2009) but within a positivist rather than realist framework. Another example, also within the positivist tradition, is Wolf-Branigin's (2013) use of agent-based modelling (ABM) to analyse how global behaviour evolves via local interactions and response to contingencies. Wolf-Branigin (2013) argues for a shift 'from a metaphorical to a mathematical approach' to complexity, and makes a case for ABM as a tool for applying complexity theory through its use of agent–client level data. He illustrates the method with a study of community inclusion of disabled people who have transitioned from institutional residences to various forms of community-based living; an ABM-based spatial analysis of housing patterns over time reveals some of the factors linked to clustering and dispersal across the locality.

Stacey's (2007) 'responsive processes' constitutes a very different approach to complexity from a broadly interpretivist perspective, drawing on Hegelian philosophy, the process sociology of Nobert Elias, and the symbolic interactionism of G.H. Mead. Stacey's critique of systems approaches has already been mentioned above (and in the Introduction). Strictly speaking, Stacey is concerned with strategic planning and management in organisations but his arguments are equally relevant for research and evaluation. He argues that complex causality should be seen as transformative rather than formative, where the latter is taken to mean the 'unfolding' of system properties that can be identified and directed from some external position. Instead, Stacey argues that the only position that anyone can take – whether a practitioner, manager, or researcher – is a participative one. Social order emerges through the interactions between people, and moreover the interaction is reflexive, i.e. people's reasons and intentions are bound up with what they perceive other people's intentions to be. What this means in research terms is a focus on reflective narratives that explore how patterns of thinking, behaviour, and interaction emerge through the interplay of multiple strategies and intentions in a particular social context. The position taken is of an 'insider', similar to the phenomenological approach, but combined with a critical focus on dialogue, conversation, and power relations.

CONCLUSION

This chapter has examined various ways in which complexity is addressed in social research and programme evaluation. The principal focus has been on theoretical and methodological approaches in the realist paradigm, looking at particular incarnations such as complex realism, critical realism, and realist evaluation. The main reason for assigning realist research such a prominent role is that it sees complex causality as the fundamental problem to be solved in social research, as opposed to being an additional challenge or a characteristic of particular contexts and interventions. Through its conceptual links with complexity theory, realism also provides a bridge between the latter's technical and abstract vocabulary, with its roots in mathematical models and algorithms, and the pragmatic process of investigating messy social problems. Another reason for focusing on realist approaches is their critical engagement with well-known methodologies in the positivist tradition such as the RCT and other experimental designs. The themes emerging from the realist critique of positivist research are closely connected to the discussion of technical rational approaches to practice in Part 1 of this book: a reduction of complex causality to linear causality, a focus on predictable relationships between variables rather than on the unpredictable behaviour of situations-in-context, and a lack of adaptability to uncertain conditions. In other words, research that overlooks complexity also serves to reinforce policy and practice that overlooks complexity. Indeed, Bhaskar (2009: 272) sees positivism as playing a role in sustaining 'an ideology of technocratic expertise and managerial authority'. Similar tensions and debates recur in the next two chapters of the book, which will look at organisations and social policy.

ORGANISING SERVICES TO MANAGE COMPLEXITY

8

CHAPTER SUMMARY

This chapter explores the challenges of addressing complexity from an organisational perspective. Two approaches to structure and management are contrasted. The first is the bureaucratic organisation, still the most common approach to delivering social work and social care services. The characteristics of bureaucracies are described and connected with the principles of scientific management and command-and-control thinking. There is a particular focus on motivation and the consequences of organising work around functions and processes, as well as the issue of performance management. The chapter then moves onto a second organisational perspective, which is socio-technical systems. The principles of a socio-technical approach are outlined with reference to the work of Trist and Ashby, before discussing the management system theories of W. Edwards Deming and John Seddon and their application to public services. Ways of overcoming the problem of control are explored along with the possibility of reconfiguring the relationship between purpose and measures. The chapter concludes with Stacey's radical take on complexity and strategic management.

INTRODUCTION

Organisations, like practitioners and researchers, seek to understand complexity. For service providers, in which most social workers are employed, complexity is inherent in the needs, motivations, expectations, and reactions of the people to whom they provide a service. Such organisations deal with a high variety of demand; people want services that work for them, which means that services have to adapt to their needs and therefore work differently for different people. Equally, services have to meet the expectations of other stakeholders: councillors, trustees, ministers, regulators, funders, taxpayers, etc. From the perspective of these groups, services work for the community as well as for individuals; the concern is with effectiveness across target populations, with value for money, and with the management of risk. As discussed in Chapter 6, bridging these different agendas has increasingly been the task of managers. Managers organise the delivery of frontline services, supervise staff, provide leadership and strategic direction, communicate institutional values and cultures, as well as presenting and justifying the organisation's activities to external parties. Theories of management are therefore relevant to the way social work agencies understand and respond to complexity. A related question is how the effectiveness of services is measured and how these indicators are used to manage performance, or to understand the factors that influence variation in performance.

In this book, it has been suggested that the ability to adapt to uncertain, variable and sometimes volatile conditions is a feature of professional responses to complexity. By the same token it becomes the responsibility of agencies as well as professional bodies to create and sustain this type of expertise. There is the usual dilemma of addressing complexity without becoming paralysed by it. On the one hand, procedures and rules help social workers to navigate the complex terrain of practice while adhering to their statutory duties and professional remits. On the other hand, an overemphasis on procedural compliance can stifle innovation and discourage creative problem-solving. Of course, complexity never goes away and unintended consequences abound. However many rules are imposed on practitioners, there will always be some discretion in how they interpret and implement the rules – what Lipsky (1980) called 'street-level bureaucracy'. An innovative practice developed one year may be fated to become next year's rule-bound orthodoxy. The struggle to continually adapt and learn without dissolving into chaos or ossifying into functional complacency is a perennial challenge for organisations, particularly in the face of external pressures from politicians, regulators, and the wider public. In describing these challenges, the chapter will start with two competing perspectives on social work organisations: as systems and as bureaucracies.

The Bureaucratic Organisation

Bureaucracy – and the derived term 'bureaucratic' – has acquired a rather bad reputation, being associated with regulatory 'red tape', procedural delays, and unresponsive services. To some extent, as will be argued later, this reputation is deserved! However, it is worth noting that bureaucracy in its original sense denoted a type of organisational structure that maximised efficiency and effectiveness. This definition stems from the German sociologist, Max Weber (1978), who was concerned with how authority was exercised in modern (or modernising) societies. His reasoning was that large industrial economies could not be governed effectively through traditional or charismatic forms of authority; these societies therefore developed a rational-legal form of public administration: the bureaucracy. Weber developed a checklist of criteria to distinguish the 'ideal type' of such an organisation:

> The rational public administration is based on written rules, an impersonal, hierarchical order, and a clear division of labor. Furthermore, bureaucrats are appointed to administrative offices because of their skills (meritocracy) and not because of their ancestry. The public servants' education is important and bureaucrats are supposed to be highly specialized professionals. Also, a career in the public sector guarantees both a fixed salary and a pension. In sum, Weberian bureaucracy consists of a hierarchically structured, professional, rule-bound, impersonal, meritocratic, appointed, and disciplined body of public servants with a specific set of competences. (Sager and Rosser, 2009: 1141)

Most social workers – or any other professional – would probably see little that is obviously objectionable about this definition. That may simply indicate that professionals have adopted a bureaucratic mindset! However, it is important to note that all organisations benefit from formal administrative structures, e.g. allocating and delegating authority, discharging responsibilities, distributing resources and information, and (if you are lucky) rotating tasks. As Freeman (1972) argued in relation to a very unbureaucratic type of organisation (campaign groups in the women's liberation movement), there is no such thing as a 'structureless' group – the absence of formal structures only fuels the development of informal ones, such as cliques and elites. The crucial point about bureaucracies is therefore not their insistence on formal structures but their emphasis on technical rationality as the means for achieving an organisation's purpose; this has implications for what structures are adopted.

Bureaucracy and organisational structure

According to Robbins (2009), organisational structure determines how jobs, roles, and tasks are managed and coordinated. Key elements include:

- *Work specialisation* – the degree to which the organisation's work is subdivided into specialist or routine tasks to be undertaken by employees
- *Departmentalisation* – the basis on which tasks are grouped together, e.g. by function, product line, geographical area
- *Chain of command* – how authority is discharged through lines of responsibility and accountability, e.g. who gives orders, who reports to whom, whose authority is needed for which decisions
- *Span of control* – the number of subordinates that a manager is able to direct; a narrow span of control leads to more vertical layers of management
- *Centralisation and decentralisation* – the degree to which decision-making is concentrated at a single point in an organisation, or distributed throughout it. Very centralised organisations often adopt a 'command and control' approach to management (see below)
- *Formalisation* – the degree to which jobs and tasks within the organisation are standardised

Given these elements, Robbins (2009) describes three structural options for organisations, each of which has a strategic implication. The first is an 'organic' structure, which is loose, relatively decentralised, and has a low level of specialisation and formalisation; according to Robbins, this type of structure is particularly suited to organisations that want to innovate. The second option is a 'mechanistic' structure, which is characterised by tight centralised controls with extensive specialisation and formalisation of work; this type of structure is suited to organisations that want to minimise costs. The third option is a mixture of organic and mechanistic characteristics, e.g. 'tight controls over current activities but looser controls over new' (Robbins, 2009: 505); this type of structure is suited to organisations that want to copy successful products and services from elsewhere. The classic Weberian bureaucracy will tend to have a mechanistic structure, while small, nimble enterprises may adopt an organic structure (at least to begin with). However, Robbins also makes the point that environmental conditions also have implications for organisational structure:

> The more scarce, dynamic and complex the environment, the more organic a structure should be. The more abundant, stable and simple the environment, the more the mechanistic structure will be preferred. (Robbins, 2009: 508)

Robbins suggests here that organisations need to be structured in such a way that there is an adaptive fit with their environment (see Case Study 8.1). Bureaucracies operating in a complex environment, which might be said to include most statutory social work agencies, therefore have something of a dilemma because the logic of technical rationality pushes them towards mechanistic rather than organic structures. However, other environmental factors may inhibit such organisations from loosening controls, such as financial constraints stemming from government austerity measures (Ferguson and Lavalette, 2013; Sidebotham, 2012), and pressure from regulators to demonstrate procedural compliance and manage institutional risk (Hood et al., 2001; Rothstein, 2006). Voluntary sector organisations, particularly those which are small and locality-based, may be more organically inclined, although Bissell (2012) argues that organisational structures in public and voluntary sector social services have converged somewhat since the 1980s due to a mutual concern with managing costs.

CASE STUDY 8.1

Armies, prisons, and schools (Wilson, 1989)

Wilson (1989) begins his account of government bureaucracies in the United States with an intriguing question. What links the success of the following three organisations: the German army that rapidly conquered France at the beginning of the Second World War; the Texas prisons in the late 1970s with much lower levels of violence and disorder than similar prisons in other states; and the 'basket-case' high school in

(Continued)

Atlanta that in a few years transformed itself into a model school? The common factor, according to Wilson, is that all three were (or became) better organisations than their peers or rivals. That does not mean they adopted the same organisational structure. On the contrary, they were structured completely differently. The German army adopted a relatively decentralised structure in which squads of lower ranking soldiers and officers had discretion to act independently in pursuit of general goals and within an overall hierarchy of discipline. The Texas prisons, on the other hand, were designed with completely the opposite intention, employing a strict, command-and-control structure to ensure 'immediate and reflexive obedience of detailed rules'. The Atlanta high school adopted yet another approach, which emphasised strong leadership but sought to imbue staff with the authority and confidence to reduce disorder and instil 'school rules and personal self-esteem'. Wilson argues that the success of these organisations was due to the adaptive fit between their 'coordinating system' and the 'critical task' or key environmental challenge they had to solve. For the German army, the critical task concerned the killing power of dug-in machine guns and artillery, which required alternative tactics to the full-frontal assaults that had failed so conclusively in the First World War. The prison's critical task was to maintain order among a large number of impulsive and aggressively inclined inmates with a small number of guards. The school's critical task was to tackle the 'fear, disorder and low morale among students and staff'. Wilson distinguishes between these critical tasks, which suggest specific organisational solutions, and more general goals, such as 'defeat the enemy', 'keep order', and 'educate our children', which are too vague to adjudicate between different methods of accomplishing them. He goes on to describe two further organisational problems: the challenge of building consensus on how the critical task is to be defined and addressed, and the challenge of gaining sufficient autonomy and external support to pursue the desired solutions.

Questions to consider

- How would you describe the organisational structure in your current place of work or study?
- Do you think there is a critical environmental task that this structure is designed to solve?

'Command and control' management

The bureaucratic concern with efficiency aligns with a traditional branch of management theory known as 'scientific management', which emerged in the work of Taylor (1914) and Fayol (1948) in the early twentieth century. Their main concern was with the productivity of workers undertaking physical activities in order to achieve organisational goals. Taylor's approach was based on close observation of the production process, which was broken down into separate work tasks in order to analyse how long tasks took to complete, what skills and training were required, what materials were needed, and what outputs were produced. Management was therefore seen in terms of command and control; managers made decisions about exactly what workers should do and used management practices to make sure those decisions were carried out:

> [Taylor's] prescription was to provide standardized descriptions of every activity, specify the skills required, define the boundaries around each activity and fit the person to the job requirement. Individual performance was to be measured against the defined standards and rewarded through financial incentive schemes. (Stacey, 2007: 36)

The Taylorist command-and-control approach was developed for mass manufacturing and arguably has limited applicability to service organisations, where it is harder to break down the work (e.g. building relationships) into specific, measurable activities. Nonetheless, its influence is evident in the 'new managerialism' (Clarke et al., 2000) that has underpinned reforms to the welfare state in recent decades (see also Chapter 6). For example, local authority social workers are generally expected to know and follow detailed procedural guidance, carry out standardised assessments, and to align their activities with electronic workflow management systems. In turn, they and their agencies are monitored for compliance with timescales and other performance indicators by internal audit functions and external regulators (Hood et al., 2016c). This type of approach relies on top-down hierarchies to enforce decisions about budgets, targets, standards, specifications, and so on, (Seddon, 2008), and has been heavily criticised for de-skilling and de-professionalising social workers (Ayre and Calder, 2010). Dustin (2016) has even expressed concerns about the 'McDonaldisation' of social work, arguing that care management approaches have resulted in the commodification of care and the routinisation of social work roles (for a more sympathetic view of care management, see Lymbery, 1998).

Management and motivation

One of the problems with Taylor's theory is its view of people as 'cogs in a machine' rather than as people with their own reasons for doing things. Accordingly, 'human relations' management theorists such as Mayo (1933) and McGregor (1960) argued that organisations needed to take account of the psychology of work, focusing particularly on what motivated people to work and how organisational assumptions about motivation affected people's attitudes. In this context it is worth recalling the distinction between intrinsic and extrinsic motivation discussed in Chapter 4. McGregor (1960) thought that organisations which assumed employees were primarily motivated by extrinsic factors would – in a kind of self-fulfilling prophecy – produce employees who did indeed behave in such a way. He called this 'Theory X', which in its extreme form is characterised by the belief that people are lazy shirkers who avoid doing work whenever possible and must be coerced into meeting the organisation's goals. Journalists working undercover in a retail sports warehouse in the UK in 2016 reported some good examples of Theory X implementation; they found that staff were 'searched daily, harangued via tannoy to hit targets and can be sacked in a "six strikes and you're out" regime' (Goodley and Ashby, 2016). This was not a scientific study, so the effects on employees' levels of intrinsic motivation and job satisfaction can only be surmised. Seddon (2008) argues that Theory X is a defining feature of command-and-control management, even if it is appears in less extreme forms, e.g. coaching sessions and performance reviews rather than tannoy announcements and daily searches!

McGregor's (1960) alternative approach was what he called 'Theory Y', which emphasises intrinsic forms of motivation. Here it is assumed that workers are naturally inclined to put effort into their jobs and will proactively pursue organisational objectives in addition to accepting directions and guidance. In other words, people do not need to be manipulated into working and their morale will often improve if they are allowed to use their own ingenuity to solve problems. Frederick Herzberg, a work psychologist who wrote about job enrichment, put it another way: 'if you want people to do a good job, give them a good job to do' (Herzberg, 1987, cited in Seddon, 2008: 75). Intrinsic motivation seems particularly important for the so-called 'caring professions', which include social work and nursing (Abbott and Wallace, 1990) and whose status and remuneration lags behind more established (and male-dominated) professions such as law and medicine (Etzioni, 1969). Bissell (2012) reviewed the literature on what motivates social workers to enter and stay in the profession, despite its parlous public image and often high levels of stress and burnout (see Chapter 5), finding that the ethical dimension of social work seems to compensate to some extent for widespread dissatisfaction with working conditions. Nonetheless, turnover and retention of staff has long been a problem in social work, particularly in statutory settings with a strong culture of bureaucratic control and compliance (Baginsky, 2013; Munro, 2010). Indeed, Curtis et al. (2009) estimated the 'expected working life' of social workers to be just eight years, much lower than healthcare professionals including nurses.

Functions and processes

Bureaucracies tend to group together key specialisms into 'functions', e.g. legal, personnel, marketing, sales, and so on. In the UK, the majority of social workers are employed in their own professional function, which may be further subdivided into service areas and teams. What most social workers experience as their organisational setting tends to be multiple teams making up the function of a much larger bureaucracy, e.g. a local authority or the National Health Service. In these organisations, there is a high degree of horizontal and vertical differentiation. The former might mean different teams covering different geographical patches as well as different aspects of provision, e.g. referral and assessment, children in need, and looked after children teams in statutory children's social care (see Case Study 8.2 below). The latter might mean long chains of approval for resources, with a view to controlling costs, so that requests made at the front line wind their way up the management hierarchy, across functions, and then back again.

According to Seddon (2008), a proliferation of functional silos is a key feature of command-and-control organisations. An unintended consequence of functions is that work tends to be divided up in a way that makes sense to the organisation but not to the service recipient. Often this follows the logic of technical efficiency underlying scientific management approaches; complex tasks are broken up into discrete tasks, each of which is processed en masse and passed onto the next stage. This 'conveyor-belt' process will be familiar to anyone who has approached a government agency with a request; the first step usually involves handing or sending paperwork to someone whose job is to check it and scan it into a computer system for processing elsewhere. Often the request goes through several further steps of verification before a final decision is made, and if any information is (or goes) missing the whole process stops while the citizen is contacted and responds. The result, needless to say, is often not to people's satisfaction; in some cases, e.g. delays to benefits claims, the system can be ruinous (O'Hara, 2015). Nonetheless, management information about performance in such organisations may well show a picture of efficiency, e.g. each step being completed in large numbers and within timescales.

An alternative to organising services around functions is to focus on processes instead, i.e. on what happens when a citizen makes contact with the agency and how long it takes for their issue to be resolved. From this perspective, organisations that successfully manage processes will improve coordination across functions and avoid fragmentation and duplication, e.g. by providing a single point of contact rather than obliging citizens to deal with several different functions. This does not necessarily involve a change in management practice; processes can still be managed via command-and-control mechanisms, such as targets for timeliness and consumer satisfaction. Sparrow (2008) observes that organisations which become preoccupied with process management may end up losing touch with their overarching purpose; resources become entirely dedicated to managing internal processes efficiently with the result that the organisation stops innovating and fails to adapt to changing environmental conditions.

Performance management

Performance management is another key characteristic of command-and-control organisations. Hood et al. (2016c: 50) define it as 'the process through which managers evaluate their employees' work and distribute rewards in order to achieve strategic goals'. It has been a feature of UK public services since the early 1980s (Baars et al., 2010; Osborne et al., 1995) but gathered pace during the New Labour administration of 1997–2010, during which the use of performance-related indicators, benchmarks, targets, and incentives in the public sector become widespread (Propper and Wilson, 2003). Hood (1991: 4) describes the 'doctrinal components' of new public management as including 'commitment to explicit standards and measures of performance', and 'greater emphasis on output controls'. Over time, these components have become associated with a regime of internal audit and external inspection, reinforced by IT-based workflow systems and the threat of sanctions for non-compliance (Bevan and Hood, 2006). Social work practice, particularly in the statutory sector, has been transformed by these developments (Shaw et al., 2009; Munro, 2004). Agencies have come under increasing pressure to measure what they do and use this information as a way of demonstrating their accountability to stakeholders, i.e. that they are using public money efficiently and providing an effective service to citizens.

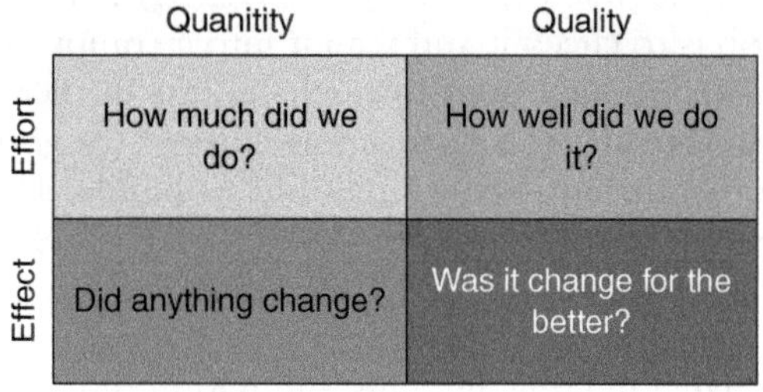

Figure 8.1 Performance-based accountability (adapted from Friedman, 1997: 4–5)

Friedman (1997, 2001) developed a framework of 'performance-based accountability' that conceptualises the relationship between process and outcomes measures. In the context of social work, processes include inputs and resources, such as numbers of staff and caseloads, as well as the time taken to complete important pieces of work, such as needs assessments. Outcomes relate to the effects of intervention. Taking the example of children who are the subject of a child protection (CP) plan, outcomes include the number of children who are stepped down from CP plans within a certain time frame, or the proportion of plans made for children who have already had this service in the past (Hood et al., 2016c). These distinctions can be used to create a typology of indicators based on how they are measuring performance, a version of which is represented in Figure 8.1, which distinguishes not only between 'effort' (i.e. inputs) and 'effect' (i.e. outcomes), but also between quantity and quality. Freidman (1997) notes that the most significant data are provided by 'quality' measures, particularly those in the bottom-right quadrant that indicate the quality of 'change for the better' produced by the service. Unfortunately, these are also the most difficult measures to obtain, partly because the nature of outcomes often takes a long time to emerge. As a result, a lot of the quality measures that organisations are likely to collect tend to be skewed towards effort ('how well did we do it') rather than effect ('change for the better'). For a more detailed discussion of these measures in relation to children's social care, the reader is referred to Hood et al. (2016c). A description of how these indicators might contribute to internal quality assurance and performance management in adult social care is given below in Case Study 8.2.

CASE STUDY 8.2

The quality assurance and performance management meeting (QAPMM)

Violet is a team manager in a statutory adult social care service providing assessments and care coordination under the Care Act to vulnerable adults and elderly citizens in the community. All the social workers in the team enter their activity onto an electronic workflow management system, iCAC, which monitors timescales and completion rates as well as costings for individual packages of care. iCAC is able to produce monthly statistics on performance on a variety of process and outcome measures, which enables senior managers to monitor teams' compliance with quality targets and budget forecasts. Every month, Violet attends a quality assurance and performance management meeting (QAPMM) for her service. In the QAPMM, every team manager is asked to present their statistics for the month and give reasons for any failure to meet with quality standards, e.g. for a minimum 80% of assessments to be completed within timescales. After the QAPMM, Violet is required to log a 'practice alert' on the iCAC system for tasks and processes that are failing to meet the required standards, and to record supervision discussions with the relevant staff. Violet is allocated an overall budget for social care provision within her team, although her own level of discretionary approval is minimal. Care packages are approved by a monthly resource panel chaired by a senior manager, which makes decisions on the basis of reports and funding calculations generated by iCAC.

Questions to consider

- What elements of command-and-control management can you identify in the case study?
- Have you experienced any of these elements in your work setting?
- What are the advantages and disadvantages of this approach?

The Organisation as System

Organisations can be seen as a type of system in that they are composed of interacting agents oriented towards a purpose. In the case of social work organisations, their purpose is first and foremost to provide a service to individuals and communities, although they may also perform a regulatory role in relation to public harms such as child abuse or crime (Sparrow, 2008). Given that there are different types of systems theory (see Introduction), seeing organisations as systems is not in itself particularly informative. As with the realist perspective explored in the previous chapter, the focus here will be on organisations as complex social systems that interact with and intervene in other complex social systems. The starting point is that organisations work through the involvement of human actors, often working in teams or other sorts of groups, and including citizens, who are enabled and constrained in their activity by the material conditions, technology, artefacts, rules, perceptions, and other characteristics of the working environment. These assumptions contribute to what is known as a 'socio-technical systems' perspective.

Socio-technical systems

Socio-technical systems theory is often associated with the work of Erik Trist, a British psychologist and organisational researcher who helped found the Tavistock Institute for Social Research. His original study (Trist and Bamforth, 1951) looked at post-war working practices in English coalmines, where a highly mechanised approach called 'longwall working' was predominant; large-scale operations were managed via command-and-control, leading to 'aggregates of men of considerable size having their jobs broken down into one-man-one-task roles, while coordination and control had been externalised in supervision, which had become coercive' (Trist, 1981: 8). However, Trist found that miners in one site, Haighmoor, had encountered a seam that could not be worked in this way, and so had evolved a new way of working based on 'relatively autonomous groups interchanging roles and shifts and regulating their affairs with a minimum of supervision' (1981: 8). Such practices had been fairly common in pre-mechanised days but had largely disappeared with the advent of longwall working. The Haighmoor miners found a way to recover their group cohesion and capacity for self-regulation without losing the benefits of mechanisation. Trist goes on to note other benefits to the new approach:

> Cooperation between task groups was everywhere in evidence; personal commitment was obvious, absenteeism low, accidents infrequent, productivity high. The contrast was large between the atmosphere and arrangements on these faces and those in the conventional areas of the pit, where the negative features characteristic of the industry were glaringly apparent. (Trist, 1981: 8)

Trist argued that such innovations showed that there was an alternative to the pervasive logic of scientific management and Weberian bureaucracy: increases in scale and use of technology did not necessarily mean more bureaucracy and command-and-control. Instead, a 'new paradigm of work' promised to integrate the social and technical aspects of organisational systems. Organisations would focus on the work system, comprising all the activities through which the organisation achieved its purpose, rather than on individual jobs and tasks. Work groups were seen as the basic operational unit, not individual job-holders, and these groups were to a large extent self-regulating rather than needing to be controlled by external supervisors. Individuals would be encouraged to develop multiple skills and use their discretion, rather than being confined to one prescribed role. In turn, this would 'increase the response repertoire of the group' (Trist, 1981: 9). The socio-technical mode of organisation therefore sought to increase internal adaptability and breadth of expertise, in contrast to the 'variety-decreasing' bureaucratic mode.

Requisite Variety

Trist's ideas are linked to another systems concept called 'requisite variety' (Ashby, 1956). The term originated in the field of cybernetics, which explores how systems respond to changes in their internal and external environment through feedback loops and other regulatory mechanisms. Variety essentially refers to information, which can never be complete for any complex system because of non-linear causality (see Introduction); operational processes therefore need to have a sufficient range of response to deal with potential variation in environmental conditions. In social work, the demands on organisations are highly variable; for example, consider the range of issues that may come to the attention of someone on the 'duty desk' of a multi-agency safeguarding team. Ashby's 'law of requisite variety' states that 'only variety destroys variety' (1956: 205), so that, as Woods et al. (2010: 11) point out, the human role in regulatory systems is 'to be resilient and robust when events and demands do not fit preconceived and routinized paths' (see Chapter 9). Without that designed-in adaptability, the organisation is exposed to potentially catastrophic failure when unforeseen events escalate out of control (Rasmussen, 1997; Reason, 1997).

Deming's management system approach

W. Edwards Deming was an American engineer and statistician who became famous as a management theorist through his work in Japan in the decades following the Second World War. Deming was a staunch opponent of functional hierarchies and command-and-control management practices. Instead, he argued that organisations should be managed as systems, and that quality could be improved without increasing costs as long as control, learning, and improvement happened where it needed to happen, i.e. on the production line (Deming, 2000). An early exponent of this type of approach was Taiichi Ohno, inventor of the Toyota Production System, which revolutionised car manufacturing in the 1960s and 1970s and was the precursor to 'lean' manufacturing models (Liker, 2004). Like Ohno, Deming believed that managers should be concerned with understanding the flow of work through the system, and the reasons for variations in quality, rather than with prescribing and monitoring individual task-performance. He showed that the majority of problems with quality were actually attributable to system conditions rather than the fault of individual workers; he therefore advised organisations to 'eliminate management by objective' and 'eliminate management by numbers and numerical targets', and to replace these methods with leadership (Deming, 2000). In other words, the fundamental task of management was to act on systems, not to try and control what individuals did.

While most of Deming's examples were from manufacturing industry, his ideas are readily transferable to public services, where bureaucracies and functional hierarchies continue to be the dominant form of provision. Seddon (2008) argues that in service organisations the 'nominal value' to be measured actually comes from the service user. The organisation should be designed in such a way that citizens can 'pull' the resources and expertise they need as quickly as possible. Socio-technical systems, because of their focus on variety and responsiveness on the frontline, stand a better chance of delivering this kind of service. Conversely, command-and-control hierarchies oblige people to adapt to functions and processes that are mainly designed to satisfy organisational aims, e.g. to control costs and manage demand. The result is sub-optimisation, or waste, as citizens struggle with the system to get what they need from it. The answer, as Seddon (2008) puts it, is to 'design against demand', i.e. gear the system towards understanding what people want from it and then giving it to them. It sounds straightforward, but actually contravenes how many services approach their end-users.

Designing against demand

Seddon (2008) suggests that a systems perspective involves thinking about an organisation 'from the outside-in, to understand customer demand and to design a system that meets it' (2008: 70). Demand is seen from the citizen's point of view, i.e. 'what do I want', rather than from the organisation's point of view, i.e. 'what do we do with this?'. This reveals another distinction: between 'value demand', which is what people need from the service, and 'failure demand', which exists because people have not been able to get what they need the first time round. An example familiar to many people will be the experience of having to ring a call centre for the umpteenth time because the promised solution to a problem has not materialised. Another example, familiar to many social workers, is the person or family who is re-referred to social services a few months after their case was closed. Within traditional management approaches, failure demand may not be visible or given much attention because it is treated the same as any other referral or client contact. This means that very high volumes of failure demand can go unnoticed and even start to overwhelm a service unless action is taken to improve system conditions (Seddon, 2008).

Another systems insight is that studying demand from the citizen's perspective will reveal some of it to be predictable over time. For example, practitioners in a community drug and alcohol team (CDAT) make an effort to find out what matters most to the people they work with and find that the most common aspirations are stable accommodation, access to employment, and reconnecting with close family members. Ideally, resources to address these problems could be 'pulled' from the organisational networks around the CDAT without the usual pathways of multiple onward referrals, lengthy waiting lists and missed clinical appointments. Having identified what was needed, practitioners could work with managers on how to design the service in a more user-centric way, e.g. employing a dedicated housing support worker or a psychologist trained in family therapy. The CDAT might also consider its response to unpredictable demand, e.g. whether its assessment processes are flexible enough to deal with unusual presenting problems, or what kind of specialist support has been found useful in the past.

As Hood (2015b) points out, designing against demand in social care settings means bringing expertise as close as possible to the point of first contact. In the UK, specialist multi-agency services tend to be targeted at groups whom mainstream services have been unable to help and who seem likely to cost the state a lot of money (Harwin et al., 2011; Local Government Leadership and City of Westminster, 2010). Using the terminology of tiered services discussed in Chapter 6, these new and luxurious forms of provision fall into the Tier 2 or Tier 3 category and therefore require onward referral from other agencies. However, this raises the question as to why expertise and resources held in secondary or tertiary services are not available within Tier 1 since that is where people come into contact with the system. In relation to children's social care, Hood (2015b) argues that mainstream services should have embedded expertise to address predictable issues such as non-engagement, parenting skills, drug and alcohol misuse, behavioural disorders, and mental health problems (C4EO, 2009). The system would then be geared towards doing preventative work with families, rather than assessing, case managing, and referring on (see Case Study 8.3).

CASE STUDY 8.3

The Vanguard Method as applied to the design and management of English and Welsh children's services departments (Gibson and O'Donovan, 2014)

Gibson and O'Donovan (2014) describe findings from their case study research into systems redesign in statutory children's social care. A small number of local authority children's services departments used Seddon's (2003) proprietary systems approach, the Vanguard Method, to transform the delivery of services in their area. The Vanguard Method begins with a process called 'Check', in which the current performance of the system is assessed. It was found that social workers were spending 60–80% of their time at their computers; failure demand in the form of cases closed then re-referred at a later date was running at up to 70% of total demand; and the average end-to-end time from the child's perspective (i.e. counting re-referrals) was 852 days. System conditions responsible for this state of affairs included an inflexible electronic workflow system, preoccupation with gatekeeping, managing demand and cutting costs, use of numerical targets to manage performance, fragmented provision with multiple transitions between teams, and services not addressing the underlying causes of problems. The first step of redesign was to remove some of these system conditions, e.g. by applying for ministerial permission to dispense temporarily with the IT system and

(Continued)

central reporting requirements. The system's purpose was redefined from the child's perspective, i.e. 'Help me to have a family who can keep me safe, happy and healthy'. New operating principles were devised with this purpose in mind, e.g. 'We will put the appropriate expertise as close as possible to the demand when it enters the system'. New measures were also derived from purpose, including 'needs met right first time' and 'number of hand-offs in a case'. The redesigned service took the form of an integrated multi-agency team based in the local community (e.g. school cluster, health centre, or children's centre) dealing with all demand at the first point of contact. The team had the core expertise to deal with frequent and predictable demand with additional expertise able to be pulled in quickly as needed. The results of the redesign were promising. Failure demand was reduced to about 25–30%, decision-making was decentralised with managers spending much more time working alongside practitioners, social workers spent 80–90% of their time out face-to-face with the people they were supposed to be helping, and end-to-end times were substantially reduced in all areas. Two of the case studies were included in the influential Munro Review of Child Protection (Munro, 2011) as examples of systems thinking in action.

Overcoming the control problem

The issue of control is perhaps the biggest stumbling block for bureaucratic organisations wanting to adopt a socio-technical systems approach. Many conventional management practices (and indeed managers) are rendered superfluous when operational processes are decentralised and decoupled from arbitrary measures and standards. Perhaps the most striking example is the practice of budgeting. Most managers consider budgets to be an indispensable tool, without which their organisation would quickly disintegrate in a blur of spiralling costs and unshackled spending. In fact, budgets are simply an offshoot of command-and-control thinking; Bogsnes (2016) and Hope and Fraser (2003) examine a number of large companies that have successfully discarded budgets in favour of alternative methods of organising resources and planning activities. Similarly, performance management in its conventional guise of target-setting and appraisal against individual objectives is largely meaningless within a socio-technical design, in which practitioners are put in charge of the work and the job of managers is to act on the system (Deming, 2000). Nonetheless, when invited to consider these arguments, managers will often cite 'losing control' as their biggest worry.

Bogsnes (2016) points out that control has a positive connotation of seeking to understand how an organisation is performing and what might help it do better. In this respect, command-and-control methods are counterproductive because they encourage people to 'game the system'. A notorious example in the UK was the parliamentary expenses scandal of 2009, in which many MPs were shown to have taken advantage of the rules to claim as much money as possible in ways that subsequently turned out to be unethical and in some cases illegal (Kelso, 2009). The problem was not a lack of rules but a lack of transparency; the system made it easy – even logical – for MPs to behave in the way they did. In contrast, Bogsnes points to the example of a multinational pharmaceutical company that reduced travel costs by the simple expedient of making all travel expenses openly visible to everyone; travel costs fell without any need for travel budgets or complicated regulations. Transparency, along with some basic values and principles, proves to be its own control mechanism. Conversely, the more rigid the prescriptions about what people can and cannot do, the more people will turn their ingenuity towards getting round the controls.

Another problem of control has already been mentioned at various points in this book, namely the futile quest to predict and micro-manage the future. Command-and-control thinking holds that ever more detailed plans and forecasts are required to reduce uncertainty and master complexity. Even when the predictions are proved wrong (as they inevitably are) the wealth of detail about now-past performance allows for a forensic examination of what went wrong. The result is a ratcheting up of the amount of detail required for the next round of forecasting, target-setting, and compliance monitoring. Although a pointless and wasteful approach to planning, this circular activity does engender a comforting illusion of control:

> When we have that binder with a voluminous and single outcome set of num-bers, it all seems less scary and more orderly and manageable. This perceived control of the future we carry with us when tomorrow becomes today. If we hit the numbers, we definitely feel in control, although it is no guarantee what-soever that we got the best possible performance. If we on the other hand didn't hit because we once again got it wrong, we feel at least somewhat in control because we can at least explain in detail both where and why! (Bogsnes, 2016: 24)

Linking measures to purpose

Seddon (2008) argues that organisations using command-and-control thinking often use the wrong measures because they start with the reporting requirements and work back from there. This is a key drawback of the performance-based accountability framework discussed earlier; it often translates into targets and standards for timescales and completion rates for particular pieces of work (see Case Study 8.2). These arbitrary measures create a de facto purpose for the organi-sation and impose constraints on method, as the work is designed around meeting the targets. In Seddon's terms, purpose comes first and – crucially – is seen from the citizen's perspective rather the organisation's. Measures are then derived from pur-pose and practitioners at the sharp end of practice are freed up to design the work, using the right measures as a guide to performance.

In the range of public services considered by Seddon (2008), one of the most important measures is 'end-to-end' time, i.e. the time that elapses from a citizen's first contact with the service to their problem being resolved. Although seemingly obvious, very few social care agencies measure this aspect of their work – timescales usually refer to discrete processes and functions, e.g. the length of time a child is on a protection plan. When practitioners and managers discover the total amount of time that their clients spend in the system waiting for a service, they are often shocked – as was the case with the Welsh children's social care agency described in Case Study 8.3. Once the right measures are in place, Seddon (2008) advocates the use of 'capability charts' to track the results of experimenting with method. Based on Deming's statistical process control, these charts are like longitudinal scatterplots that track the system's performance and variation over time. Instead of gearing performance management towards matching arbitrary targets or responding to individual data points (e.g. a 'drop' in performance this month), managers focus on the system conditions that increase capability and reduce variation.

Gibson (2016: 35) discusses measures in people-centred services, and argues that good measures should satisfy the following criteria:

- relate to purpose from the citizen's point of view
- show variation over time
- help people to learn, understand and improve the system
- are in the hands of the people doing the work
- are used by leaders to take effective action on the system

Under this definition there is a distinction to be made between 'individual measures' and 'system measures'. System measures provide an overall picture of capability and the impact of system conditions. They are what we usually think of as performance indicators and consist of quantitative data, e.g. end-to-end times, or volume of repeat demand. Individual measures, on the other hand, indicate whether a social care agency is helping citizens with the problems that matter to them. This type of information is generally qualitative, as it requires practitioners to find out what matters to people – it cannot be collected in the form of a-priori categories or a 'common assessment framework' (White et al., 2009). Gibson (2016) describes gathering this information as an ongoing record of progress that is specific to each person:

> The individual identifies what matters to them – for example, 'I'd like to be able to cook meals for myself' – and rates on a scale of 1 to 10 how near they are towards achieving that. The organisation then works with the person to understand and achieve the goal. (Gibson, 2016: 36)

A summary of this 'what matters conversation' might resemble a 'spidergram', similar to the outcomes star tool used by some social care agencies (MacKeith, 2011) but generated entirely by the citizen (see Figure 8.2 for an example). The cumulative knowledge acquired through this type of qualitative measure enables agencies to gather first-hand knowledge from citizens about the demand for services in their locality. As patterns start to be identified, the organisation brings in the necessary resources and expertise to address the demand. Gibson (2016) gives the example of loneliness, which is experienced by many vulnerable adults and might be caused by a number of factors such as lack of family relationships,

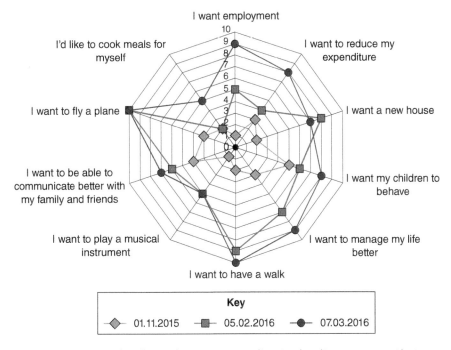

Figure 8.2 An example of a spidergram: a qualitative leading measure that demonstrates (over time) how well a system is helping an individual to achieve their purpose (reproduced with permission from Gibson, 2016: 36)

friendships or support networks. If the aspiration to be more connected to others is widely expressed in the community, locality workers can pull in the resources to make that happen, e.g. setting up community groups or improving access to public transport, and identify some relevant system measures to track overall progress. The point is that system measures should be derived from individual measures. Most statutory social care agencies have it the other way round, in that citizens are obliged to align themselves with preordained categories of 'need' and to make do with the services they get.

REFLECTIVE EXERCISE 8.1

Look back at Case Study 8.2, which described a command-and-control approach to managing adult social care. Given what you have read so far in this chapter, what do you think an alternative 'socio-technical' approach to adult social care might look like?

COMPLEX RESPONSIVE PROCESSES

Stacey's (2007) complex responsive processes approach has already been mentioned in the previous chapter. It has much in common with the socio-technical systems perspective described above and is similarly critical of command-and-control assumptions. However, Stacey takes issue with the idea of organisations as systems and this leads him to be sceptical about the possibility of system design. He describes organisations as 'iterated patterns of interactions between people', which take the form of social objects, i.e. 'generalised tendencies, on the part of large numbers of people, to act in similar ways in similar situations' (Stacey, 2007: 433). This collective activity is then idealised as an 'imaginative whole' that provides 'powerful experiences of "we" identity to members'. The imaginative whole may have 'cult values' attached to it (visions, slogans, etc.) or may be thought of as a system, but for Stacey this is a fundamentally ideological activity. When managers implement an organisational strategy, they may declare (or believe) that they are designing a system that will run in accordance with their intention. What they are actually doing is engaging in an interplay of intentions with other people in local interactions. The strategy self-organises from that point on, and 'is basically expressed as narratives of identity' and as 'power relations felt as the dynamics of inclusion and exclusion'.

Stacey's take on organisational dynamics and strategic management is a more radical take on complexity than the other perspectives discussed in this chapter. The language is conceptually difficult and lacks the pragmatic incisiveness of writers such as Trist, Deming, and Seddon. However, there are a number of crucial insights that should not be overlooked. One is that managers are active participants in the systems on which they seek to act; there is no external position from which to direct a process of transformation. Managers have to leave their offices and immerse themselves in the service they manage, lest they end up with delusions of control over their 'imaginative wholes'. However well designed or well intentioned, strategies have a life of their own, and this requires an organisational focus on dialogue and reflection rather than control and compliance (see Chapter 5). It also means that organisations have to come to terms with the inevitability of surprises as well as with 'the anxiety of not knowing' (Stacey, 2007: 448). If innovation and creativity are treated as a one-off activity, a way of generating the ideal design, the sclerosis of functionality and performance management will follow. Instead, organisations should plan for long-term unpredictability!

CONCLUSION

This chapter has examined the implications of complexity for the management and administration of social services. Such services are accountable to a number of stakeholders, including taxpayers and elected officials. From the citizen's perspective, their purpose should be to find out what people in the community want from them and make the necessary resources and expertise readily available. In systemic terms, services need to have the 'requisite variety' to deal with the complexity of demand. The problem in many bureaucratic organisations is that resources are mar-shalled behind successive thresholds or 'tiers' of provision, which inadvertently split the work into fragmented pieces of assessment and intervention. This can cause delays in meeting need and high levels of 'failure demand' that can overwhelm front-line services. Alternative forms of provision based on socio-technical principles try to place the expertise needed to solve problems near the 'front' of the system where users first come into contact with services. Of course, this may well prove easier said than done. As Wilson (1989) points out, organisations that wish to experiment with method must also build consensus on what is to be done and why it is necessary. The interface between organisations and their wider institutional and political con-text is therefore a crucial factor in efforts to address complexity, and it is to this context that our attention turns in the next chapter.

DEVELOPING POLICIES FOR SOCIAL PROBLEMS

9

CHAPTER SUMMARY

This chapter broadens the scope of analysis to consider what complexity means for social policy. It begins by exploring non-linear effects and unintended consequences in a range of policy areas, including housing, social care, and public health interventions. Some key principles of holistic policymaking are described before turning to the development of risk regulation regimes, which have become increasingly important in social work. Different policy approaches to human error are compared, drawing on socio-technical systems ideas to consider the interface between policy and research evidence. The chapter concludes with a discussion of top-down and bottom-up approaches to policy implementation and the importance of stimulating innovative solutions to complex social problems.

INTRODUCTION

As its title suggests, the chapter's starting point is to assume that social policy aims to address and alleviate social problems, such as poverty, inequality, or exclusion. Social problems are bound up with how societies are organised and how citizens, families, and communities relate to each other. Accordingly they cannot be reduced to individual decisions and attitudes for they emerge from interconnectedness.

For example, most measures of poverty are relative rather than absolute; thresholds such as average household income, or the affordability of a 'basket of goods', work by positioning the individual in relation to others in their society (Harkness et al., 2012). Indeed, from a humanist rather than economic perspective, the indignity of poverty is perhaps its truest measure (Masenya, 2013). Social problems are extremely complex, not least because of the sheer scale and density of networks in modern societies. The United Kingdom, for example, is currently composed of around 65 million people living in four different countries, who are linked to each other, as well as to other countries in the world, via political, economic, cultural, and family ties.

Such a high degree of interconnectedness means that events on one side of the world can have serious repercussions on the other. A notorious example was the sudden collapse of the subprime mortgage market in the United States in 2007. This 'local' difficulty quickly turned into an international banking crisis and a global economic downturn; many countries, including the UK, were forced to bail out their banking sector with public funds and then implemented austerity measures in order to reduce their budget deficits. The resulting cuts to government expenditure continue to affect most parts of the UK, especially the economically deprived regions that are more reliant on the statutory sector for employment and services (Jordan and Drakeford, 2012; O'Hara, 2015). In turn, the human consequences of austerity are mainly borne by the vulnerable people and families with whom social workers are often involved and at whom statutory interventions are usually targeted (Sidebotham, 2012).

The complexity of social problems creates similar difficulties for policymakers as it does for practitioners, managers, and researchers. Non-linear causality means that policies designed with specific objectives can have all sorts of unanticipated effects, requiring yet more policies to undo the damage. While unintended consequences may become evident over time, by definition they are hard to predict in advance. This points to another difficulty in social policy, which is that policymakers must deal with an uncertain future while simultaneously reassuring the public that they are taking steps to address specific problems. Particularly when called on to address emotive and sensitive issues, such as deaths from child abuse, politicians may even vow that such things must 'never happen again'. The public – abetted by the media – both demands such certainties and is unforgiving when reality proves otherwise.

Political and institutional pressures must therefore be considered part of the 'psychosocial rationality' of policy decisions (see Chapter 3). On the one hand, election results, resignations, and reshuffles contribute to ministerial turnover and 'policy churn', resulting in greater volatility and yet more unintended consequences. On the other hand, promising policy ideas are overlooked or discarded because they do not fit in with the party line on a given issue, whether it be 'tough on crime', or 'reduce benefits'. The interface between evidence and policy is therefore beset with ambiguity and contradiction; policymakers make use of research to design social interventions (evidence-based policy) but also selectively interpret and even manufacture evidence to support what they want to do (policy-based evidence). Finally, there is the question of implementation, which in social work is increasingly linked to the activity of powerful state regulators and the dilemma of control vs innovation.

POLiCY effects and consequences

From a systems perspective, policies may be seen as an effort to achieve a specific output with a specific input. In this sense, inputs might include additional financial resources to enable the roll-out of a new social programme, or the mandate to implement new legislation and statutory guidelines. Outputs (or outcomes) are usually defined in relation to specific groups of people, e.g. a reduction in teenage pregnancies, or fewer elderly adults requiring accident and emergency hospital services. However, since change in complex systems is non-linear, the effects of policies are unpredictable and may quickly diverge from what was intended. Furthermore, sensitivity to initial conditions means that interventions in one part of the system may have unforeseen effects elsewhere. Concerns about unintended consequences are often cited in relation to the ecological and environmental impact of human activities. For example, Case Study 9.1 describes how efforts by the World Health Organisation to eradicate malaria in the 1950s became associated with a host of unintended consequences, including crushed eggs, collapsing roofs, and even parachuting cats!

CASE STUDY 9.1

Malaria eradication and parachuting cats
(O'Shaughnessy, 2008)

O'Shaughnessy (2008) reviews the practice of using DDT to control malaria, which was widely pursued by the World Health Organisation in the 1950s and still continues in some areas today. The practice is controversial because its public health benefits, i.e. the reduction in deaths and illnesses caused by malaria-carrying mosquitoes, may be counteracted by its adverse impact on the local ecology. When sprayed in high enough concentration on walls and under beds, DDT leaves a persistent residue that is toxic enough to kill insects coming into contact with it. This makes DDT an effective means of eradicating mosquitoes but can also lead to harmful ecological effects, often linked to its ingestion by other animals and its accumulation higher up in the food chain. For example, it was found in the 1950s that birds of prey in areas with heavy insecticide use produced eggs with shells so thin that they were crushed when adult birds covered them. Other ecological consequences were more indirect. For example, in British Guyana, eradication of the malarial mosquito led to an increase in the human population that in turn resulted in a change in agricultural practices, as cattle herding was replaced with rice cultivation. A different type of malarial mosquito that fed on cattle then suffered a scarcity of food and switched to human blood instead, leading to a higher incidence of the disease than ever before. An entirely different problem was experienced in Thailand and Indonesia, where most houses in rural areas had thatched roofs; caterpillars that fed on the thatch learned to avoid the DDT residues but the parasitic wasps that killed the caterpillars did not. As a result the number of caterpillars multiplied and villagers found their roofs collapsing in on them. The most notorious incident occurred in Borneo, where domestic cats began dying as a result of eating lizards who had themselves eaten DDT-poisoned insects. The lack of cats then led to an explosion in rat numbers and associated diseases. In a widely reported but possibly apocryphal story, the government began shipping crates of live cats to affected villages, with those in remote areas receiving their cats via parachute drop!

The current housing crisis in the UK, which affects the lives of many recipients of social services, is often attributed to the unintended consequences of government housing policies (Mullins and Pawson, 2005; Meek, 2014; Robertson, 2017). In particular, the national shortage of social housing arguably has its roots in a single policy from 1980: the famous 'Right to Buy' for council tenants introduced during Margaret Thatcher's first term in office. This policy effectively privatised large swathes of the public housing stock built up since the Second World War, as councils were prohibited from borrowing to build new homes. In the decades that followed, the expected private sector investment in social housing never materialised, while financial liberalisation encouraged mortgage lending and a series of asset bubbles that vastly inflated property prices and rental charges. Housing benefit – a welfare payment introduced in 1982 – swelled in size and now consumes over £14 billion of government expenditure (Department for Work and Pensions, 2016). In recent years, austerity policies designed to curb this growth, including a benefits cap and a 'bedroom tax', have caused even more hardship for families struggling to avoid debt, eviction, and homelessness (O'Hara, 2015).

Haynes (2007) analyses another pattern of unintended consequences and complex change, this time in adult social care policy. Here the 'small change with large consequences' was Rhodes Boyson's amendment of social benefits regulations in 1983, which allowed people to use government benefits to pay for their care in a private residential home. This meant that elderly people no longer had to rely on local authority provision, while equivalent benefits for carers looking after family members in their home were comparatively small. The change precipitated a large-scale privatisation of the residential care sector: the number of local authority care homes fell sharply between 1980 and 1991, while in the absence of any investment in home care services there was huge increase in private residential provision. Social security payments for residential care rose accordingly from £6 million in 1978 to £499 million in 1986 (Haynes, 2007: 2002). Following the Griffiths report on community care (Griffiths, 1988), the government reformed what was seen as a dysfunctional market through the 1990 NHS and Community Care Act, aiming to increase the diversity of services, split purchaser and provider functions, and oblige local authorities to manage costs. The focus on marketisation led in turn to an increased emphasis on user choice and involvement, which eventually transformed the sector again through new policies such as direct payments and personalisation (Duffy et al., 2010;

West, 2013). Haynes (2007) concludes that while successive governments were certainly able to influence the environment for social care and steer it towards a more marketised model of delivery, the market itself did not tend towards stable equilibrium but rather towards dynamic patterns of change:

> Using markets to deliver social care services set a new course of events where the overall sense of long-term direction (diversity of services, potential to respond to individuality, new choices for some social groups) could be forecast, but where the pace of change, quantities of services and the detail of what would happen were very difficult to predict. This is a challenging environment for government agencies to manage. (Haynes, 2007: 204).

Fragmented vs holistic policy-making

Vester (2007) points out that unintended consequences are the inevitable result of applying linear thinking to complex adaptive systems. As noted in earlier chapters, this approach is typified by splitting up an overall problem into separate tasks for which technical solutions are perceived to exist, e.g. the psychiatric diagnosis of a homeless person, or the educational achievement of a looked after child. In policy terms, the categories are much broader but the logic is the same. Vester cites a well-known experiment by Dörner (1996), who set up a computer simulation to test the results of development initiatives in a fictional African region called Tanaland (the underlying data and premises were based on real case studies). A team of 12 experts from different specialisms were given the job of improving the lives of the people of Tanaland. Financial resources (World Bank loans) could be used for development projects such as sinking wells, changing agricultural practices, introducing new forms of medical care, promoting particular industries, and so on. By coordinating the decisions made at various levels in these different areas, and reviewing outcomes at regular intervals, Tanaland could be steered towards a brighter future. After the simulation had been run for an extended period, the results were unambiguous:

> Instead of people's lives becoming steadily better, which had been the aim, brief periods of improvement were succeeded by disasters and famines. Herds shrank to a fraction of their former size, food sources became exhausted, and finance dried up; loans could no longer be repaid. What was striking was that everyone involved in the experiment, experts included, created chaos and ran the country into the ground – although they had wanted the best. (Vester, 2007: 36)

According to Vester, what catastrophic policy interventions often have in common is a lack of attention to the interconnectedness of complex systems. The search for manageable problems, each with their own technical solution, results in a patchwork of measures, whose repercussions ripple through the system in an unpredictable way. The alternative is to maintain focus on the system as a whole. Vester suggests the following principles for holistic policy-making:

- *Goal definition* – the overarching goals of policies, and the measures used to monitor success and failure, have to align with overall system parameters rather than an arbitrary part of them. A set of holistic organising principles should counteract the tendency to define problems around the perspective and capabilities of a single discipline or area of expertise (cf. the relationship between purpose and measures discussed in Chapter 8).
- *Understand system dynamics* – understanding how elements in a system interconnect is just as (if not more) important than amassing large amounts of data on separate elements. Information about contexts, relationships, and dynamics is often qualitative, which means that policymakers (and researchers) have to overcome their preference for neat statistical tables when it comes to analysing problems (see Chapter 7).
- *Avoid irreversible emphasis* – initial success in a particular problem area can lead policymakers to seize on that area as *the* problem to be solved. Maintaining a holistic perspective allows policymakers to keep track of other problem areas as well as the wider consequences of any interventions adopted.
- *Explore side-effects* – exploring side-effects counteracts the tendency to single-mindedly pursue technical solutions to individual problems. This could include 'what-if' scenarios that consider the systemic consequences of a proposed intervention, and actively searching for unintended consequences in pilot projects rather than just testing for change in selected outcomes.
- *Don't oversteer* – complex system effects are often interpreted as if they were linear consequences of a policy intervention, e.g. initial progress leads to a 'full steam ahead' response, whereas unexpected setbacks mean the brakes are slammed on. Similarly, if a relatively minor action does not seem to change the system then it may be assumed that more vigorous intervention is required. None of these responses is appropriate and will often lead to more severe repercussions further down the line.
- *Avoid authoritarian impulses* – social workers are familiar with this issue through their training in professional ethics and anti-oppressive practice. On a policy level, bureaucratic authority and political power can conjure a misplaced sense of control over systems, often fuelled by the desire for prestige and status through 'high impact' projects. Vester argues that in complex systems the most effective approach is actually 'to swim with the current rather than against it, making changes as you go' (2007: 38).

RiSK, ReGULatiON aND BLaMe

The connection between complexity and risk has been discussed in previous chapters, and hinges on the difficulty of predicting the nature and likelihood of outcomes in situations where levels of uncertainty are high. It has been argued by sociologists such as Beck (1992) and Giddens (1990) that contemporary societies have become increasingly preoccupied with the control of risks, stemming from deep-rooted anxiety about technological and social change and its potential for catastrophe. Governments have accordingly developed risk regulation regimes in many areas of life, from waste disposal to child protection, in order to reduce the likelihood of harm to human health and welfare. According to Majone (1994), regulation has become one of the main activities and policy levers of the state, whose role as employer and service provider has been increasingly ceded to the market. Regulatory activity has also been linked to audit culture (Power, 1997), which fits in with the command-and-control management philosophy discussed in Chapter 8. From this perspective, governments control the regulators, who control organisations through inspections and other compliance processes, while organisations use their internal audit and quality assurance functions to manage the performance of professionals and other frontline staff. Nonetheless, risk regulation regimes take various forms and differ widely in the strictness of their rules and attitudes to compliance and enforcement (Hood et al., 2001).

Regulation and social work

Sparrow (2008) argues that regulatory activity is fundamentally about the reduction of harms. In the social sphere, this means controlling specific risks to the public, usually around health, safety, and the environment;[1] it includes a wide range of harms ranging from contamination of rivers by industrial pollutants to the repair of potholes in roads and pavements. Regulation necessarily involves the imposition of duties on others (e.g. compliance with rules, engagement with inspections) and more often than not is an involuntary and unpleasant experience for those being regulated. These characteristics distinguish regulation from activities designed to promote general health and wellbeing, which fall more easily into the category of services received by willing clients. The problem for many regulators, as Sparrow sees it, is that they have conflated harm reduction with the construction of social goods; this has led them to adopt a 'customer service' model of regulation based on management concepts and methods imported from the private sector, e.g. process improvement, quality assurance, and performance management (Sparrow, 2000). Organising the practice of regulation in this way makes it harder for regulators to innovate and adapt new strategies to tackle specific harm-reduction problems that do not fit into their existing processes. The problem of child sexual exploitation, highlighted in recent reports as a blind-spot for statutory protective services (Jay, 2014; Ofsted, 2016), might be seen as a case in point.

  Sparrow's analysis is pertinent for social work, which tends to subsume its regulatory role within a broader remit to promote positive outcomes for citizens, families, and communities. This gives rise to the mixture of 'care and control' or 'prevention and protection' characteristic of many types of social work provision (Hood, 2016b). Moreover, the combination of marketisation and 'new public management' reforms over recent decades has led many social work agencies to adopt what might

---

[1]Sparrow (2000) distinguishes between social and economic regulation, where the latter is focused on ensuring competitive markets, fair trade practices, and consumer protections in a given industry.

be termed a customer service ethos, i.e. a commitment to efficient and effective 'user-centric' provision, reinforced by the principles of transparency and account-ability. This is linked to another feature of contemporary social work, which is the phenomenon of double or even triple regulation, i.e. where social workers act as regulators while being regulated themselves (Webb, 2006). At the time of writing, a child and family social worker in the UK contributes to the regulation of certain aspects of public and private life, such as abusive or neglectful parenting or youth involvement in gangs; their adherence to ethical standards of work is enforced by the professional regulator (currently the Health and Care Professions Council) while their organisation is regulated by Ofsted, the statutory inspector for local authority children's services.

Multiple layers of regulation are consistent with the technical rational approach to complexity described in earlier chapters, where the focus is on containing volatile and potentially dangerous energies within successive bands of protection (Woods et al., 2010). One unintended consequence is that more and more activities are drawn into the regulatory net; in the UK, for example, it has been found that local authorities' use of protective interventions to deal with child welfare issues has been rapidly outpacing growth in demand for services (Hood et al., 2016b). Another potential effect is what Bardach and Kagan (2002) call 'regulatory unreasonable-ness', which may take many forms including inflexible application of over-inclusive, centrally formulated rules, or particular incidences of oppressive behaviour from enforcement officials. Power (2004) has referred to the proliferation of control processes in organisational culture as 'the risk management of everything', arguing that regulation regimes should to some extent be seen as a 'responsibility-shifting strategy' designed by governments seeking protection from blame. According to Rothstein et al. (2006), regulation has become 'colonised' by risk concepts, which allow agencies to account for their inability to control the 'regulated objects', i.e. the public harms they seek to reduce. Since regulators cannot control societal risks, they become increasingly concerned with managing 'institutional risks', i.e. 'threats to both regulator and regulated organisations such as delivery failure, budget overruns, liabilities and loss of reputation' (2006: 92). If a mismatch develops between societal and institutional risk, e.g. because of public expectations or political sensitivities about the regulated area, blame avoidance starts to take the place of the regulator's core business.

Blame culture

Many social workers have experienced the feeling that they are 'damned if they do and damned if they don't' when making decisions about risk.[2] This is a symptom of blame culture, which could be seen as the 'dark side' of accountability – a prod-uct of pervasive institutional and professional anxiety about being held accountable

---

[2]This was also the title of an episode of 'Protecting Our Children', a BBC2 documentary on child protection social work, shown on 30 January 2012.

for an uncertain future. Blame culture affects individuals and organisations in various ways; they may be singled out for criticism in serious case reviews (Fish et al., 2008) or have to endure punitive and demoralising forms of inspection (Perryman, 2007). It also affects regulators, who are condemned for being oppressive but also for not identifying poor practice (Craven and Tooley, 2016). In response, social workers may resort to the kind of defensive routines analysed by Isabel Menzies (see Chapter 6), while agencies and regulators become preoccupied with managing institutional risk. The result is an increase in what Hood and Rothstein (2001) call 'protocolization' (otherwise known as back covering), i.e. rules and procedures designed to demonstrate 'bureaucratically rational "due diligence" defences in the face of increased accountability pressures' (Rothstein et al., 2006: 97). As Munro (2010) argued in relation to child protection, while the ostensible aim of these measures is to improve professional practice so that past mistakes are not repeated, their actual effect can be to de-skill and demoralise the workforce. This results in different mistakes being made and a further ratcheting up of blame and prescription.

Theoretically, the cycle can be broken by applying what Argyris and Schön (1978) call 'double-loop learning', which examines the underlying system conditions that shape organisational and professional practice. However, the scope of this analysis needs to go beyond the organisation to encompass the policy domain in which complex social problems are constructed as regulatory issues. As Hood (2002) points out, policymakers have an extra incentive to delegate responsibility in areas where the consequences of being blamed for failure are perceived to outweigh the rewards of claiming credit for success. The regulatory role of social work, which includes making highly sensitive decisions on issues such as compulsory hospitalisation or the removal of children, arguably fall into this category. The result is a proliferation of regulatory supervision, which operates in the name of accountability but ironically often serves to obscure it (see also Hood, 2015b).

The scandal-reform cycle

Scandals and their institutional counterpart, the Inquiry, have long formed part of the policy context to social work (Stanley and Manthorpe, 2004). In politically sensitive areas such as child maltreatment, violent crime, and institutional abuse, a recurrent cycle of scandal and reform has gradually shaped the nature of professional work in those fields. According to Sass and Crosbie (2013), the scandal-reform cycle can perform a stabilising function in democracies by identifying deviant actors, holding them to account and upholding social norms and values. On the other hand, it involves complex social processes that can just as easily prove disruptive and volatile.

In Figure 9.1, Sass and Crosbie's model is adapted to show how the scandal-reform cycle operates in social work. First, a critical incident is identified by the media as being both newsworthy and illustrative of a particular narrative around professional or institutional failings. Unfortunately for social workers, the narrative of social workers 'not doing their jobs properly' seems to be particularly favoured

Reforms
to system

Critical
incident

Inquiry
held

Reported
by media

Public is
outraged

Figure 9.1   The scandal-reform cycle in social work (adapted from Sass and Crosbie, 2013: 853)

by the press (Jones, 2014). Media reporting of the incident then generates public outrage by tapping into more widely held anxieties and insecurities, although this will depend on a number of other factors including whether the public accepts the media's chosen narrative (Sass and Crosbie, 2013). As the scandal develops, policymakers will be forced to take steps to avoid being blamed for institutional failings as well as to reassure stakeholders and voters that the incident in question will never happen again. The next step is often to set up an independent review or public inquiry, which will not report until after the scandal has died down. The report will conclude with a list of recommendations and reforms to the system, which are largely accepted by policymakers in order to close the cycle – until the next scandal breaks.

In the UK, a longstanding scandal-reform cycle in child protection (Munro, 2004) has been driven in recent years by the tragic deaths of two children: Victoria Climbié in 2000 and Peter Connelly ('Baby P') in 2007. Both Victoria and Peter died as a result of injuries caused by severe abuse and neglect suffered while in the care of their families, and both lived and died in the same area, the London Borough of Haringey. The media stoked huge public interest in these cases after it was revealed that the children had had extensive contact with a number of professionals, including social workers, doctors, and police officers, in the period leading up to their deaths. Media coverage focused relentlessly on the failure of social workers to protect the children from abuse, and in the case of Peter Connelly successfully campaigned for the government to sack the Director of Children's Services in Haringey (Jones, 2014). The public inquiry into the death of Victoria Climbié reported in 2003 with a comprehensive account of the institutional and professional failures contributing to Victoria's death and made more than 100 recommendations for reforms to the child protection system (Laming, 2003). All were accepted by the government of the time and were incorporated into its next piece of major legislation, the 2004 Children Act. After the Baby P scandal erupted, the author of the Climbié report, Lord Laming, was commissioned to undertake a progress report into how his recommendations had been implemented in child protection services across the country (Laming, 2009). Sadly, there has been no shortage of further deaths, scandals, and inquiries since then (Morris, 2013).

One effect of the scandal-reform cycle is that it tends to focus policymakers' attention on risks that are low in probability but have very serious consequences, such as deaths from child abuse or violent assaults committed by people with a mental illness (Holloway, 1996). Since these risks are often managed by agencies that have a broader preventative remit in providing services to a wide range of people, sectors such as social care can become skewed towards the business of assessing high risk individuals within a group otherwise characterised by vulnerability and need. The greater the institutional anxiety about risk, the more emphasis is placed on surveillance and assessment rather than help and support. Compounding the emphasis on risk regulation is the tendency for serious case reviews and inquiries to fall into the trap of hindsight bias (see Chapter 3); such reports tend to present a detailed explanation of human error on the part of practitioners and managers and on this basis make procedural recommendations that add to the protocolisation and prescription of work (Fish et al., 2008; Cooper, 2004).

Human error

Woods et al. (2010) present two contrasting 'stories' about failure in complex regulatory systems such as passenger air travel or nuclear power generation. The first story may be familiar to social workers as the 'you don't want your name in the Daily Mail' warning. In this story, human beings are prone to errors, such as negligence or oversight, during the course of their work; while people sometimes get away with their mistakes, at other times these errors can have serious and even fatal consequences. Safe systems therefore do their best to minimise human error by means of multiple protective layers, e.g. checklists, guidelines, procedures, automated processes, and information technology (see Figure 9.2). When failures do happen, a review is carried out to identify what mistakes were made and how to ensure they do not happen again. Analysis of human error may go beyond frontline practitioners to establish the culpability of managers, e.g. those who have not provided consistent supervision or have failed to implement risk management strategies. In this story, it is always possible to identify a linear sequence of events from errors to consequences to failure. Moreover, as Woods et al. point out, 'saying what people should have done is a satisfying way to describe failure' (2010: 7). As illustrated by Figure 9.2, safety in this story is generally to be found *behind* all the layers of procedures and compliance processes that have been established to protect us from human error.

The second story about failure is that performance is shaped by system conditions; any single incident emerges from the interaction of multiple factors, vulnerabilities,

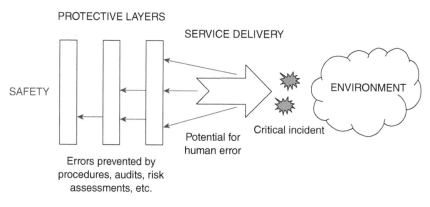

Figure 9.2   Protecting ourselves from human error

and events, often over a long period of time. Since failures emerge from these dynamics, saying what people should have done 'does not explain why it made sense for them to do what they did' (Woods et al., 2010: 7). For example, Laming's (2003) report into the death of Victoria Climbié painstakingly describes the multiple missed opportunities for professional intervention that might have saved her life; however, the report largely constructs these errors as an inexplicable series of aberrations rather than as the product of multiple underlying causes, including the emotional and psychological dimension of child protection work (Cooper, 2004; Ferguson, 2005). From a socio-technical perspective, human expertise is the linchpin rather than the weak link of the system, for safety depends on how well the system is able to adapt to complexity (see Figure 9.3). Human practitioners work

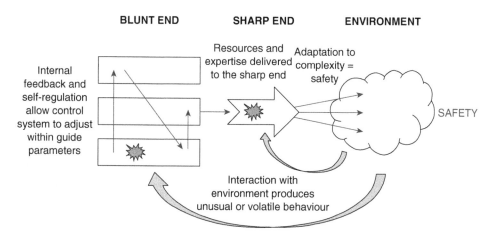

Figure 9.3   Successful adaptation to complexity

with artefacts such as procedures and risk assessment tools in order to adapt to conditions at the 'sharp end' of the system. The 'blunt end' of the system, composed of management and administrative functions, provides resources to and imposes constraints on what happens at the sharp end. The overall system needs to be able to adjust for deviation in work practices so that errors do not lead to system failure. Another crucial insight is that safe systems, i.e. those with a good track record, have a tendency to migrate towards the boundaries of acceptable performance. This may be because of complacency or resource pressures or simply because small changes in initial conditions are working their way through the system. Control theory should therefore be geared as much towards modelling the dynamics of normal working processes as establishing the reason for erroneous actions and assessments (Rasmussen, 1997; Perrow, 1984).

Cybernetic concepts of self-regulation and feedback are fundamental for thinking about error in systemic terms (Vester, 2007). A starting point is Murphy's Law – anything that can go wrong, will go wrong – which encourages us to develop resilient systems that are tolerant of error, rather than failsafe systems that never go wrong (Perrow, 1984). In this sense, self-regulation is akin to the thermostat function in an air-conditioned room (see Introduction), or the role of parasitic wasps in controlling thatch-eating caterpillars in Borneo (Case Study 9.1). In the natural world, multiple, interconnected feedback loops allow ecological systems to be self-regulating within quite wide parameters of deviation from the norm, i.e. error. When these regulatory mechanisms are removed or disrupted, new types of positive feedback loops may be unleashed that will eventually wreak havoc. Awareness of these interconnecting mechanisms leads us to interpret system behaviour more cautiously, and to take a more informed approach to policy experiments. It can also lead to some quite counter-intuitive findings. For example, some experts in wildfire control argued in the 1980s that consistently suppressing outbreaks of fire (in wilderness areas) removed a regulatory mechanism that prevented excess fuel build-up, so that human firefighting actually led to less frequent but more devastating wildfires (Johnson et al., 2001).[3] Vester (2007: 44) even rephrases Murphy's Law as follows: 'Even if something that really should go wrong turns out not to have gone wrong, you'll find that things would be better if it had'!

POLICY AND EVIDENCE

The term 'evidence-based policy' seems to suggest a linear relationship between policymakers and research evidence, in which 'good evidence will produce changes in policy and that these changes will in turn change practice on the ground' (Coote et al., 2004: 69). The idea is that researchers and other qualified experts fill a gap in knowledge so that policymakers can make informed decisions (Black, 2001).

---

[3]Johnson et al. (2001) point to evidence that this theory only seems to hold true in certain ecological systems; it is not a 'law' but what was termed a 'demi-regularity' in Chapter 8.

However, for this process to work in a straightforward way, there needs to be consensus in a particular policy domain about how to define a problem and its solution, what constitutes good evidence, and how to choose between different options and recommendations. Such consensus is unlikely to exist around contentious social problems such as poverty, homelessness, drug addiction, or child abuse; moreover, as we saw in Chapter 7, researchers are the first to disagree on how to evaluate complex interventions! Another thorny question is what to do about evidence that challenges entrenched political narratives, vested interests, and power relations (Hunter, 2009). After all, politicians and civil servants are prone to the same cognitive biases as everyone else (see Chapter 3); the temptation might be for policymakers to seek out evidence that suits the story they want to tell and ignore findings that contradict their preconceived views. As Keynes acerbically noted eighty years ago: '[t]here is nothing a government hates more than to be well-informed, for it makes the process of arriving at decisions much more complicated and difficult' (Keynes, 1937/2012: 409).

Coote et al. (2004) reviewed a number of major social programmes in the UK that received government investment in the early 2000s. The study explored the role of evidence in these policy decisions, including the ongoing process of evaluation after programmes were up and running. Perhaps unsurprisingly, they found that centrally mandated initiatives such as Sure Start, an early intervention programme for young children (Glass, 1999), were 'designed, by and large, on the basis of informed guesswork and expert hunches, enriched by some evidence and driven by political and other imperatives' (Coote et al., 2004: 47). According to the authors this was not necessarily a bad thing, since any available evidence was likely to be fragmented and diffused across a wide range of disparate studies, none of them focused on the same policy question.[4] Desire on the part of policymakers to act (or be perceived as acting) swiftly and decisively meant that gradual and painstaking evidence-gathering was sometimes eschewed in favour of rapid policy trials, i.e. pilots. The review also suggested that evidence-based policy approaches are often in conflict with efforts to promote innovation through local control of decision-making. All these issues are germane to the discussion below.

Analysing the policy–evidence interface

Bowen and Zwi (2005: 602) set out six different policymaking strategies for the use of research evidence:

- *Knowledge-driven*: new empirical evidence about a social problem is directly applied to policy, using effective strategies for transferring research into practice
- *Problem-solving*: systematic review of research evidence leads to practical recommendations that help solve a policy problem

---

[4]This issue was also discussed in Chapter 7 in relation to realist synthesis (Pawson, 2006).

- *Interactive*: knowledge goes beyond research to include other sources such as politics and interests, reflecting the complexity of the policymaking process
- *Political*: research evidence must serve a political purpose, e.g. demonstrate proof for a predetermined decision or problem area
- *Enlightenment*: research cumulatively shapes the concepts and perspectives that permeate the policy process over time, influencing how people think about social issues
- *Tactical*: evidence is used to support and justify government inaction, or rejection of and delay in commitment to a policy issue

These models provide a critical lens for analysing the policy–evidence interface in health and social care. Hunter (2009) argues that while the knowledge-driven and problem-solving models of evidence-based policy are widely embraced, they do not always reflect the reality of implementation and ignore the potential for bias and partiality that are explicit in the political and tactical models. In his view, the interactive approach is the most promising for connecting research with policy because it calls for the co-production of knowledge rather than assuming that the interests of stakeholders are sufficiently aligned for knowledge to be created in one place and transferred and applied elsewhere. Hunter (2009) recommends a 'compact' between researchers and policymakers, in which the former become actively engaged in communication and implementation rather than seeing their job as just to investigate and publish (see also Letherby and Bywaters, 2006); in turn, policymakers commit themselves to continually testing polices against available evidence, rather than looking for quick fixes, and to accepting research findings even if they challenge political orthodoxies.

The dangers of a disconnect between researchers and policymakers are illustrated in Case Study 9.2, which also demonstrates how essential it is to go back to the primary research in order to find out how plausible the evidence for an 'evidence-based' policy really is. In their most recent work, Wastell and White (2017) apply a similar critique to the way findings from epigenetics research are beginning to influence social policy, with some disturbing consequences. Epigenetics is the study of environmental influences on gene expression that leads to changes in organisms. Like neuroscience, it is a relatively new field of research and it is even more reliant on animal experiments (usually on laboratory rats) in its quest for biological explanations of social behaviour. As it stands, there are enormous gaps and uncertainties in our knowledge of epigenetic mechanisms in humans, let alone their potential contribution to complex developmental processes throughout someone's lifetime. Nonetheless, Wastell and White (2017) show that even a shaky evidence base can be a powerful tool when allied to widely accepted policy principles, e.g. that social problems can be addressed by changing poor decisions and bad behaviour linked to psychological and cognitive deficits in the individual. What epigenetics then adds to the picture is the idea that these deficits (and their effects on personality and behaviour) can be transmitted epigenetically to the next generation via the 'uterine environment', i.e. pregnant women's wombs. From there, it is only a short conceptual step to public health and child welfare interventions targeting the epi-genome, arguably a form of neo-eugenics (Leroi, 2006).

CASE STUDY 9.2

Neuroscience and the politics of early intervention (Wastell and White, 2012)

Wastell and White (2012) undertake a critical examination of the evidence base for social policies in the UK promoting early intervention to improve the lives of disadvantaged children. In this context, early intervention means a focus on young children (particularly those aged under three) rather than a rapid response to the problems experienced by families. The rationale is that the first three years of life are critical for subsequent healthy development, so that irreparable damage can be caused by deficits in the home environment and particularly by neglectful parenting. It therefore makes sense for welfare services to target children in this age group, and their parents, and to take a more robust approach to protecting children from the risk of developmental harm. Wastell and White point out that neuroscience research is increasingly being used to justify these policies. Neuroscience is the study of the development and functioning of the brain at the molecular level of neurones and synapses. As a biological science, it adds a 'medical' edge to psychosocial theories such as attachment, exemplified by the use of brain images to illustrate the damage caused by neglect and maltreatment. However, Wastell and White show that policymakers have consistently simplified and exaggerated the inferences that can be drawn from provisional (and often disputed) findings in this nascent field of research. In fact, most studies have concluded that the infant brain is not readily susceptible to permanent and irreversible damage from psychosocial deprivation but is generally characterised by plasticity and resilience. The authors go on to argue that neuroscience has been co-opted and bowdlerised in policy discourse, using the polemical power of brain images to obscure the contradictions and uncertainties in the primary research. The result for social workers and other professionals working with children has been to push practice towards 'standardised, targeted interventions rather than simpler forms of family and community support, which can yield more sustainable results'.

Of course, not all policy–evidence interfaces have such far-reaching and worrying implications. Nonetheless, given the sensitive and contentious domains of practice in which social workers tend to operate, it is worth maintaining a critical stance vis-à-vis policy statements that claim a firm basis in empirical evidence. This seems particularly important when research findings are presented with a high degree of certainty, and when complex social issues are boiled down to technical problems for which a standard solution is at hand, e.g. parenting programmes or compulsory medication regimes. Perhaps we should be more sceptical when the words 'research shows that…' appear in a policy document; in most cases, a comprehensive review of the literature is unlikely to reflect the rhetorical certitude of the policy. A critical stance also leads us to consider the first principles on which the evidence base is constructed, e.g. how effectiveness has been understood in evaluation design (see Chapter 7), whether moral and ethical issues have been explored, or unintended consequences taken into account.

Pilot programmes

Pilot programmes, sometimes also called trials or feasibility studies (Thabane et al., 2010), are a familiar part of evidence-based policy in health and social care (Coote et al., 2004). They involve testing out a small-scale, exploratory version of a new programme (or an approach that is new to the organisation at least). Pilot programmes are usually harnessed to some form of evaluation, looking at effectiveness, viability, cost/benefit analysis, implementation fidelity, and process management. Pilots enable policymakers to manage the risk of implementing new programmes and identify problems before committing more substantial resources to them. If the pilot fails to live up to expectations, wider adoption or 'roll-out' of the programme may be put on hold until an improved model of implementation (or another model of intervention) can be developed and tested. Ideally, pilots should help policymakers to study programme theories in context and adapt them to local contingencies; as noted in Chapter 7, this means going beyond the standard 'does it work?' formulation to ask other sorts of questions:

*   Are the programme's aims and objectives clear, realistic, and aligned with the priorities of its beneficiaries?
*   What is the programme's theory of change? Are the chosen measures of success appropriate?
*   Are roles and responsibilities clearly set out and is the right expertise available to achieve the programme's goals?
*   Are all stakeholders fully involved in the programme's development and evaluation?
*   What are the unintended consequences of programme implementation and have contextual factors (including cultural differences) been taken into account?
*   How is the project being funded? What happens when this funding runs out? What happens if implementation costs are much higher than expected?

Of course, one difficulty with pilots is that they are embedded in the policy-making process and so the 'lessons learned' from undertaking them may fall on deaf ears. This is the 'doomed to succeed' syndrome that has characterised many flagship government projects over the years; certainly when it comes to grandiose IT systems, no amount of piloting has been able to stop the headlong rush into gross incompetence and mismanagement (Bacon, 2013). Another difficulty is common to all evaluations of complex interventions, namely the extent to which findings are transferable to other contexts. For example, as Pawson (2013) points out, pilot programmes may benefit from a 'showcasing effect' because they are novel ideas that are initially taken up by people who are enthusiastic about them. Later on, as the intervention becomes routinised, enthusiasm wanes and the programme may become less capable of inspiring change. Another perennial problem is that of implementing 'evidence-based' programmes in social and cultural contexts that are very different from where the original evidence was produced (Shaw et al., 2009). Grant and Hood (2017) discuss the example of a sugar tax, a public health policy that was advocated by the Chief Medical Officer for England on the basis that 'we know it works because there is rigorous evidence from Mexico' (2017: 4). In other words, there could be no doubt that findings from a Mexican pilot study were directly applicable to an entirely different country and healthcare system! Of course, the primary research itself makes no such claims (Colchero et al., 2016); the authors themselves point out that they had insufficient data to model such a complex phenomenon as sugar consumption, nor could they report on the extent to which overall consumption had changed, as opposed to just the purchase of sugary drinks.[5]

In social work, the label 'evidence-based intervention' is sometimes used to denote a programme that has 'passed' its pilot stage and continues to prove effective when implemented on a wider scale. Evaluation through an RCT or quasi-experimental design (see Chapter 7) is a particularly sought-after criterion in this respect (see Allen, 2011: 120). However, as Featherstone et al. (2014) point out, one problem with defining the concept of evidence-based interventions so strictly is that that the majority of social programmes will not meet the criteria and may consequently fail to receive support. Small, local projects designed to serve a specific purpose in the community are unlikely to be honoured with an RCT-type evaluation – and even if they are the contextual factors that contributed to their success will be ironed out and ignored (see Chapter 7). Overly centralised government implementation of evidence-based policy may therefore have the unintended consequence of stifling innovation.

Policy innovation or policy control?

The interface between research, policy, and practice is shaped by messy dynamics of persuasion and coercion, resistance and subversion. Some policy documents openly assume a top-down implementation model (Sabatier, 1986); for example, Allen (2011) argues that funding for early intervention should be directed towards programmes that have been rigorously evaluated and found to be effective, and sets out specific criteria for what is (and is not) an evidence-based intervention. This particular view of evidence-based policy chimes with new public management approaches to public services, which emphasise the need for accountability and efficiency (see Chapter 7). In a top-down implementation model, regulatory regimes may require organisations and practitioners to demonstrate their use of evidence-based models of practice, so that adoption of certain interventions becomes a way of complying with regulatory standards. The result may be a highly standardised form of

---

[5]For example, Mexican consumers may simply have responded to higher prices by switching to an alternative type of sugary drink, such as the homemade fruit infusions known as 'agua fresca'.

provision, which is not adaptable enough to deal with the complexity of issues at the sharp end of practice (Featherstone et al., 2014).

A bottom-up view of evidence-based policy reverses the order of influence. While the principles remain the same, it is left to organisations and communities to implement them as they see fit, i.e. to identify a social problem, design an intervention to tackle it, track measures of success and failure, and adapt or change the approach depending on what progress is made. The role of the regulator moves away from compliance and enforcement and towards what Bardach and Kagan term 'the inspector as consultant' (2002: 150), i.e. providing advice to organisations and supporting them to meet the strategic aims and objectives set out in the broader policy framework. The role of government, meanwhile, is to set those strategic aims and not to get involved in operational management and decision-making. This bottom-up approach to evidence-based policy should encourage innovation, as long as policymakers are prepared to accept that experiments may fail as well as succeed – something that may be politically difficult when the sector is in the grip of a scandal-reform cycle.

Sparrow (2008) points out that innovation is often the exception rather than the rule in public services – one-off creative forays that are lauded and imitated if they turn out to be a success (or ignored if not). He suggests that organisations that are geared towards continuous process improvement are particularly prone to seeing innovation as atypical and as extra work; the all-consuming focus on what happens to incoming demand makes it harder to search actively for problems that are not currently being addressed. This is a particular issue for social work agencies that play a regulatory role in relation to public and private life, particularly if they are dealing with what Sparrow (2008) calls 'invisible harms', where referrals represent only a small proportion of the actual problem (e.g. domestic violence) or where the agency faces conscious opposition (e.g. organised child sexual exploitation networks). Performing a regulatory role through (or as part of) a customer service process may unwittingly hold back innovation and therefore hinder the agency from serving the community.

Aside from regulation, a decentralised, bottom-up approach to innovation has long been a feature of community social work. Diers (2004) and McKnight (2011) discuss a range of citizen-led approaches to community organising and neighbourhood planning, which they suggest provides evidence for a restructuring of the relationship between local communities and the state. Diers argues that statutory agencies have become accustomed to treating citizens as 'nothing more than customers' and neighbourhoods only as places 'with needs' (2004: 172). This is counterproductive because it ignores the latent resources within communities, which can be tapped if local authorities are willing to listen to and act on what is important for citizens, rather than just imposing their own agenda on them. In turn, this requires professional agencies to act more as facilitators than as experts, providing tools and resources but not taking over activities that community organisations can do for themselves (see also Davis, 2016).

CONCLUSiON

This chapter has explored various ways of analysing complexity in the domain of social policy. Retrospective analysis of policy effects often sheds light on unintended consequences and explains why new initiatives do not have the desired effects. A more difficult task is to apply these lessons prospectively in order to avoid further cascades of unwanted outcomes. Cybernetic concepts such as feedback loops are helpful in understanding why some systems are stable while others seem to spiral out of control. They also help us to identify self-reinforcing policy cycles, such as the scandal-reform loop in child protection and its impact on risk regulation, blame culture, and procedural forms of practice. While innovation and creativity are essential for social services to adapt to the complex conditions they face, their capacity to innovate may be stifled by an all-encompassing focus on process improvement and a drift towards standardisation under the guise of evidence-based policy. An alternative approach to evidence-based policy is to allow services the freedom to experiment and find ways of achieving common social goals in very different communities and local contexts.

CONCLUSION: FINAL REFLECTIONS

CHAPTER SUMMARY

This final chapter looks ahead to the future of social work in a fast-changing policy and practice environment. Some broad implications are drawn from the topics discussed in the book. Complex problems often create a sense of disconnect between citizens, social workers, managers, and policymakers. This is partly because paradoxical patterns of interaction and intention are a feature of complex behaviour. It is argued that current models of policy and practice have become highly intolerant of paradox and skewed towards analytic approaches that rely on processing ever greater quantities of data. Shifting the balance towards systems thinking may prove a difficult culture shift in many social work settings but is essential for a people-centred profession.

INTRODUCTION

This book has examined various aspects of social work through the lens of complexity. The chapters in Part 1 have considered some of the practice issues that arise when working with complex cases; those in Part 2 have explored complexity in social work's institutional and political context. Ordering the chapters in this way reflects the way that practitioners tend to see their work. Most social workers want knowledge that is useful to them in their everyday practice, e.g. what to do in order to change their client's behaviour, what counts as 'best practice' in their area, what new tools they should learn to use. However, such questions also inspire others, e.g. what do we mean by change when it comes to human beings; does 'best practice' mean the same as 'what works'; is a social worker more or less than the tools they employ? To think about these questions as a practitioner it is necessary to understand how politicians, regulators, researchers, and senior managers think about them. It is also important to understand how all these perspectives relate to the concerns of individual citizens. We may find at the outset that they hardly relate at all.

'The Disconnect'

Most social workers will sometimes – or perhaps even regularly – perceive a disconnect between what they think is important, what their clients or service users think is important, and what managers and policy leaders think is important. Sometimes the disparity may be about resources and the clash between utilitarian and deontological ethics (see Chapter 5). Sometimes it is about process and the clash between lengthy assessment procedures and the more spontaneous dynamics of dialogue and relationship building (see Chapter 4). At other times the disconnect seems even more profound: it is almost as if citizens, professionals, and officials are talking in different languages about completely different things. Social workers have become accustomed to mediating between the person and the system ('I need you to help me fill in this form so that I can get you the help you need'). Yet if the gap is too great, this mediating role may take up all the available time, or social workers may end up unwittingly antagonising people with bureaucratic demands and professional jargon ('This meeting is to discuss concerns about your parenting'). If mediation fails, the person is seen as not meeting the system's requirements ('I am writing to inform you that as you did not attend your last two appointments we are closing your case').

Some of this disconnect is arguably rooted in the ambivalent relationship between individuals and the state. Consider that perennial social problem: the teenager. In the UK, young people aged 16–24 who are 'not in education, employment or training' (NEET) are often targeted for statutory intervention (Social Exclusion Unit, 1999). Young people who are classified as NEET are more likely than the average citizen to experience problems in later life, such as imprisonment, addiction, and mental illness. Governments are keen to help them – but not just for humanist reasons. From a social investment perspective (Fawcett et al., 2004) targeting interventions at the NEET group is seen as cost-effective if the result is adults who are able to contribute to the economy and pay taxes instead of costing the state money. Reducing the number of young people who are NEET has therefore become a key metric in UK social policy, influencing the direction of government funding, regulatory scrutiny, key performance indicators, and organisational priorities (Yates and Payne, 2006). But this is not how young people or the professionals working with them think about their problems. While tracking an aggregate measure might make sense on a policy level, pushing it down to the organisational level – for example, in the form of targets – is likely to alter managerial priorities and distort frontline practice. As Yates and Payne (2006) point out: 'evidence suggests that adherence to NEET-reduction targets encourages a "fire-fighting" approach to working with young people rather than focusing support and intervention on areas where they may be most productive'.

A related example is the educational achievement of children and young people in the care system, a longstanding area of concern in social policy. In the UK, educational outcomes for 'looked after children' in every local authority have been monitored and reported to government for many years (Brodie, 2010). Now imagine you are a social worker. One of the young people you work with is a 16-year-old boy who has been in care since he was five years old, experienced multiple changes of foster placement, and is currently in residential care. It is his last year of secondary education but he has been excluded from school and is now enrolled in a pupil referral unit, which he rarely attends; he has been absconding from the children's home and is believed to be spending time with an older peer group who may be gang-affiliated. You receive a phone call from your service manager wanting to know how many GCSEs the young person has been entered for.[1] He is not satisfied with your answer, and asks whether an incentive can be offered to this young person in order for them to sit some more exams.[2]

POINT FOR REFLECTION

As a social worker, what would be your reaction to this query? Why might a service manager be interested in the number of exams this young person has been entered for? Do you think that doing GCSEs is a priority for the young person right now? If not, why not? Has there been a 'failure' to promote his educational aspirations and achievement and if so where does the blame lie?

When there is a divergence of perspectives on an issue like this, it is tempting to think that somebody must be right and therefore other people must be wrong. In the example above, perhaps the service manager is right to push for the young person to sit as many GCSE exams as possible. But why this particular issue and this particular measure? If it is about educational achievement, why not focus on maximising his performance in the exams that he does intend to sit? If it is about general welfare and development, should the current priority be his absconding from home and the risk of being exploited by older peers? As noted at various points during this book, complex problems are characterised by a lack of consensus on how to define them and what a solution looks like. In the absence of certainties based on

---

[1]GSCEs are the school exams taken at the end of secondary education (11–16) in the UK.

[2]This example is based on the author's own experience.

technical knowledge and expertise, political and regulatory pressures can substitute a more pragmatic form of certainty, i.e. what gets measured is what matters (Bevan and Hood, 2006). The resulting forms of provision may be disconnected from what citizens and communities actually want from them but *are* responsive to public demands for accountability and control. As noted in Chapter 8, this disconnect is linked to one of the key dilemmas faced by public services, namely how to address the competing goals and priorities of different stakeholders, each of which construes the 'public' and how to serve it in different ways.

Towards paradox

Smith and Lewis (2011: 387) define paradox as 'contradictory yet interrelated elements that exist simultaneously and persist over time; such elements seem logical when considered in isolation, but irrational, inconsistent, and absurd when juxtaposed'. Their definition highlights two components of paradox: first, the underlying tension between elements that seem contradictory or incompatible, and second, responses that embrace those tensions simultaneously. Complex systems are inherently paradoxical: self-organising behaviour emerges from intentional actions, unstable order emerges from stable disorder, internal plurality (e.g. functions, processes, hierarchical levels) is shaped by external contingency. In social systems such behaviour manifests itself as a messy sort of interdependence, a confluence of tactical inventions that may seem entirely at odds with each other but with hindsight seem to cohere into an adaptive strategy. In Chapter 8 we saw that public services strive to be many things to many people: efficient and effective, accountable for failure, customer-friendly, tough on crime, ethically beyond reproach, and politically malleable. In earlier chapters, social workers were likewise seen to be constantly grappling with paradox via the familiar dichotomies of care and control, certainty and uncertainty, facts and values, thought and feeling (Howe, 2014).

Smith and Lewis (2011) suggest that paradoxes tend to invoke strategies of acceptance, synthesis, and separation. A common institutional response is 'spatial separation', allocating different organisational units to elements that are in tension with each other. For example, the separation of 'purchaser' and 'provider' functions in health and social care arguably reflects in structural terms the tensions of marketisation in public services, e.g. cost and quality, choice, and prescription. Conversely, organisations may choose 'temporal separation', i.e. concentrating for a period of time on one pole of the dichotomy with a view to switching if conditions change. For example, the accelerating use of child protection interventions in English children's social care could be seen as an adaptive strategy to manage institutional risk by emphasising 'control' at the expense of 'care' (Hood et al., 2016c). This is a type of contingency approach, in which the question is less about ideal solutions ('is care or control more effective?') and more about what current conditions demand ('will more control solve this particular problem?'). The drawback with such approaches is that they have a relatively short time horizon and may therefore overlook issues relating to longer-term sustainability, including unintended consequences as discussed in Chapter 9.

Another approach to paradox is dialectical synthesis, in which the tension between opposing theses is resolved through a new concept that accommodates both of them. This is the approach used by Howe (2014), who explores a range of dichotomous debates within the profession of social work. For example, the merits of considering social work in terms of 'art' or 'science' are respectively discussed and the attributes of both are then incorporated into the idea of social work as a 'craft': 'Science helps us to make sense of the general. Art gives us licence to be creative with the particular. Craft blends the two' (Howe, 2014: 125).

The metaphor seems an apt one. Craftwork demands skill, commitment, and judgement, as well as an 'intimate connection between head and hand, thought and concrete action, problem-solving and problem-finding' (Howe, 2014: 123). To flourish as a craftsman or craftswoman, social workers need to be situated within 'open knowledge systems', which are open to new problems and solutions and tolerant of exceptions, resistance, and ambiguity. Organisations that allow social workers to practise their craft are open to improvisation and invention rather than seeking to organise practice as a means to a fixed end.

It is tempting to believe that most dilemmas in social work have an equally elegant solution. Howe's notion of the 'compleat' social worker[3] could be viewed as an ideal form of practice, achievable in principle as long as the right professionals are employed in the right organisations. However, the problem with resolution through synthesis is that the new integrative concept will eventually (or rapidly) be faced with its own antithesis. For example, is the concept of social work as a 'craft' reconcilable with the idea of social work as 'care management' if the latter means that most face-to-face work is done by support workers while professionals are stuck behind their desks (Jones et al., 2013)? Smith and Lewis (2011) refer to 'latent tensions', which persist because of complexity and adaptation; such tensions may become salient because environmental conditions change or because people start to think differently about what they do. Complex systems never stand still, and so even the best solutions have a sell-by date.

Separation and synthesis both seek to resolve paradox. The third approach, acceptance, encourages us to live with it. According to Smith and Lewis (2011: 385), living with paradox requires people to 'shift their expectations for rationality and linearity to accept paradoxes as persistent and unsolvable puzzles'. It means working through the tensions that give rise to paradox, and therefore requires the capacity to acknowledge and deal with the strong emotions that such work entails (see Chapter 5). Acceptance enables an insight into the interrelationship between elements, the realisation that focusing on just one side will only accentuate the need for the other. The oscillation between prevention and protection in child safeguarding is a case in point – as the pendulum swings too far one way, calls to redress the balance inevitably emerge (Department of Health, 1995; Hood, 2016c). Accepting paradox therefore encourages people to consider both/and possibilities rather than always tying themselves to an either/or choice. The shift towards paradox is a shift towards interrelatedness and interconnection. In other words, it requires us to do more systems thinking.

---

[3]This is not a typo – Howe's reason for the spelling is explained in the book!

Systems thinking

In a general sense, systems thinking means attending to the relationships between elements in a system rather than separating out those elements for individual analysis. The aim is to grasp essential patterns of the complex whole rather than breaking it down into simpler, more manageable parts. Its dichotomous 'other half' is sometimes called analytic thinking, a version of which was discussed in Chapter 3. Cultural psychology research has found certain forms of analytic thinking to be more prevalent in Western (i.e. European and North American) cultures than in East Asian cultures, which exhibit a greater tendency towards 'holistic thinking' (Nisbett et al., 2001; Choi et al., 2007). In this context, holistic thinking has a similar meaning to systems thinking, but is specifically associated with cultural differences in cognition or thinking style (see Table 10.1).

Table 10.1 Cultural differences in holistic and analytic thinking styles (Choi et al., 2007)

	Holistic thinking (East Asian cultures)	Analytic thinking (Western cultures)
Field vs parts	Attention is oriented towards the relationship between parts and the field to which they belong. Allows people to see the 'whole picture' with more ease than they can see individual parts.	Attention is oriented towards the object itself rather than the field to which it belongs. Allows people to separate out objects from the field in which they are embedded
Causality	Causal relationships are assumed to be interactional, i.e. emerging from the interactions between an object or agent and its surroundings.	Causal relationships are assumed to be dispositional, i.e. produced by the characteristics and internal dispositions of the object or agent.
Cyclic vs linear	Complex interactions between interconnected elements are likely to produce constant change. When predicting future events, it is assumed there will be cyclical patterns of change with constant fluctuations.	Because objects are independent, their basic properties do not change dramatically over time. When predicting the future, it is assumed there will be linear patterns of change or stability that follow on from past events.
Paradox	When two contradictory opposites exist, a compromise is reached that assumes that both propositions may be true at the same time and one may even turn into the other (yin/yang approach).	Contradictions are resolved by choosing one of the two opposite propositions. There is a preference for non-contradictory arguments (either yin or yang).

The cultural take on holistic and analytic thinking reminds us that one is not ideologically better than the other. Analytic thinking, for example, lends itself to methodical, step-by-step problem-solving and is the basis for innumerable science discoveries and their technical applications in everyday life. Yet as Kuhn (1996) argued, the idea of scientific progress as an accumulation of incremental advances is only true within an established paradigm, such as Newtonian mechanics.[4] When a new paradigm or 'big picture' emerges, such as relativistic or quantum mechanics, there is a rupture with the existing way of doing things; often a wave of hostility and opposition from scientists must be overcome before the new paradigm is accepted and the incremental approach to scientific inquiry can resume. Analytic thinking gets you only so far before the need for a holistic rethink becomes apparent.

Another implication of the analytic-holistic distinction is that system-level phenomena, such as feedback loops or unpredictable fluctuations in behaviour, benefit from system-level analysis and intervention. Arguably the most pressing challenges faced by human civilisation, such as climate change and various forms of ecological and economic crisis, have emerged because of our civilisation's unprecedented global scale and interconnectivity. Yet our approach to solving those problems remains resolutely embedded within analytic categories (disciplines, professions, sectors, etc.) that originally developed in the West and were exported to the rest of the world during its period of political and economic hegemony. The 'Tanaland' example discussed in Chapter 9 is a striking example of what happens when a systemic issue (development) is tackled with a multitude of interventions within separate expert domains (farming, medicine, finance, etc.). Of course, the cultural component of this example will not be lost on readers: Western experts solving 'Africa's problems' has been a recurring theme in the history of foreign aid and development (Mayo, 2009; Tarp, 2003). Similar attitudes may be evident in the internationalisation of social policy, where the traffic of ideas seems to flow in one direction, i.e. from 'developed' to 'developing countries', with the concomitant challenges of transferability and implementation (Barrientos and Hulme, 2008).

Vester (2007) has argued that our predilection for linear thinking makes us ill-equipped to understand the effects of our actions in an age of extreme global interconnectedness. When it comes to system-level problems, our tendency is to intervene on a piecemeal basis in separate domains, each linked to an established base of knowledge and expertise (see Chapter 6). The result is a chain reaction of unintended consequences and short-term fixes that lead us further and further away from the equilibrium state we originally had in mind. As Ulrich (2005) points out in his review of Vester's work, efforts to work in a more holistic way are hindered by an institutional infrastructure built around category-specific expertise and a preoccupation with data:

---

[4]Mechanics is the study of how objects move under the influence of forces. Classical mechanics is based largely on the theories of Isaac Newton. Newtonian mechanics was superseded in the twentieth century by new approaches based on quantum physics and Einstein's theories of relativity.

Despite customary lip service to holistic, inter- and transdisciplinary thinking, decision makers both in the public and in the private sector still mostly try to grasp complex problems by structuring them along administrative (bureaucratic) and professional (disciplinary) boundaries and then accumulating and processing a lot of data on the thus-defined problems. (Ulrich, 2005: 5)

Analytic problem-solving has therefore become congruent with large-scale data gathering and processing. Indeed, what has been called the 'Big Data' revolution is arguably one of the defining socio-economic trends of the twenty-first century (Mayer-Schonberger and Cukier, 2014). Advances in computer science now allow corporations and governments to analyse vast quantities of data in increasingly sophisticated ways. Their overall aim is deceptively simple: to produce and refine algorithms. In general terms, an algorithm is a set of rules or procedures for solving a problem or making a decision. While considerable effort and creativity are needed to begin with, once the algorithm is in place its steps can be automated. Algorithms are therefore a way of 'taming' complex problems, processing enormous amounts of data in order to produce the optimal solution. In this sense, our brains use algorithms to interpret and act on sensory data; the cognitive heuristics and biases discussed in Chapter 3 could be seen as algorithms that have been refined over the course of our evolutionary history. Likewise the risk matrices and actuarial assessment tools discussed in the same chapter are algorithmic: follow these steps, add up the scores and see the result. The belief is that with enough data and enough processing power to improve algorithms, all problems will eventually prove to be technical. The problems experienced by human beings and the societies they live in – the most complex known to us – only seem messy and intractable because current data flows are insufficiently dense or networked to produce the algorithms we need.

Seen in this light, the proliferation of information technology in human services forms part of a Big Data revolution, designed to augment (and perhaps eventually replace) human judgement with ever more powerful algorithms. While this may seem somewhat futuristic, social workers who have been in the profession for many years will certainly have noticed what Parton (2008) has called a 'shift from the social to the informational', one symptom of which has been the increasing amount of time devoted to inputting data on computers. In the long run, this shift could profoundly affect how professionals perceive people and knowledge about people. Most of us would probably say that *knowing a person* is very different from knowing things about them – it is a deeper understanding formed during the course of a relationship and is best expressed through narrative (Howe, 1996). However, algorithms do not need to know people in this humanist sense because individuals are just a set of data points: demographic characteristics, health indicators, educational achievement, psychological diagnosis, history of care, etc. From this perspective, the task of assessment is not to present a holistic account of people's subjective and social selves; it is to gather relevant information that can be categorised and classified in a form amenable to statistical analysis.

Apart from the ethical implications of what Harari (2016) has called 'dataism', there are reasons to be sceptical about its real-world applications. The most sophisticated algorithms known to humankind may be almost invincible at chess but are pretty useless at stacking shelves.[5] The problem is perhaps not the inhu-man algorithms so much as their all-too-human developers and implementers; a well-known maxim in computer sciences is 'garbage in – garbage out', which could certainly apply to many IT-based innovations in social work over the years (Wastell and White, 2010). Moreover, Vester (2007) argues that the current fetish for big data entirely misses the point of systems thinking, which is to *reduce* the amount of information we process in order to see overall patterns and interconnections that are otherwise buried in detail. In social work, the traditional method of achieving a holistic view of another person is to build some sort of relationship with them (see Chapter 4). For now at least, algorithms that can successfully replicate and replace human relationships remain the preserve of science fiction.

A final point is about eclecticism. Social work is often characterised as an eclectic profession because it uses theories and ideas from a range of disciplines as a source of knowledge (Payne, 2015); this allows practitioners to apply different theories in particular cases and to tailor their approach accordingly. The drawback of eclecticism is that social workers cannot point to an array of technical expertise in one specific domain – leaving them vulnerable to the charge of 'jack of all trades, master of none'. Of course, many social workers do go on to specialise in specific areas of practice, although in doing so they may remove themselves from the more generic forms of case-work in which eclecticism is practised. Yet despite – even because of – its drawbacks, it could be argued that an eclectic approach is very useful for systems thinking. It offers a number of theoretically informed perspectives on the 'big picture' while inhibiting the desire to drill down prematurely into a single patch of detail. Eclecticism also invites a certain humility, a willingness to confer with others and hand over technical tasks to those with the expertise to carry them out. In short, social workers are trained to be systems thinkers – and this is precisely what should be valued about them.

CONCLUSiON

Overall, this book has attempted both an exposition and a critique. The former has aimed to highlight the potential of social work to contribute to our understanding and response to complex social problems, whether at the level of individuals, com-munities, or societies. The latter has been directed at overly reductive and linear approaches to complexity, which have come to dominate the profession's institu-tional context. Preference has accordingly been given to approaches that encourage systems thinking across practice, research, management, and policy. This concluding chapter has tried to adopt a broader perspective on the analytic vs holistic debate, suggesting that the dichotomy reflects the paradoxical demands placed on social workers and their agencies rather than a straightforward either/or choice. The chal-lenge in the current context is to find the right balance, and particularly to ensure that technology does not get in the way of talking to people and getting to know them. For complexity in social work is where it has always been: between people.

---

[5]www.youtube.com/watch?v=JzlsvFN_5HI

References

Abbott, A. (1988) *The System of the Professions*. Chicago: University of Chicago Press.

Abbott, A. (2001) *Chaos of Disciplines*. Chicago: University of Chicago Press.

Abbott, A. (2003) Understanding transference and countertransference: Risk management strategies for preventing sexual misconduct and other boundary violations in social work practice. *Psychoanalytic Social Work,* 10: 21–41.

Abbott, P. and Wallace, C. (1990) *The Sociology of the Caring Professions*. Basingstoke: The Falmer Press.

Abrams, L.S. and Moio, J.A. (2009) Critical race theory and the cultural competence dilemma in social work education. *Journal of Social Work Education,* 45: 245–61.

Akhtar F. (2016) Preparing the ethical tookit: balancing rights and responsibilities. In: Davies, K. and Jones, R. (eds) *Skills for Social Work Practice*. London: Sage.

Aldrich, H.E. (1972) An organisational environment perspective on cooperation and conflict between organisations in the manpower and training system. In: Neghandi, A. (ed.) *Interorganisation Theory*. Kent, OH: Kent State University Press.

Aldrich, H. (1976) Resource dependence and interorganizational relations: Local employment service offices and social services sector organizations. *Administration Society,* 7L 419–54.

Allen, G. (2011) *Early Intervention – The Next Steps*. London: Cabinet Office.

Allen, G. (2012) *Early Intervention: Smart Investment, Massive Savings. The Second Independent Report to Her Majesty's Government* [Online]. London: Cabinet Office. Available: www.cabinetoffice.gov.uk/sites/default/files/resources/earlyintervention-smart investment.pdf [Accessed 13/07/2012].

Allen, P. (1998) Evolving complexity in social science. In: Altman, G. and Koch, W. (eds) *Systems: New Paradigms for the Human Sciences*. New York: Walter de Gruyter, 3–38.

Allport, G.W. (1954) *The Nature of Prejudice*. New York: Doubleday.

Anderson, J.A., Meyer, R.D., Sullivan, W.P. and Wright, E.R. (2005) Impact of a system of care on a community's children's social services system. *Journal of Child and Family Studies,* 14: 505–20.

Anning, A., Cottrell, D., Frost, N., Green, J. and Robinson, M. (2006) *Developing Multiprofessional Teamwork for Integrated Children's Services*. Maidenhead: Oxford University Press.

Archer, M. (1998) Realism in the social sciences. In: Archer, M., Bhaskar, R., Collier, A. et al. (eds) *Critical Realism: Essential Readings*. London: Routledge.

Argyris, C. (1992) *On Organizational Learning*. Boston, MA: Blackwell.

Argyris, C. and Schön, D.A. (1974) *Theory in Practice: Increasing Professional Effectiveness*. San Francisco: Jossey-Bass.

Argyris, C. and Schön, D.A. (1978) *Organisational Learning: A Theory of Action Perspective*. Reading, MA: Addison-Wesley.

Armitage, P. (1983) Joint working in primary health care. *Nursing Times,* 79: 75–8.

Ashby, W.R. (1956) *An Introduction to Cybernetics*. London: Chapman & Hall.

Audit Commission (2002) *Integrated Services for Older People: Building a Whole System Approach in England*. London: Audit Commission.

Ayre, P. and Calder, M.C. (2010) The de-professionalisation of child protection: Regaining our bearings. In: Ayre, P. and Preston-Shoot, M. (eds) *Children's Services at the Crossroads: A Critical Evaluation of Contemporary Policy for Practice*. Lyme Regis: Russell House Publishing.

Ayre, P. and Preston-Shoot, M. (eds) (2010) *Children's Services at the Crossroads: A Critical Evaluation of Contemporary Policy for Practice*. Lyme Regis: Russell House Publishing.

Baars, I.J., Evers, S.M., Arntz, A. et al. (2010) Performance measurement in mental health care: Present situation and future possibilities. *The International Journal of Health Planning and Management,* 25: 198–214.

Babcock, J.C., Green, C.E. and Robie, C. (2004) Does batterers' treatment work? A meta-analytic review of domestic violence treatment. *Clinical Psychology Review,* 23: 1023–53.

Bacon, R. (2013) *Conundrum: Why Every Government Gets Things Wrong – And What We Can Do About It*. Biteback Publishing.

Baginsky, M. (2013) *Retaining Experienced Social Workers in Children's Services: The Challenge Facing Local Authorities in England*. Available at: www.kcl.ac.uk/sspp/policy-institute/scwru/pubs/2013/reports/baginsky13retaining.pdf.

Bailey, R. and Brake, M. (1975) *Radical Social Work*. London: Edward Arnold.

Baird, C. and Wagner, D. (2000) The relative validity of actuarial- and consensus-based risk assessment systems. *Children and Youth Services Review,* 22: 839–71.

Baltes, P. (1987) Theoretical propositions of life-span developmental psychology: On the dynamics between growth and decline. *Developmental Psychology,* 23: 611–26.

Bandman, E. and Bandman, B. (1995) *Critical Thinking in Nursing* (2nd edn). Norwalk, CT: Appleton and Lange.

Bandura, A. and Schunk, D. (1981) Cultivating competence, self-efficacy, and intrinsic interest through proximal self-motivation. *Journal of Personality and Social Psychology* 41: 586.

Banks, S. (2006) *Ethics and Values in Social Work*. Basingstoke: Palgrave Macmillan.

Barad K. (2007) *Meeting the Universe Halfway: Quantum Physics and the Entanglement of Matter and Meaning*. Durham, NC: Duke University Press.

Barber, J.G. (1991) *Beyond Casework*. Basingstoke: Macmillan.

Bardach, E. and Kagan, R.A. (2002) *Going by the Book: The Problem of Regulatory Unreasonableness*. Brunswick, NJ: Transaction Publishers.

Barnes, V. (2016) Skills For Interprofessional Social Work Practice. In: Daviers, K. and Jones, R. (eds) *Skills for Social Work Practice*. London: Sage.

Barr, H. (2013) Toward a theoretical framework for interprofessional education. *Journal of Interprofessional Care,* 27(1): 4–9.

Barr, H., Koppel, I., Reeves, S., Hammick, M. and Freeth, D. (2005) *Interprofessional Education: Assumption, Argument and Evidence*. Oxford: Blackwell.

Barrientos, A. and Hulme, D. (2008) *Social Protection for the Poor and Poorest: Concepts, Policies and Politics*. Basingstoke: Palgrave Macmillan.

Barrowclough, C., Haddock, G., Tarrier, N. et al. (2001) Randomized controlled trial of motivational interviewing, cognitive behavior therapy, and family intervention for patients with comorbid schizophrenia and substance use disorders. *American Journal of Psychiatry,* 158: 1706–13.

Beck, U. (1992) *Risk Society: Towards a New Modernity*. London: Sage.

Beck, U., Giddens, A. and Lash, S. (1994) *Reflexive Modernization: Politics, Tradition and Aesthetics in the Modern Social Order*. Cambridge: Polity Press.

Belbin, R. (1981) *Management Teams: Why They Succeed or Fail*. London: Heinemann.

Benabou, R. and Tirole, J. (2003) Intrinsic and extrinsic motivation. *The Review of Economic Studies*, 70: 489–520.

Beresford, P., Croft, S. and Adshead, L. (2008) 'We don't see her as a social worker': A service user case study of the importance of the social worker's relationship and humanity. *British Journal of Social Work*, 38: 1388–407.

Bevan, G. and Hood, C. (2006) What's measured is what matters: Targets and gaming in the English public health care system. *Public Administration*, 84: 517–38.

Bhaskar, R. (1978) *A Realist Theory of Science*. Brighton: Harvester Press.

Bhaskar. R. (2009) *Scientific Realism and Human Emancipation*. Abingdon: Routledge.

Bilson, A. and Martin, K. (2016) Referrals and child protection in England: One in five children referred to children's services and one in nineteen investigated before the age of five. *British Journal of Social Work*, 47(3): 793–811.

Bion, W. (1962) *Learning from Experience*. London: Heinemann.

Bissell, G. (2012) *Organisational Behaviour for Social Work*. Bristol: Policy Press.

Black, N. (2001) Evidence based policy: Proceed with care. *BMJ : British Medical Journal*, 323: 275–9.

Boddy, J., Potts, P. and Statham, J. (2006) *Models of Good Practice in Joined-up Assessment: Working for Children with 'Significant and Complex Needs'*. London: University of London, Institute of Education, Thomas Coram Research Unit.

Bogo, M. and McKnight, K. (2006) Clinical supervision in social work: A review of the research literature. *The Clinical Supervisor*, 24: 49–67.

Bogsnes, B. (2016) *Implementing Beyond Budgeting: Unlocking the Performance Potential*. Hoboken, NJ: John Wiley & Sons.

Bond, J., Cartlidge, A.M., Gregson, B.A., Barton, A., Phillips, P., Armitage, P., Brown, A. and Reedy, B. (1987) Interprofessional collaboration in primary health care. *Journal of the Royal College of General Practitioners*, 37: 158–61.

Borton, T. (1970) *Reach, Touch and Teach*. London: Hutchinson.

Bowen, S. and Zwi, A.B. (2005) Pathways to 'evidence-informed' policy and practice: a framework for action. *PLoS medicine* 2: e166.

Bower, M. and Trowell, J. (1995) *The Emotional Needs of Young Children and Their Families: Using Psychoanalytic Ideas in the Community*. New York: Routledge.

Brandell, J. (2013) *Psychodynamic Social Work*. New York: Columbia University Press.

Brandon, M. (2009) Child fatality or serious injury through maltreatment: Making sense of outcomes. *Children and Youth Services Review*, 31: 1107–112.

Brandon, M., Bailey, S., Belderson, P., Gardner, R., Sidebotham, P., Dodsworth, J., Warren, C. and Black, J. (2008) *Understanding Serious Case Reviews and Their Impact: A Biennial Analysis of Serious Case Reviews 2005–07*. London: Department for Children, Schools and Families.

Brehmer, B. (1999) Reasonable decision making in complex environments. In: Juslin, P. and Montgomery, H. (eds) *Judgment and Decision Making: Neo-Brunswikian and Process-Tracing Approaches*. Hove: Pychology Press, 9–21.

Bride, B. (2007) Prevalence of secondary traumatic stress among social workers. *Social Work* 52: 63–70.

Brodie, I. (2010) *Knowledge Review: Improving Educational Outcomes for Looked After Children and Young People*. London: C4EO.

Bronfenbrenner, U. (1979) *The Ecology of Human Development*. Cambridge, MA: Harvard University Press.

Brown, K. and White, K. (2006) *Exploring the Evidence Base for Integrated Children's Services* [Online]. Available: www.openscotland.gov.uk/publications [Accessed 21/10/09].

Brown, R., and Williams, J. (1984) Group identification: The same thing to all people? *Human Relations,* 37, 547–64.

Bryman, A. (1988) *Quantity and Quality in Social Research.* London: Routledge.

Byrne, D. (1998) *Complexity and the Social Sciences.* London: Routledge.

Byrne, D. (2009a) Case-based methods: Why we need them; what they are; how to do them. In: Byrne, D. and Ragin, C. (eds) *The Sage Handbook of Case-Based Methods.* London: Sage.

Byrne, D. (2009b) Complex realist and configurational approaches to cases. In: Byrne, D. and Ragin, C. (eds) *The Sage Handbook of Case-Based Methods.* London: Sage.

Byrne, D. and Ragin, C. (2009) *The Sage Handbook of Case-Based Methods.* London: Sage.

Bywaters, P. (2017) *Identifying and Understanding Inequalities in Child Welfare Intervention Rates: Comparative Studies in Four UK Countries.* Briefing Paper 2: UK Four Country Quantitative Comparison. Coventry: Child Welfare Inequalities Project

Bywaters, P., Kwhali, J., Brady, G. et al. (2016) *Out of Sight, Out of Mind: Ethnic Inequalities in Child Protection and Out-of-Home Care Intervention Rates.* Available at: http://bjsw. oxfordjournals.org/content/early/2016/12/02/bjsw.bcw165.abstract.

Cameron, A. and Lart, R. (2003) Factors promoting and obstacles hindering joint working: A systematic review of the research evidence. *Journal of Integrated Care,* 11, 9–17.

Canavan, J., Coen, L., Dolan, P. and Whyte, L. (2009) Privileging practice: Facing the challenge of integrated working for outcomes for children. *Children & Society,* 23: 377–88.

Carney, T. (2005) Complex needs at the boundaries of mental health, justice and welfare: Gatekeeping issues in managing chronic alcoholism treatment. *Current Issues in Criminal Justice,* 17: 347.

Carnwell, R. and Buchanan, J. (eds) (2005) *Effective Practice in Health, Social Care and Criminal Justice: A Partnership Approach.* Buckingham: Open University Press.

Carpenter, J., Webb, C., Bostock, L. et al. (2012) Effective Supervision in Social Work and Social Care. [Online]. Available from: www.thehealthwell.info/node/366402 [Accessed: 29th October 2017].

Carter, B. and Sealey, A. (2009) Reflexivity, realism and the process of casing. In: Byrne, D. and Ragin, C. (eds) *The Sage Handbook of Case-Based Methods.* London: Sage.

Carter, S., Cook, J., Sutton-Boulton, G., et al. (2016) Social pedagogy as a model to provide support for siblings of children with intellectual disabilities: A report of the views of the children and young people using a sibling support group. *Journal of Intellectual Disabilities,* 20: 65–81.

Case, S. and Haines, K. (2014) Youth justice: From linear risk paradigm to complexity. In: Pycroft, A. and Bartollas, C. (eds) *Applying Complexity Theory.* Bristol: Policy Press.

Centre for Excellence and Outcomes in Children and Young People's Services (C4EO) (2009) *Safeguarding Briefing 1: Effective Interventions for Complex Families Where There are Concerns about, or Evidence of, a Child Suffering Significant Harm.* Available at: www. archive.c4eo.org.uk/themes/safeguarding/files/safeguarding_briefing_1.pdf.

Chaffin, M. and Friedrich, B. (2004) Evidence-based treatments in child abuse and neglect. *Children and Youth Services Review,* 26: 1097–113.

Chamberlain, P., Leve, L.D. and DeGarmo, D.S. (2007) Multidimensional treatment foster care for girls in the juvenile justice system: 2-year follow-up of a randomized clinical trial. *Journal of Consulting and Clinical Psychology,* 75: 187.

Chard, A. and Ayre, P. (2010) Mangerialism – at the tipping point? In: Ayre, P. and Preston-Shoot, M. (eds) *Children's Services at the Crossroads: A Critical Evaluation of Contemporary Policy for Practice.* Lyme Regis: Russell House Publishing.

Choi, I., Koo, M. and Choi, J.A. (2007) Individual differences in analytic versus holistic thinking. *Personality and Social Psychology Bulletin,* 33: 691–705.

Cilliers, P. (1998) *Complexity and Postmodernism: Understanding Complex Systems.* London: Routledge.

Cilliers, P. (2005) Complexity, deconstruction and relativism. *Theory Culture Society,* 22: 255–67.

Clark, P.G., Cott, C. and Drinka, T.J.K. (2007) Theory and practice in interprofessional ethics: A framework for understanding ethical issues in health care teams. *Journal of Interprofessional Care,* 21: 591–603.

Clarke, J., Gewirtz, S. and Mclaughlin, E. (eds) (2000) *New Managerialism, New Welfare?* London: Sage.

Cochrane, A. (2000) Local government: Managerialism and modernisation. In: Clarke, J., Gewirtz, S. and McLaughlin, E. (eds) *New Managerialism, New Welfare?* London: Sage.

Colchero, M.A., Popkin, B.M., Rivera, J.A., et al. (2016) Beverage purchases from stores in Mexico under the excise tax on sugar sweetened beverages: Observational study. *British Medical Journal,* 352: h6704.

Collier, A. (1994) *Critical Realism: An Introduction to Roy Bhaskar's Philosophy.* London: Verso.

Conway, P. (2009) Falling between minds: The effects of unbearable experiences on multi-agency communication in the care system. *Adoption and Fostering,* 33: 18–29.

Cook, K.S. (1977) Exchange and power in networks of interorganizational relations. *The Sociological Quarterly,* 18: 62–82.

Cooper, A. (2004) Surface and depth in the Victoria Climbié Inquiry Report. *Child & Family Social Work,* 10: 1–9.

Cooper, A., Hetherington, R., Bairstow, S., Pitts, J. and Spriggs, A. (1995) *Positive Child Protection: A View from Abroad.* Lyme Regis: Russell House Publishing.

Coote, A., Allen, J. and Woodhead, D. (2004) *Finding out What Works: Building Knowledge about Complex, Community-Based Initiatives.* London: Kings Fund.

Coveney, P. and Highfield, R. (1995) *Frontiers of Complexity: The Search for Order in a Chaotic World.* New York: Ballantine Books.

Craig, P., Dieppe, P., Macintyre, S., et al. (2008) Developing and evaluating complex interventions: The new Medical Research Council guidance. *BMJ* 337: a1655.

Craven, B.M. and Tooley, J.N. (2016) Safeguarding children: Ofsted and regulatory failure. *Economic Affairs,* 36: 64–79.

Crawford, K. (2012) *Interprofessional Collaboration in Social Work Practice.* London, Sage.

Currer, C. (2007) *Loss and Social Work.* Exeter: Learning Matters.

Curtis, L., Moriarty, J. and Netten, A. (2009) The expected working life of a social worker. *British Journal of Social Work,* 40: 1628–43.

Damasio, A. (2006) *Descartes' Error: Emotion, Reason and the Human Brain.* London: Random House.

Danermark, B., Ekstrom, M., Jacobsen L, et al. (2002) *Explaining Society: Critical Ralism in the Social Sciences.* Abingdon: Routledge.

Danvers, L., Freshwater, D., Cheater, F., et al. (2003) Providing a seamless service for children with life-limiting illness: Experiences and recommendations of professional staff at the Diana Princess of Wales Children's Community Service. *Journal of Clinical Nursing,* 12: 351–9.

Davis, R. (2016) *Responsibility and Public Services.* Axminster: Triarchy Press.

Dawson, S. (2007) Interprofessional working: Communication, collaboration... perspiration! *International Journal of Palliative Nursing,* 13: 502–5.

D'Cruz, H., Gillingham, P. and Melendez, S. (2007) Reflexivity, its meanings and relevance for social work: A critical review of the literature. *British Journal of Social Work,* 37: 73–90.

Deming, W.E. (2000) *Out of the Crisis*. Cambridge, MA: MIT Press.

Department for Children, Schools and Families (DCSF) (2010) *Children's Trusts: Statutory guidance on cooperation arrangements, including the Children's Trust Board and the Children and Young People's Plan*. London: The Stationery Office.

Department for Education (2015) *Working Together to Safeguard Children: A guide to inter-agency working to safeguard and promote the welfare of children*. London: The Stationery Office.

Department for Work and Pensions (2016) Benefit expenditure by country and region, 1996/97 to 2015/16. Available at: www.gov.uk/government/publications/benefit-expenditure-and-caseload-tables-2016.

Department of Health (1991) *Report of the Inquiry into the Removal of Children from Orkney*. London: HMSO.

Department of Health (1995) *Messages from Research*. London: HMSO.

Department of Health and Social Security (1987) *Report of the Inquiry into Child Abuse in Cleveland*. London: HMSO.

Devaney, J. (2004) Relating outcomes to objectives in child protection. *Child and Family Social Work, 9*: 27–38.

Dewey, J. (1997) *How We Think*. New York: Dover Publications.

Diers, J. (2004) *Neighbor Power: Building Community the Seattle Way*. University of Washington Press.

Dingwall, R., Eekelaar, J. and Murray, T. (1983) *The Protection of Children*. Oxford, Basil Blackwell.

Doel, M. and Marsh, P. (1992) *Task Centred Social Work*. Aldershot: Ashgate.

Dolgoff, R., Harrington, D. and Loewenberg, F.M. (2012) *Ethical Decisions for Social Work Practice*. Nashville, TN: Broadman & Holman Publishers.

Dominelli, L. (2002) *Anti Oppressive Social Work Theory and Practice*. Basingstoke: Palgrave Macmillan.

Dominelli, L. and Hoogvelt, A. (1996) Globalization and the technocratization of social work. *Critical Social Policy, 16*: 45–62.

Dörner, D. (1996) *The Logic of Failure: Recognizing and Avoiding Error in Complex Situations*. New York: Basic Books.

Doueck, H.J., Levine, M. and Bronson, D.E. (1993) Risk assessment in child protective services: An evaluation of the Child at Risk Field System. *Journal of Interpersonal Violence, 8*: 446–67.

Dowie, J. (1993) Clinical decision analysis: Background and introduction. In: Llewelyn, H. and Hopkins, A. (eds) *Analyzing How We Reach Clinical Decisions*. London: Royal College of Physicians, 7–25.

Dreyfus, H. and Dreyfus, S. (1986) *Mind Over Machine: The Power of Human Intuition*. Oxford: Basil Blackwell.

Duffy, S., Waters, J. and Glasby, J. (2010) Personalisation and adult social care: Future options for the reform of public services. *Policy & Politics, 38*: 493–508.

Dustin, D. (2016) *The McDonaldization of Social Work*. Abingdon: Routledge.

Easton, C., Featherstone, G., Poet, H., Aston, H., Gee, G. and Durbin, B. (2012) *Supporting Families with Complex Needs: Findings from LARC 4*. Slough: NFER.

Eastwood, J.G., Kemp, L.A. and Jalaludin, B.B. (2016) Realist theory construction for a mixed method multilevel study of neighbourhood context and postnatal depression. *SpringerPlus, 5*: 1081.

Egan, G. (2013) *The Skilled Helper: A Problem-Management and Opportunity-Development Approach to Helping.* Belmont, CA: Brooks/Cole.

Eichsteller, G. and Holthoff, S. (2012) The art of being a social pedagogue: Developing cultural change in children's homes in Essex. *International Journal of Social Pedagogy,* 1: 30–45.

Elliot, E. and Kiel, D.L. (1997) Nonlinear dynamics, complexity and public policy. In: Eve, R.A., Horsfall, S. and Lee, M.E. (eds) *Chaos, Complexity, and Sociology: Myths, Models, and Theories.* Thousand Oaks, CA: Sage.

Engels, C. (1994) A functional anatomy of teamwork. In: Leathard, A. (ed.) *Going Interprofessional: Working Together for Health and Welfare.* London: Routledge.

Engeström, Y. (ed.) (1999) *Perspectives on Activity Theory.* New York: Cambridge University Press.

Engeström, Y. (2001) Expansive learning at work: Toward an activity theoretical reconceptualization. *Journal of Education & Work,* 14: 133–56.

Eraut, M. (2000). Non-formal learning and tacit knowledge in professional work. *British Journal of Educational Psychology,* 70(1): 113–36.

Etzioni, A. (1969) *The Semi-Professions and their Organisation.* New York: Free Press/ Macmillan.

Evans, J. (2003) In two minds: dual-process accounts of reasoning. *Trends in Cognitive Sciences,* 7: 454–9.

Eve, R.A., Horsfall, S. and Lee, M.E. (1997) *Chaos, Complexity, and Sociology: Myths, Models, and Theories.* Thousand Oaks, CA: Sage.

Everson, S.A., Maty, S.C., Lynch, J.W., et al. (2002) Epidemiologic evidence for the relation between socioeconomic status and depression, obesity, and diabetes. *Journal of Psychosomatic Research,* 53: 891–5.

Farmakopoulou, N. (2002) What lies underneath? An inter-organisational analysis of collaboration between education and social work. *British Journal of Social Work,* 32: 1051–66.

Fawcett, B., Featherstone, B., and Goddard, J. (2004) *Contemporary Child Care Policy and Practice.* Basingstoke: Palgrave Macmillan.

Fayol, H. (1948) *Industrial and General Management.* London: Pitman.

Featherstone, B., White, S. and Morris, K. (2014) *Re-imagining Child Protection: Towards Humane Social Work with Families.* Bristol: Policy Press.

Ferguson, H. (2001) Social work, individualization and life politics. *British Journal of Social Work,* 31: 41–55.

Ferguson, H. (2003) In defence (and celebration) of individualization and life politics for social work. *The British Journal of Social Work,* 33: 699–707.

Ferguson, H. (2005) Working with violence, the emotions and the psychosocial dynamics of child protection: Reflections on the Victoria Climbié case. *Social Work Education,* 24: 781–95.

Ferguson, H. (2009) Performing child protection: Home visiting, movement and the struggle to reach the abused child. *Child & Family Social Work,* 14: 471–80.

Ferguson, H. (2010) The understanding systemic caseworker: The (changing) nature and meanings of working with children and families. In: Ayre, P. and Preston-Shoot, M. (eds) *Children's Services at the Crossroads: A Critical Evaluation of Contemporary Policy for Practice.* Lyme Regis: Russell House Publishing.

Ferguson, H. (2011) *Child Protection Practice.* Basingstoke: Palgrave Macmillan.

Ferguson, I. and Lavalette, M. (2013) Crisis, austerity and the future (s) of social work in the UK. *Critical and Radical Social Work,* 1: 95–110.

Fischhoff, B. (1975) Hindsight is not equal to foresight: The effect of outcome knowledge on judgment under uncertainty. *Journal of Experimental Psychology: Human perception and performance,* 1: 288.

Fish, S., Munro, E., and Bairstow, S. (2008) *Learning Together to Safeguard Children: Developing a Multi-agency Systems Approach for Case Reviews.* London: SCIE.

Fook, J. (1999) Critical reflectivity in education and practice. In: Pease, B. and Fook, J. (eds) *Transforming Social Work Practice: Postmodern Critical Perspectives.* St Leonards, Australia: Allen & Unwin.

Fook, J. (2002) Theorizing from practice: Towards an inclusive approach for social work research. *Qualitative Social Work,* 1: 79–95.

Fook, J. and Askeland, G. (2006) The 'critical' in critical reflection. In: White, S., Fook, J. and Gardner, F. (eds) *Critical Reflection in Health and Social Care.* Maidenhead: Open University Press, 40–55.

Fook, J. and Gardner, F. (2007) *Practising Critical Reflection: A Resource Handbook.* London: McGraw-Hill Education (UK).

Fook, J., Ryan, M. and Hawkins, L. (2000) *Professional Expertise: Practice, Theory and Education for Working In Uncertainty.* London: Whiting & Birch Ltd.

Fook, J., White, S. and Gardner, F. (2006) Critical reflection: A review of contemporary literature and understandings. In: White, S., Fook, J. and Gardner, F. (eds) *Critical Reflection in Health and Social Care.* Maidenhead: Open University Press, 3–20.

Forrester, D. (2010) Playing with fire or rediscovering fire? The perils and potential for evidence-based practice in child and family social work. In: Ayre, P. and Preston-Shoot, M. (eds) *Children's Services at the Crossroads: A Critical Evaluation of Contemporary Policy for Practice.* Lyme Regis: Russell House Publishing.

Forrester, D. (2012) Evaluation research. In: Gray, M., Midgley, J. and Webb, S.A. (eds) *The Sage Handbook of Social Work.* London: Sage.

Forrester, D. and Harwin, J. (2011) *Parents Who Misuse Drugs and Alcohol: Effective Interventions in Social Work and Child Protection.* Chichester: Wiley-Blackwell.

Forrester, D., Kershaw, S., Moss, H., et al. (2008) Communication skills in child protection: How do social workers talk to parents? *Child & Family Social Work,* 13: 41–51.

Forrester, D., Westlake, D. and Glynn, G. (2012) Parental resistance and social worker skills: Towards a theory of motivational social work. *Child & Family Social Work,* 17: 118–29.

Freeman, J. (1972) The tyranny of structurelessness. *Berkeley Journal of Sociology,* 17: 151–64.

Freidson, E. (2001) *Professionalism: The Third Logic.* Cambridge: Polity Press.

French, J. and Raven, B. (1968) The bases of social power. In: Cartwright, D. and Zander, A. (eds) *Group Dynamics: Research and Theory.* New York: Harper and Row, 259–69.

Friedman, M. (1997) *A Guide to Developing and Using Performance Measures in Results-Based Budgeting.* Washington, DC: Finance Project.

Friedman, M. (2001) *The Results and Performance Accountability Implementation Guide.* Available at: www.raguide.org.

Frost, N. (2005) *Professionalism, Partnership and Joined Up Thinking.* Dartington: Research in Practice.

Gambrill, E. (1999) Evidence-based practice: An alternative to authority-based practice. *Families in Society: The Journal of Contemporary Social Services,* 80: 341–50.

Garrett, P.M. (2003) The trouble with Harry: Why the 'new agenda of life politics' fails to convince. *British Journal of Social Work,* 33: 381–97.

Gerdes, K. and Segal, E. (2011) Importance of empathy for social work practice: Integrating new science. *Social Work,* 56: 141–8.

Gerrits, L. and Verweij, S. (2015) Taking stock of complexity in evaluation: A discussion of three recent publications. *Evaluation,* 21: 481–91.

Gibbs, G. (1988) *Learning by Doing: A Guide to Teaching and Learning Methods.* London: FEU.

Gibson, J. (2016) Why better measures lead to better lives. In: Caulkin, S., Pell, C., O'Donovan, B., et al. (eds) *The Vanguard Periodical: The Vanguard Method in People Centred Services.* Buckingham: Vanguard Consulting Ltd, 34–7.

Gibson, J. and O'Donovan, B. (2014) The Vanguard Method as applied to the design and management of English and Welsh children's services departments. *Systemic Practice and Action Research,* 27: 39–55.

Giddens, A. (1990) *The Consequences of Modernity.* Cambridge: Polity Press.

Gigerenzer, G. and Gaissmaier, W. (2011) Heuristic decision making. *Annual Review of Psychology,* 62: 451–482.

Gilligan, C. (1993) *In a Different Voice: Psychological Theory and Women's Development.* Cambridge, MA: Harvard University Press.

Gillingham, P. and Humphreys, C. (2010) Child protection practitioners and decision-making tools: Observations and reflections from the front line. *British Journal of Social Work,* 40: 2598–616.

Gitterman, A. and Germain, C. (2008) *The Life Model of Social Work Practice: Advances in Theory and Practice.* New York: Columbia University Press.

Glaser, B.G. and Strauss, A. (1967) *Discovery of Grounded Theory: Strategies for Qualitative Research.* Mill Valley, CA, Sociology Press.

Glass, N. (1999) Sure Start: The development of an early intervention programme for young children in the United Kingdom. *Children & Society,* 13: 257–64.

Glendinning, C. (2002) Partnership between health and social services: Developing a framework for evaluation. *Policy and Politics,* 30: 115–27.

Glendinning, C., Clarke, S., Hare, P., Maddison, J. and Newbronner, L. (2008) Progress and problems in developing outcomes-focused social care services for older people in England. *Health & Social Care in the Community,* 16: 54–63.

Glover, J. (2009) *Bouncing Back: How Can Resilience Be Promoted in Vulnerable Children and Young People?* Ilford: Barnado's.

Goldstein, E. (1995) *Ego Psychology and Social Work Practice.* New York: Simon and Schuster.

Goldstein, H. (2002) The literary and moral foundations of the strengths perspective. In: Saleebey, D (ed.) *The Strengths Perspective in Social Work Practice.* New York: Longman, 23–47.

Goldstein, J. (1999) Emergence as a construct: History and issues. *Emergence,* 1: 49–72.

Goodley, S.and Ashby, J. (2016) Revealed: How Sports Direct effectively pays below minimum wage. Available at: www.theguardian.com/business/2015/dec/09/how-sports-direct-effectively-pays-below-minimum-wage-pay.

Goodman, S. and Trowler, I. (2012) *Social Work Reclaimed.* London: Jessica Kingsley.

Gould, N. (2004) Introduction: The Learning Organization and Reflective Practice – the Emergence of a Concept. In: Gould, N. and Baldwin, M. (eds) *Social Work, Critical Reflection and the Learning Organization.* Aldershot: Ashgate, 1–9.

Gould, N. and Baldwin, M. (2016) *Social Work, Critical Reflection and the Learning Organization.* Abingdon: Routledge.

Grant, R.L. and Hood, R. (2017) Complex systems, explanation and policy: Implications of the crisis of replication for public health research. *Critical Public Health,* 27 (5): 525–532.

Granville, J. and Langton, P. (2002) Working across boundaries: Systemic and psychodynamic perspectives on multi-disciplinary and inter-agency practice. *Journal of Social Work Practice,* 16: 23–7.

Gray, M. (2011) Back to basics: A critique of the strengths perspective in social work. *Families in Society: The Journal of Contemporary Social Services,* 92: 5–11.

Gregson, B.A., Cartlidge, A.M. and Bond, J. (1992) Development of a measure of professional collaboration in primary health care. *Journal of Epidemiology and Community Health,* 46: 48–53.

Griffiths, R. (1988) *Community Care: Agenda for Action: A Report to the Secretary of State for Social Services.* London: HM Stationery Office.

Grove, W.M. and Meehl, P.E. (1996) Comparative efficiency of informal (subjective, impressionistic) and formal (mechanical, algorithmic) prediction procedures: The clinical–statistical controversy. *Psychology, Public Policy, and Law,* 2: 293.

Guba, E.G. and Lincoln, Y. (2005) 'Paradigmatic controversies, contradictions and emerging confluences'. In: Denzin, N. and Lincoln, Y. (eds), *The Sage Handbook of Qualitative Research,* Third Edition. Thousand Oaks: CA, Sage, pp. 191–215.

Haidt, J. (2001) The emotional dog and its rational tail: A social intuitionist approach to moral judgment. *Psychological Review,* 108: 814–34.

Haidt, J. (2008) Morality. *Perspectives on Psychological Science,* 3: 65–72.

Hall, A. (2003) Some ethical issues arising from interprofessional working. In: Leathard, A. (ed.) *Interprofessional Collaboration: From Policy to Practice in Health and Social Care.* Hove: Routledge.

Hallett, C. and Birchall, E. (1995) *Interagency Coordination in Child Protection.* London: HMSO.

Hammersley, M. (2005) Should social science be critical? *Philosophy of the Social Sciences,* 35: 175–95.

Hammick, M., Freeth, D., Copperman, J. and Goodsman, D. (2009) *Being Interprofessional.* Cambridge: Polity Press.

Harari, Y.N. (2016) *Homo Deus: A Brief History of Tomorrow.* London: Vintage.

Harkness, S., Gregg, P. and MacMillan, L. (2012) Poverty: The role of institutions, behaviours and culture. *Joseph Rowntree Foundation.* URL (consulted 5 May 2013): www. jrf.org.uk/report/poverty-role-institutions-behaviours-and-culture

Harré, R. (1970) *The Principles of Scientific Thinking.* Chicago: University of Chicago Press.

Harvey, D.L. (2009) Complexity and Case. In: Byrne, D. and Ragin, C. (eds) *The Sage Handbook of Case-Based Methods.* London: Sage.

Harvey, D.L. and Reed, M. (1996) Social science as the study of complex systems. In: Kiel, D.L. and Elliot, E. (eds) *Chaos Theory in the Social Sciences: Foundations and Applications.* Ann Arbor: The University of Michigan Press.

Harwin, J., Ryan, M., Tunnard, J., et al. (2011) *The Family Drug & Alcohol Court (FDAC) Evaluation Project.* London: Brunel University.

Hassett, P. and Stevens, I. (2014) Child protection practice and complexity. In: Pycroft, A. and Bartollas, C. (eds) *Applying Complexity Theory.* Bristol: Policy Press.

Hawkins, P. and Shohet, R. (2012) *Supervision in the Helping Professions.* London: McGraw-Hill Education (UK).

Hawton, K.I., Comabella, C.C., Haw, C. and Saunders, K. (2013) Risk factors for suicide in individuals with depression: A systematic review. *Journal of Affective Disorders,* 147: 17–28.

Haynes, P. (2007) Chaos, complexity and transformations in social care policy in England. *Public Money and Management,* 27: 199–206.

Heath, L. and Tindale, R.S. (2013) Heuristics and biases in social settings: An introduction. In: Heath, L., Tindale, R.S., Edwards, J., Posavac, E., Bryant, F., Henderspm-King, E., Suarez-Balcazar, Y. and Myers, J. (eds) *Applications of Heuristics and Biases to Social Issues*. London: Springer.

Henderson, K. and Matthew-Byrne, J. (2016) Developing communication and interviewing skills. In: Davies, K. and Jones, R. (eds) *Skills for Social Work Practice*. London: Sage.

Hepworth, D., Rooney, R., Rooney, G., Strom-Gottfried, K. and Larsen, J. (2006) *Direct Social Work Practice (International Edition)*. Belmont, CA: Brooks/Cole.

Hester, M. (2011) The three planet model: Towards an understanding of contradictions in approaches to women and children's safety in contexts of domestic violence. *British Journal of Social Work*, 41: 837–53.

Hewitt, G., Sims, S. and Harris, R. (2014) Using realist synthesis to understand the mechanisms of interprofessional teamwork in health and social care. *Journal of Interprofessional Care*, 28: 501–6.

Hewitt, G., Sims, S. and Harris, R. (2015) Evidence of communication, influence and behavioural norms in interprofessional teams: A realist synthesis. *Journal of Interprofessional Care*, 29: 100–5.

Higgs, J., Jones, M.A., Loftus, S., et al. (2008) *Clinical Reasoning in the Health Professions*. Oxford: Butterworth Heinemann.

Holloway, F. (1996) Community psychiatric care: From libertarianism to coercion. 'Moral Panic' and mental health police in Britain. *Health Care Analysis*, 235–43.

Honey, P. and Mumford, A. (2000) *The Learning Styles Helper's Guide*. Maidenhead: Peter Honey Publications.

Hood, C. (1991) A public management for all seasons? *Public Administration*, 69: 3–19.

Hood, C. (2002) The risk game and the blame game. *Government and Opposition*, 37: 15–37.

Hood, C. and Rothstein, H. (2001) Risk regulation under pressure: Problem solving or blame shifting? *Administration & Society*, 33: 21–53.

Hood, C., Rothstein, H. and Baldwin, R. (2001) *The Government of Risk: Understanding Risk Regulation Regimes*. Oxford: Oxford University Press.

Hood, R. (2012) A critical realist model of complexity for interprofessional working. *Journal of Interprofessional Care*, 26: 6–12.

Hood, R. (2013) 'Complexity and Interprofessional Working in Children's Services.' PhD Thesis. Royal Holloway, University of London, UK.

Hood, R. (2014) How professionals talk about complex cases: A critical discourse analysis. *Child & Family Social Work*, Epub ahead of print 9 January 2014. DOI: 10.1111/cfs.12122.

Hood, R. (2015a) How professionals experience complexity: An interpretative phenomenological analysis. *Child Abuse Review*, 24: 140–52.

Hood, R. (2015b) A socio-technical critique of tiered services: Implications for interprofessional care. *Journal of Interprofessional Care*, 29: 8–12.

Hood, R. (2016a) Assessment for social work practice. In: Davies, K. and Jones, R. (eds) *Skills for Social Work Practice*. London: Sage.

Hood, R. (2016b) Prevention and protection: The development of safeguarding in children's services. *Policy & Social Work Practice*. London: Sage.

Hood, R., Gillespie, J. and Davies, J. (2016a) A conceptual review of interprofessional expertise in child safeguarding. *Journal of Interprofessional Care*, 30: 493–8.

Hood, R., Goldacre, A., Grant, R., et al. (2016b) Exploring demand and provision in English child protection services. *British Journal of Social Work*, 46: 923–41.

Hood, R., Grant, R., Jones, R., et al. (2016c) A study of performance indicators and Ofsted ratings in English child protection services. *Children and Youth Services Review,* 67: 50–6.

Hood, R., Price, J., Sartori, D., Maisey, D., Johnson, J. and Clark, Z. (2017) Collaborating across the threshold: The development of interprofessional expertise in child safeguarding. *Journal of Interprofessional Care,* 31(6): 705–13.

Hope, J. and Fraser, R. (2003) *Beyond Budgeting: How Managers Can Break Free from the Annual Performance Trap.* Boston, MA: Harvard Business Press.

Hornby, S. and Atkins, J. (2000) *Collaborative Care: Interprofessional, Interagency and Interpersona.* Oxford: Blackwell Science.

Horwath, J. (2007) *Child Neglect: Identification and Assessment.* Basingstoke: Palgrave Macmillan.

Houston, S. (2010) Prising open the black box: Critical realism, action research and social work. *Qualitative Social Work,* 9: 73–91.

Howe, D. (1996) Surface and depth in social work practice. In: Parton, N. (ed.) *Social Theory, Social Change and Social Work.* London: Routledge, 77–97.

Howe, D. (1998) Relationship-based thinking and practice in social work. *Journal of Social Work Practice,* 12: 45–56.

Howe, D. (2005) *Child Abuse and Neglect: Attachment, Development and Intervention.* Basingstoke: Palgrave Macmillan.

Howe, D. (2014) *The Compleat Social Worker.* Basingstoke: Palgrave Macmillan.

Hudson, B. (2007) Pessimism and optimism in inter-professional working: The Sedgefield Integrated Team. *Journal of Integrated Care,* 21: 3–15.

Hughes, L. and Pengelly, P. (1997) *Staff Supervision in a Turbulent Environment: Managing Process and Task in Front-line Services.* London: Jessica Kingsley.

Hunter, D. (2009) Relationship between evidence and policy: A case of evidence-based policy or policy-based evidence? *Public Health,* 123: 583–6.

International Federation of Social Work (IFSW) (2014) Global definition of the social work profession. Available at: http://ifsw.org/policies/definition-of-social-work/.

Irvine, R., Kerridge, I., Mcphee, J. and Freeman, S. (2002) Interprofessionalism and ethics: Consensus or clash of cultures? *Journal of Interprofessional Care,* 16: 199–210.

Ixer, G. (1999) There's no such thing as reflection. *British Journal of Social Work,* 29: 513–27.

Jack, G. and Gill, O. (2003) *The Missing Side of the Triangle: Assessing the Importance of Family and Environmental Factors in the Lives of Children.* Barkingside: Barnardo's.

Janis, I. (1982) *Groupthink: Psychological Studies of Policy Decisions and Fiascoes.* Boston, MA: Houghton Mifflin.

Jay, A. (2014) *Independent Inquiry into Child Sexual Exploitation in Rotherham.* Available at: www.rotherham.gov.uk/downloads/file/1407/independent_inquiry_cse_in_rotherham.

Johns, C. (2000) *Becoming a Reflective Practitioner.* Oxford: Blackwell Science.

Johnson, E., Miyanishi, K. and Bridge, S. (2001) Wildfire regime in the boreal forest and the idea of suppression and fuel buildup. *Conservation Biology,* 15: 1554–7.

Johnson, K., Bogie, A., Wagner, D., et al. (2010) *Developing an Actuarial Risk Assessment to Inform the Decisions Made by Adult Protective Service Workers.* Oakland, CA: National Council on Crime and Delinquency.

Jones, M. (2004) Supervision, Learning and Transformative Practices. In: Gould, N. and Baldwin, M. (eds) *Social Work, Critical Reflection and the Learning Organization.* Aldershot: Ashgate, 1–9.

Jones, R. (2014) *The Story of Baby P: Setting the Record Straight.* Bristol: Policy Press.

Jones, R., Bhanbhro, S.M., Grant, R., et al. (2013) The definition and deployment of differential core professional competencies and characteristics in multiprofessional health and social care teams. *Health & Social Care in the Community,* 21: 47–58.

Jones T. (1991) Ethical decision making by individuals in organizations: An issue-contingent model. *Academy of Management Review*, 16: 366–395.

Jordan, B. and Drakeford, M. (2012) *Social Work and Social Policy Under Austerity*. Basingstoke: Palgrave Macmillan.

Kadushin, A. and Harkness, D. (2014) *Supervision in Social Work*. New York: Columbia University Press.

Kahneman, D. (2011) *Thinking, Fast and Slow*. London: Palgrave Macmillan.

Kahneman, D., Slovic, P. and Tversky, A. (1990) *Judgment Under Uncertainty: Heuristics and Biases*. Cambridge: Cambridge University Press.

Keene, J. (2001) *Clients with Complex Needs: Interprofessional Practice*. Oxford: Blackwell Science.

Kelso, A. (2009) Parliament on its knees: MPs' expenses and the crisis of transparency at Westminster. *The Political Quarterly*, 80: 329–38.

Kemp, A.M., Dunstan, F., Harrison, S., Morris, S., Mann, M., Rolfe, K., Datta, S., Thomas, D.P., Sibert, J.R. and Maguire, S. (2008) Patterns of skeletal fractures in child abuse: systematic review. *BMJ*, 337: a1518.

Kendall, S., Rodger, J. and Palmer, H. (2010) The use of whole family assessment to identify the needs of families with multiple problems. Research report DFE-RR045. London: Department for Education.

Kendrick, A. and Smith, M. (2002) Close enough? Professional closeness and safe caring. *Scottish Journal of Residential Child Care*, 1: 46–54.

Kessler, R.C., McGonagle, K.A., Swartz, M., Blazer, D.G. and Nelson, C.B. (1993) Sex and depression in the National Comorbidity Survey I: Lifetime prevalence, chronicity and recurrence, *Journal of Affective Disorders*, 29(2): 85–96.

Keynes, J.M. (2012) *The Collected Writings of John Maynard Keynes* (Volume 21). Cambridge: Cambridge University Press.

Kiel, D.L. and Elliot, E. (1996) *Chaos Theory in the Social Sciences: Foundations and Applications*. Ann Arbor: The University of Michigan Press.

Kinchin, I. and Cabot, B. (2010) Reconsidering the dimensions of expertise: From linear stages towards dual processing. *London Review of Education*, 8: 153–166.

Kinman, G. and Grant, L. (2011) Exploring stress resilience in trainee social workers: The role of emotional and social competencies. *British Journal of Social Work*, 41: 261–75.

Kinsella, E.A. (2007) Technical rationality in Schön's reflective practice: Dichotomous or non-dualistic epistemological position. *Nursing Philosophy*, 8: 102–13.

Kirk, S. (2008) Transitions in the lives of young people with complex healthcare needs. *Child: Care, Health and Development*, 34: 567–75.

Klein, M. (1946) Notes on some schizoid mechanisms. *The International Journal of Psycho-analysis*, 27: 99–110.

Knott, C. and Scragg, T. (2016) *Reflective Practice in Social Work*. Exeter: Learning Matters.

Kolb, D. (1984) *Experiential Learning: Experiences as the Source of Learning and Development*. Englewood Cliffs, NJ: Prentice Hall.

Kroll, B. (2010) Only Connect... Building relationships: working with hard-to-reach people. In: Ruch, G., Turney, D. and Ward, A.(eds) *Relationship-Based Social Work: Getting to the Heart of Practice*. London: Jessica Kingsley.

Kuhn, T. (1996) *The Structure of Scientific Revolutions*. Chicago: University of Chicago Press.

Laird, S. (2014) Training social workers to effectively manage aggressive parental behaviour in child protection in Australia, the United States and the United Kingdom. *British Journal of Social Work*, 44: 1967–83.

Laming, L. (2003) *The Victoria Climbié Inquiry*. Available at: www.gov.uk/government/uploads/system/uploads/attachment_data/file/273183/5730.pdf

Laming, L. (2009) *The Protection of Children in England :A Progress Report*. London: The Stationery Office.

Larson, M.S. (1977) *The Rise of Professionalism: A Sociological Analysis*. London: University of California Press.

Law, J., McCann, D. and O'May, F. (2011) Managing change in the care of children with complex needs: Healthcare providers' perspectives. *Journal of Advanced Nursing*, 67: 2551–60.

Lawson, T. (1997) *Economics and Reality*. Abingdon: Routledge.

Leathard, A. (2003) Models for interprofessional collaboration. In: Leathard, A. (ed.) *Interprofessional Collaboration: From Policy to Practice in Health and Social Care*. Hove: Routledge.

Leathard, A. and Mclaren, S. (2002) Ethics and interprofessional care. *Journal of Interprofessional Care*, 16: 197–8.

Leroi, A.M. (2006) The future of neo-eugenics. *EMBO reports*, 7: 1184–7.

Letherby, G. and Bywaters, P. (2006) *Extending Social Research: Application, Implementation and Publication*. Maidenhead: Open University Press.

Levine, S. and White, P. (1961) Exchange as a conceptual framework for the study of inter-organizational relationships. *Administrative Science Quarterly*, 5: 583–601.

Levy, R. (2010) New public management. *Public Policy and Administration*, 25: 234–40.

Lewicki, R.J., Weiss, S.E. and Lewin, D. (1992) Models of conflict, negotiation and third party intervention: A review and synthesis. *Journal of Organizational Behavior*, 13: 209–52.

Liker, J.K. (2004) *Becoming Lean: Inside Stories of US Manufacturers*. New York: Productivity Press.

Limbrick, P. (2004) *Early Support for Children with Complex Needs: Team around the Child and the Multi-agency Keyworker*. Worcester: Interconnections.

Lipsky, M. (1980) *Street Level Bureaucracy: Dilemmas of the Individual in Public Services*. New York: Russell Sage Foundation.

Lloyd, C., King, R. and Chenoweth, L. (2002) Social work, stress and burnout: A review. *Journal of Mental Health*, 11: 255–65.

Local Government Leadership and City of Westminster (2010) *Repairing Broken Families and Rescuing Fractured Communities: Lessons from the Front Line*. London: Local Government Leadership and City of Westminster.

Lord, P., Southcott, C. and Sharp, C. (2011) *Targeting Children's Ccentre Services on the Most Needy Families* (LGA Research Report). Slough: NFER.

Loxley, A. (1997) *Collaboration in Health and Welfare: Working with Difference*. London: Jessica Kingsley.

Luft, J. (1970) *Group Processes: An Introduction to Group Dynamics*. Palo Alto, CA: National Press Books.

Lymbery, M. (1998) Care management and professional autonomy: The impact of community care legislation on social work with older people. *The British Journal of Social Work*, 28: 863–78.

MacKeith, J. (2011) The development of the outcomes star: A participatory approach to assessment and outcome measurement. *Housing, Care and Support*, 14: 98–106.

Mainstone, F. (2014) *Mastering Whole Family Assessment in Social Work: Balancing the needs of children, adults and their families*. London: Jessica Kingsley.

Majone, G. (1994) The rise of the regulatory state in Europe. *West European Politics*, 17: 77–101.

Mann, K., Gordon, J. and Macleod, A. (2009) Reflection and reflective practice in health professions education: A systematic review. *Advances in Health Sciences Education*, 14: 595.

Masenya, M. (2013) Eating the louse and its larva! The indignity of poverty as embedded within selected African and Old Testament Proverbs. *Scriptura,* 111: 452–9.

Maslow, A. (1970) *Motivation and Personality* (2nd edn). New York: Harper & Row.

Masten, A. (2001) Ordinary magic: Resilience processes in development. *American Psychologist,* 56: 227–38.

Maxwell, J. (2012) *A Realist Approach for Qualitative Research.* London: Sage.

Maxwell, N., Scourfield, J., Le-Zhang, M., et al. (2016) *Independent evaluation of the front-line pilot.* London: Department for Education.

Mayer-Schonberger, V. and Cukier, K. (2014) *Big Data: A Revolution That Will Transform How We Live, Work, and Think.* New York: Houghton Mifflin Harcourt.

Mayo, E. (1933) *The Human Problems of an Industrial Civilization.* New York: Viking Press.

Mayo, E. (2009) Can the West save Africa? *Journal of Economic Literature,* 47: 373–447.

McCarthy, M., Schellinger, J., Smith, R.R., Behimer, G., Hargraves, D. and Scherra, K. (2017) Comparison of service effectiveness for youth with depressed versus nondepressed caregivers. *Research on Social Work Practice,* 27(4): 413–422.

McGregor, D. (1960) *The Human Side of Enterprise.* New York: McGraw Hill.

McKnight, J. (2011) *The Abundant Community: Awakening the Power of Families and Neighborhoods.* ReadHowYouWant.com.

McMahon, L. (2010) Long-term complex relationships. In: Ruch, G., Turney, D. and Ward, A. (eds) *Relationship-Based Social Work: Getting to the Heart of Practice.* London: Jessica Kingsley.

McNeece, C. and Thyer, B. (2004) Evidence-based practice and social work. *Journal of Evidence-Based Social Work,* 1: 7–25.

McPeck, J.E. (2016) *Critical Thinking and Education.* Abingdon: Routledge.

Meehl, P. (1954) *Clinical versus Statistical Prediction: A Theoretical Analysis and a Review of the Evidence.* Minneapolis: University of Minnesota Press.

Meek, J. (2014) *Private Island: Why Britain Now Belongs to Someone Else.* London: Verso Press.

Mendoza, N., Rose, R., Geiger, J., et al. (2016) Risk assessment with actuarial and clinical methods: Measurement and evidence-based practice. *Child Abuse & Neglect,* 61: 1–12.

Menzies, I. (1960) A case-study in the functioning of social systems as a defence against anxiety: A report on a study of the nursing service of a general hospital. *Human Relations,* 13: 95–121.

Menzies Lyth, I. (1988) *Containing Anxiety in Institutions.* London: Free Association Press.

Merton, R. (1968) *Social Theory and Social Structure.* New York: Free Press.

Mezirow, J. (1991) *Transformative Dimensions of Adult Learning.* San Francisco, CA: Jossey-Bass.

Miller, S.C. (2013) *The Ethics of Need: Agency, Dignity, and Obligation.* London: Routledge.

Miller, W. and Rollnick, S. (2002) *Motivational Interviewing: Preparing People for Change.* New York: Guilford Press.

Milner, J. and O'Byrne, P. (2015) *Assessment in Social Work.* London: Palgrave Macmillan.

Minuchin, S. (1974) *Families and Family Therapy.* Cambridge, MA: Harvard University Press.

Mohaupt, J., Van Soeren, M., Andrusyszyn, M.A., Macmillan, K., Devlin-Cop, S. and Reeves, S. (2012) Understanding interprofessional relationships by the use of contact theory. *Journal of Interprofessional Care,* 26(5), 370–375.

Molander, A. (2016) *Discretion in the Welfare State: Social Rights and Professional Judgment.* Abingdon: Routledge.

Molin, R. (1988) Treatment of children in foster care: Issues of collaboration. *Child Abuse and Neglect,* 12: 241–50.

Morris, S. (2013) Daniel Pelka: Professionals failed 'invisible' murdered boy, report says. Available at: www.theguardian.com/society/2013/sep/17/professionals-failed-report-daniel-pelka.

Morris, T. (2006) *Social Work Research Methods: Four Alternative Paradigms.* Thousand Oaks, CA: Sage.

Morrison, T. (1996) Partnership and collaboration: Rhetoric and reality. *Child Abuse and Neglect,* 20: 127–40.

Mowbray, C.T., Holter, M.C., Teague, G.B., et al. (2003) Fidelity criteria: Development, measurement, and validation. *American Journal of Evaluation,* 24: 315–40.

Mowles, C. (2014) Complex, but not quite complex enough: The turn to the complexity sciences in evaluation scholarship. *Evaluation* 20: 160–75.

Moynihan, D.P. (2009) The network governance of crisis response: Case studies of incident command systems. *Journal of Public Administration Research and Theory,* 19: 895–915.

Mukamel, D., Temkin-Greener, H., Delavan, R., Peterson, D., Gross, D., Stephen, K. and Williams, T.F. (2006) Team performance and risk-adjusted health outcomes in the program of all-inclusive care for the elderly (PACE). *The Gerontologist,* 46: 227–37.

Mullen, E.J. (2001) *Toward Outcomes Measurement in Human Services.* New York: Center for the Study of Social Work Practice, Columbia University.

Mullins, D. and Pawson, H. (2005) 'The land that time forgot': Reforming access to social housing in England. *Policy & Politics,* 33: 205–30.

Munro, E. (1996) Avoidable and unavoidable mistakes in child protection work. *British Journal of Social Work,* 26(6): 793–808.

Munro, E. (2004) The impact of child abuse inquiries since 1990. In: Stanley, N. and Manthorpe, J. (eds.) *The Age of the Inquiry: Learning and Blaming in Health and Social Care.* London: Routledge.

Munro, E. (2008) *Effective Child Protection.* London: Sage.

Munro, E. (2009) Managing societal and institutional risk in child protection. *Risk Analysis,* 29: 1015–23.

Munro, E. (2010) *The Munro Review of Child Protection Part One: A Systems Analysis.* London: Department for Education.

Munro, E. (2011) *The Munro Review of Child Protection: Final Report. A Child-Centred System.* London: TSO.

Munro, E. and Fish. S. (2015) *Hear No Evil, See No Evil. Understanding Failure to Identify and Report Child Sexual Abuse in Institutional Contexts.* Sydney: Royal Commission into Institutional Responses to Child Sexual Abuse.

Murphy, D., Duggan, M. and Joseph, S. (2013) Relationship-based social work and its compatibility with the person-centred approach: Principled versus instrumental perspectives. *British Journal of Social Work,* 43: 703–19.

Neukrug, E., Bayne, H., Dean-Nganga, L., et al. (2013) Creative and novel approaches to empathy: A neo-Rogerian perspective. *Journal of Mental Health Counseling,* 35: 29.

Newhill, C. (1995) Client violence toward social workers: A practice and policy concern for the 1990s. *Social Work,* 40: 631–6.

Nisbett, R.E., Peng, K., Choi, I., et al. (2001) Culture and systems of thought: Holistic versus analytic cognition. *Psychological Review,* 108: 291–310.

Nurius, P. and Gibson, J. (1990) Clinical observation, inference, reasoning, and judgment in social work: An update. *Social Work Research Abstracts,* 26: 18–25.

Nybell, L. (2001) Meltdowns and containments. Constructions of children at risk as complex systems. *Childhood,* 8: 213–30.

O'Brien, M., Bachmann, M.O., Jones, N.R., Reading, R., Thoburn, J., Husbands, C., Shreeve, A. and Watson, J. (2009) Do integrated children's services improve children's outcomes? Evidence from England's Children's Trust Pathfinders. *Children & Society*, 23: 320–35.

Office for National Statistics (ONS) (2014) *2011 Census Glossary of Terms*. Available at: www.ons.gov.uk/ons/guide-method/census/2011/census-data/2011-census-data/2011-first-release/2011-census-definitions/2011-census-glossary.pdf.

Ofsted (2016) *Annual Report into Children's Social Care 2016*. Available at: www.gov.uk/government/uploads/system/uploads/attachment_data/file/574464/Ofsted_social_care_annual_report_2016.pdf

O'Hara, M. (2015) *Austerity Bites: A Journey to the Sharp End of Cuts in the UK*. Bristol: Policy Press.

Osborne, S.P., Bovaird, T., Martin, S., et al. (1995) Performance management and accountability in complex public programmes. *Financial Accountability & Management*, 11: 19–37.

O'Shaughnessy, P.T. (2008) Parachuting cats and crushed eggs: The controversy over the use of DDT to control malaria. *American Journal of Public Health*, 98: 1940–8.

Osmo, R. and Landau, R. (2001) The need for explicit argumentation in ethical decision-making in social work. *Social Work Education*, 20: 483–92.

Ovretveit, J. (1996) Five ways to describe a multidisciplinary team. *Journal of Interprofessional Care*, 10: 163–171.

Ovretveit, J. (1997) How to describe interprofessional working. In: Ovetreit, J., Mathias, P. and Thompson, T. (eds) *Interprofessional Working for Health and Social Care*. Basingstoke: Palgrave.

Owens, P. and Petch, H. (1995) Professionals and management. In: Owens, P., Carrier, J. and Horder, J. (eds) *Interprofessional Issues in Community and Primary Health Care*. Basingstoke: Macmillan.

Parker, G. (1990) *Team Players and Teamwork*. San Francisco, CA: Jossey-Bass.

Parkinson, C. (2010) Sustaining relationships: Working with strong feelings. 2: Hoplessness, depression and despair. In: Ruch, G., Turney, D. and Ward, A. (eds) *Relationship-Based Social Work: Getting to the Heart of Practice*. London: Jessica Kingsley.

Parton, N. (2008) Changes in the form of knowledge in social work: From the 'social' to the 'informational'? *British Journal of Social Work* 38: 253–69.

Parton, N. (2011) Social work, risk and 'the blaming system'. In: Cree, V. (ed.) *Social Work: A Reader*. Abingdon: Routledge.

Pawson, R. (2006) *Evidence-Based Policy: A Realist Perspective*. London: Sage.

Pawson, R. (2013) *The Science of Evaluation: A Realist Manifesto*. London: Sage.

Pawson, R. and Manzano-Santaella, A. (2012) A realist diagnostic workshop. *Evaluation*, 18: 176–91.

Pawson, R. and Tilley, N. (1997) *Realistic Evaluation*. London: Sage.

Pawson, R., Greenhalgh, T., Harvey, G. and Walshe, K. (2005) Realist review – a new method of systematic review designed for complex policy interventions. *Journal of Health Services Research & Policy*, 10: 21–34.

Payne, M. (2000) *Teamwork in Multiprofessional Care*. London: Macmillan.

Payne, M. (2015) *Modern Social Work Theory* (4th edn). Basingstoke: Palgrave Macmillan.

Pence, E. and Paymar, M. (1993) *Education Groups for Men Who Batter: The Duluth Model*. New York: Springer.

Perrow, C. (1984) *Normal Accidents. Living With High-Risk Technologies*. New York: Basic Books.

Perryman, J. (2007) Inspection and emotion. *Cambridge Journal of Education*, 37: 173–90.

Pincus, A. and Minahan, A. (1973) *Social Work Practice: Model and Method*. Itasca, IL: Peacock.

Popper, K.. (2005 [1935]) *The Logic of Scientific Discovery*. London: Routledge.

Power, M. (1997) *The Audit Society: Rituals of Verification*. Oxford: Oxford University Press.

Power, M. (2004) *The Risk Management of Everything*. London: Demos.

Prigogine, I. and Lefever, R. (1973) Theory of dissipative structures. In: Haken, H. (ed.), *Synergetics*. Stuttgart: BG Teubner, 124–35.

Prigogine, I. and Stengers, I. (1984) *Order Out of Chaos*. New York: Bantam.

Prochaska, J. and Diclemente, C. (1986) Toward a Comprehensive Model of Change. In: Miller, W.R. and Heather, N. (eds) *Treating Addictive Behaviors: Processes of Change*. Boston, MA: Springer US, 3–27.

Propper, C. and Wilson, D. (2003) The use and usefulness of performance measures in the public sector. *Oxford Review of Economic Policy*, 19: 250–67.

Pumariega, A.J. (1997) Community-based systems of care for children's mental health services. *Journal of the Association for Academic Minority Physicians: The official publication of the Association for Academic Minority Physicians*, 8: 67–73.

Ragin, C. (1992) 'Casing', and the process of social inquiry. In: Ragin, C.C. and Becker, H.S. (eds) *What is a Case? Exploring the Foundations of Social Inquiry*. Cambridge: Cambridge University Press.

Ragin, C.C. and Becker, H.S. (1992) *What is a Case? Exploring the Foundations of Social Inquiry*. Cambridge: Cambridge University Press.

Rahim, M.A. (1983) A measure of styles of handling interpersonal conflict. *Academy of Management Journal*, 26: 368–76.

Rankin, J. and Regan, S. (2004) *Meeting Complex Needs: The Future of Social Care*. Southampton: Institute for Public Policy Research.

Raphael, B. and Wilson, J. (2000) *Psychological Debriefing: Theory, Practice, and Evidence*. Cambridge: Cambridge University Press.

Rasmussen, J. (1997) Risk management in a dynamic society: A modelling problem. *Safety Science*, 27: 183–213.

Rawson, D. (1994) Models of inter-professional work: Likely theories and possibilities. In: Leathard, A. (ed.) *Going Inter-Professional: Working Together for Health and Welfare*. London and New York: Routledge.

Ray, T. (1992) An approach to the synthesis of life. In: Langton, G., Taylor, C., Doyne Farmer, J., et al. (eds) *Artificial Life II*. Reading, MA: Addison-Wesley.

Reamer, F.G. (1983) Ethical dilemmas in social work practice. *Social Work*, 28: 31–35.

Reason, J. (1997) *Managing the Risks of Organizational Accidents*. Brookfield, VT: Ashgate.

Reder, P. and Duncan, S. (1999) *Lost Innocents: A Follow-up Study of Fatal Child Abuse*. Abingdon: Routledge.

Reder, P. and Duncan, S. (2004) From Colwell to Climbié: Inquiring into fatal child abuse. In: Revans, R.W. (1980) *Action Learning: New Techniques for Management*. London: Blond and Biggs.

Reed, M. and Harvey, D.L. (1992) The new science and the old: Complexity and realism in the social sciences. *Journal for the Theory of Social Behaviour*, 22: 353–80.

Reeves, S. and Freeth, D. (2003) New forms of technology, new forms of collaboration? In: Leathard, A. (ed.) *Interprofessional Collaboration: From Policy to Practice in Health and Social Care*. Hove: Routledge.

Reeves, S. and Harris, R. (2016) Interprofessional teamwork in health and social care: Key tensions and future possibilities. In: Plümacher, M. and Abel, G. (eds) *The Power of Distributed Perspectives*. Berlin: De Gruyter.

Reeves, S., Lewin, S., Espin, S. and Zwarenstein, M. (2011) *Interprofessional Teamwork for Health and Social care*. London: John Wiley.

Revans, R.W. (1980) *Action Learning: New Techniques for Management*. London: Blond and Biggs.

Reynolds, C.W. (1987) Flocks, herds and schools: A distributed behavioral model. *Computer Graphics*, 21: 25–34.

Ringstad, R. (2005) Conflict in the workplace: Social workers as victims and perpetrators. *Social Work*, 50: 305–13.

Rittel, H, and Webber, M. (1973) Dilemmas in a general theory of planning. *Policy Sciences* 4: 155–69.

Robbins, S.P. (2009) *Organizational Behavior* (13th edn). Harlow: Pearson Education.

Robertson, M. (2017) The great British housing crisis. *Capital & Class*, 41: 195–215.

Robinson, M., Atkinson, M. and Downing, D. (2008) *Supporting Theory Building in Integrated Services Research*. Slough: NFER.

Rocco-Briggs, M. (2008) 'Who owns my pain?' An aspect of the complexity of working with looked after children. *Journal of Child Psychotherapy*, 34: 190–206.

Rodgers, C. (2002) Defining reflection: Another look at John Dewey and reflective thinking. *Teachers College Record*, 104: 842–66.

Rogers, A. and Welch, B. (2009) Using standardized clients in the classroom: An evaluation of a training module to teach active listening skills to social work students. *Journal of Teaching in Social Work*, 29: 153–68.

Rogers, C.R. (1957) The necessary and sufficient conditions of therapeutic personality change. *Journal of Consulting Psychology*, 21: 95–103.

Rogers C. (1973) The interpersonal relationship: The core of guidance. In: Maslowski, R. and Morgan, L. (eds) *Interpersonal Growth and Self Actualization in Groups*. New York: Arno Press, 176–89.

Rose, J. (2011) Dilemmas of inter-professional collaboration: Can they be resolved? *Children & Society*, 25: 151–63.

Rosenberg, M. (2015) *Nonviolent Communication: A Language of Life: Life-Changing Tools for Healthy Relationships*. Encinitas, CA: PuddleDancer Press.

Rossi, P. (1987) The iron law of evaluation and other metallic rules. In: Miller, J.H. and Lewis, M. (eds) *Research in Social Problems and Public Policy*. Greenwich, CT: JAI Press, 3–20.

Rothstein, H. (2006) The institutional origins of risk: A new agenda for risk research. *Health, Risk and Society*, 8: 215–21.

Rothstein, H., Huber, M. and Gaskell, G. (2006) A theory of risk colonization: The spiralling regulatory logics of societal and institutional risk. *Economy and Society*, 35: 91–112.

Ruble, T.L. and Thomas, K.W. (1976) Support for a two-dimensional model of conflict behavior. *Organizational Behavior and Human Performance*, 16: 143–55.

Ruch, G. (2005) Relationship-based practice and reflective practice: Holistic approaches to contemporary child care social work. *Child & Family Social Work*, 10: 111–23.

Ruch, G. (2007) Reflective practice in contemporary child-care social work: The role of containment. *British Journal of Social Work*, 37: 659–80.

Ruch, G. (2010a) The contemporary context of relationship-based practice. In: Ruch, G., Turney, D., and Ward, A. (eds) *Relationship-Based Social Work: Getting to the Heart of Practice*. London: Jessica Kingsley.

Ruch, G. (2010b) Theoretical Frameworks Informing Relationship-Based Practice. In: Ruch, G., Turney, D. and Ward, A. (eds) *Relationship-Based Social Work: Getting to the Heart of Practice*. London: Jessica Kingsley.

Ruch, G., Turney, D. and Ward, A. (eds) (2010) *Relationship-Based Social Work: Getting to the Heart of Practice*. London: Jessica Kingsley.

Rutter, L. and Brown, K. (2015) *Critical Thinking and Professional Judgement for Social Work*. London: Learning Matters.

Ryan, R.M. and Deci, E.L. (2000) Intrinsic and extrinsic motivations: Classic definitions and new directions. *Contemporary Educational Psychology*, 25: 54–67.

Ryan, S., Wiles, D., Cash, S., et al. (2005) Risk assessments: Empirically supported or values driven? *Children and Youth Services Review*, 27: 213–25.

Ryde, J. (2009) *Being White in the Helping Professions: Developing Effective Intercultural Awareness*. London: Jessica Kingsley.

Sabatier, P.A. (1986) Top-down and bottom-up approaches to implementation research: A critical analysis and suggested synthesis. *Journal of Public Policy*, 6: 21–48.

Sager, F. and Rosser, C. (2009) Weber, Wilson, and Hegel: Theories of modern bureaucracy. *Public Administration Review*, 69: 1136–47.

Sanderson, I. (2006) Complexity, 'practical rationality' and evidence-based policy making. *Policy and Politics*, 34: 115–32.

Sass, J. and Crosbie, T. (2013) Democracy and scandal: A research agenda. *Comparative Sociology*, 12: 851–62.

Sayer, A. (2010) *Method in Social Science: A Realist Approach*. London: Routledge.

Schön, D.A. (1987) *Educating the Reflective Practitioner: Toward a New Design for Teaching and Learning in the Professions*, San Francisco: Jossey-Bass.

Schön, D.A. (1991) *The Reflective Practitioner: How Professionals Think in Action*. Aldershot: Avebury Academic Publishing.

Scott, K.L. and Crooks, C.V. (2007) Preliminary evaluation of an intervention program for maltreating fathers. *Brief Treatment and Crisis Intervention*, 7: 224.

Seddon, J. (2003) *Freedom from Command and Control*. Buckingham: Vanguard Consulting.

Seddon, J. (2008) *Systems Thinking in the Public Sector*. Axminster: Triarchy Press.

Segal, H. (2012) *Introduction to the Work of Melanie Klein*. London: Karnac Books.

Senge, P. (1990) *The Fifth Discipline: The Art and Practice of the Learning Organization*. New York: Doubleday.

Senge, P. (2006 [1994]) *The Fifth Discipline Fieldbook: Strategies and Tools for Building a Learning Organization*. New York: Doubleday.

Shaw, I., Bell, M., Sinclair, I., et al. (2009) An exemplary scheme? An evaluation of the Integrated Children's System. *British Journal of Social Work*, 39: 613–26.

Shaw, I., Morris, K. and Edwards, A. (2009) Technology, social services and organizational innovation or how great expectations in London and Cardiff are dashed in Lowestoft and Cymtyrch. *Journal of Social Work Practice*, 23: 383–400.

Shell, G.R. (2001) Teaching ideas: Bargaining styles and negotiation: The Thomas-Kilmann Conflict Mode Instrument in negotiation training. *Negotiation Journal*, 17: 155–74.

Shlonsky, A. and Wagner, D. (2005) The next step: Integrating actuarial risk assessment and clinical judgment into an evidence-based practice framework in CPS case management. *Children and Youth Services Review*, 27: 409–27.

Sidebotham, P. (2012) Safeguarding in an age of austerity. *Child Abuse Review*, 21: 313–17.

Sims, S., Hewitt, G. and Harris, R. (2015a) Evidence of a shared purpose, critical reflection, innovation and leadership in interprofessional healthcare teams: A realist synthesis. *Journal of Interprofessional Care*, 29: 209–15.

Sims, S., Hewitt, G. and Harris, R. (2015b) Evidence of collaboration, pooling of resources, learning and role blurring in interprofessional healthcare teams: A realist synthesis. *Journal of Interprofessional Care*, 29: 20–25.

Skjorshammer, M. (2001) Cooperation and conflict in a hospital: Interprofessional differences in perception and management of conflicts. *Journal of Interprofessional Care*, 15: 7–18.

Sloper, P. (2004) Facilitators and barriers for co-ordinated multi-agency services. *Child: Care, Health and Development*, 30: 571–80.

Smethurst, C. and. Long, R. (2013) Negotiation Skills. In: Mantell, A. (ed.) *Skills for Social Work Practice* (2nd edn). London: Sage/Learning Matters.

Smith, M. (2005) *Surviving Fears in Health and Social Care: The Terrors of Night and the Arrows of Day*. London: Jessica Kingsley.

Smith, M. (2010) Sustaining relationships: Working with strong feelings. 1: Anger, aggression and hostility. In: Ruch, G., Turney, D. and Ward, A. (eds) *Relationship-Based Social Work: Getting to the Heart of Practice*. London: Jessica Kingsley.

Smith, P. and Bryan, K. (2005) Participatory evaluation: Navigating the emotions of partnerships. *Journal of Social Work Practice*, 19: 195–209.

Smith, R. (2008) *Social Work and Power*. Basingstoke: Palgrave Macmillan.

Smith, W.K. and Lewis, M.W. (2011) Toward a theory of paradox: A dynamic equilibrium model of organizing. *Academy of Management Review*, 36: 381–403.

Social Exclusion Unit (1999) *Bridging the Gap: New Opportunities for 16–18 Year Olds Not in Education, Employment or Training*. London: HMSO.

Sparrow, M.K. (2000) *The Regulatory Craft: Controlling Risks, Solving Problems, and Managing Compliance*. Washington, DC: Brookings Institution Press.

Sparrow, M.K. (2008) *The Character of Harms: Operational Challenges in Control*. Cambridge: Cambridge University Press.

Stacey, R.D. (2007) *Strategic Management and Organisational Dynamics: The Challenge of Complexity to Ways of Thinking about Organisations* (5th edn). Harlow: Pearson.

Stanley, N. and Manthorpe, J. (eds) (2004) *The Age of the Inquiry: Learning and Blaming in Health and Social Care*. London: Routledge.

Stanovich, K. and West, R. (2000) Advancing the rationality debate. *Behavioral and Brain Sciences*, 23: 701–17.

Steckley, L. (2010) Containment and holding environments: Understanding and reducing physical restraint in residential child care. *Children and Youth Services Review*, 32: 120–8.

Steiner, J. (2003) *Psychic Retreats: Pathological Organizations in Psychotic, Neurotic and Borderline Patients*. Abingdon: Routledge.

Stevenson, O. (1994) Child protection: Where now for inter-professional work? In: Leathard, A. (ed.) *Going Inter-Professional*. New York: Routledge.

Stewart, P. (2001) Complexity theories, social theory, and the question of social complexity. *Philosophy of the Social Sciences*, 31: 323–60.

Stone, J.A.M., Haas, B.A., Harmer-Beem, M.J. and Baker, D.L. (2004) Utilization of research methodology in designing and developing an interdisciplinary course in ethics. *Journal of Interprofessional Care*, 18: 57–62.

Suter, E., Arndt, J., Arthur, N., Parboosingh, J., Taylor, E. and Deutschlander, S. (2009) Role understanding and effective communication as core competencies for collaborative practice. *Journal of Interprofessional Care*, 23: 41–51.

Sword, W., Clark, A.M., Hegadoren, K., et al. (2012) The complexity of postpartum mental health and illness: A critical realist study. *Nursing Inquiry*, 19: 51–62.

Tarp, F. (2003) *Foreign Aid and Development: Lessons Learnt and Directions for the Future*. Abingdon: Routledge.

Taylor, B. (2010) *Professional Decision Making in Social Work Practice*. Exeter: Learning Matters.

Taylor, B. (2017) Heuristics in professional judgement: a psycho-social rationality model. *The British Journal of Social Work*, 47: 1043–60.

Taylor, B., Killick, C. and McGlade, A. (2015) *Understanding and Using Research in Social Work*. London: Sage.

Taylor, F.W. (1914) *The Principles of Scientific Management*. London: Harper & Brothers.

Thabane, L., Ma, J., Chu, R., et al. (2010) A tutorial on pilot studies: The what, why and how. *BMC Medical Research Methodology*, 10: 1.

Thagard, P.R. (1978) The best explanation: Criteria for theory choice. *The Journal of Philosophy*, 75: 76–92.

Thelen, E and Smith, L.B. (1994) *A Dynamic Systems Approach to the Development of Cognition and Action*. Cambridge, MA: MIT Press.

Thompson, N. (2016) *Anti-Discriminatory Practice: Equality, Diversity and Social Justice*. Basingstoke: Palgrave Macmillan.

Thompson, S. and Thompson, N. (2008) *The Critically Reflective Practitioner*. Basingstoke: Palgrave Macmillan.

Thrift, N. (1999) The place of complexity. *Theory, Culture & Society*, 16: 31–69.

Toulmin, S.E. (1958) *The Uses of Argument*. Cambridge: Cambridge University Press.

Toulmin, S.E. (1970) *An Examination of the Place of Reason in Ethics*. Cambridge: Cambridge University Press.

Trevithick, P. (2003) Effective relationship-based practice: A theoretical exploration. *Journal of Social Work Practice*, 17: 163–76.

Trist, E. (1981) *The Evolution of Socio-Technical Systems: A Conceptual Framework and an Action Research Programme*. Toronto: Ontario Quality of Working Life Centre.

Trist, E.L. and Bamforth, K.W. (1951) Some social and psychological consequences of the Longwall Method of coal-getting: An examination of the psychological situation and defences of a work group in relation to the social structure and technological content of the work system. *Human Relations*, 4: 3–38.

Tronto, J. (1993) *Moral Boundaries: A Political Argument for an Ethic of Care*. New York: Routledge.

Trowell, J. (1995) Key psychoanalytic concepts. In: Bower, M. and Trowell, J. (eds) *The Emotional Needs of Young Children and their Families: Using Psychoanalytic Ideas in the Community*. New York: Routledge.

Turnell, A. and Edwards, S. (1999) *Signs of Safety: A Solution Oriented Approach to Child Protection Casework*. London: W.W. Norton.

Turney, D. (2010) Sustaining relationships: Working with strong feelings. 3: Love and positive feelings. In: Ruch, G., Turney, D. and Ward, A. (eds) *Relationship-Based Social Work: Getting to the Heart of Practice*. London: Jessica Kingsley.

Turney, D. (2012) A relationship-based approach to engaging involuntary clients: The contribution of recognition theory. *Child & Family Social Work*, 17: 149–59.

Ulrich, W. (2005) The art of interconnected thinking: Frederic Vester's biocybernetic systems approach. *Journal of Research Practice* 1: Article R2.

Ungar, M., Liebenberg, L. and Ikeda, J. (2012) Young people with complex needs: Designing coordinated interventions to promote resilience across child welfare, juvenile corrections, mental health and education services. *British Journal of Social Work*: bcs147.

University of York (2000) *Facts, Feelings and Feedback: A Collaborative Model for Direct Observation*. York: University of York.

Van de Luitgaarden, G,M. (2009) Evidence-based practice in social work: Lessons from judgment and decision-making theory. *British Journal of Social Work*, 39: 243–60.

van der Put, C., Assink, M. and Stams, G. (2016) Predicting relapse of problematic child-rearing situations. *Children and Youth Services Review,* 61: 288–95.

Vester, F. (2007) The art of interconnected thinking. *Ideas and Tools for Tackling Complexity.* Munich: MCB-Verlag.

Waldrop, M. (1994) *Complexity: The Emerging Science at the Edge of Order and Chaos.* London: Penguin.

Ward, H. and Rose, W. (2002) *Approaches to Needs Assessment in Children's Services.* London: Jessica Kingsley.

Warmington, P., Daniels, H., Edwards, A., Brown, S., Leadbetter, J., Martin, D. and Middleton, D. (2004) *Learning in and for interagency working. Interagency Collaboration: A review of the literature.* Bath: University of Bath.

Wastell, D. and White, S. (2010) Technology as magic: Fetish and folly in the IT-enabled reform of children's services. In: Ayre, P. and Preston-Shoot, M. (eds) *Children's Services at the Crossroads: A Critical Evaluation of Contemporary Policy for Practice.* Lyme Regis: Russell House Publishing.

Wastell, D. and White, S. (2012) Blinded by neuroscience: Social policy, the family and the infant brain. *Families, Relationships and Societies,* 1: 397–414.

Wastell, D. and White, S. (2017) *Blinded by Science: The Social Implications of Epigenetics and Neuroscience.* Bristol: Policy Press.

Webb, A. (1991) Coordination: A problem in public sector management. *Policy & Politics,* 19: 229–42.

Webb, S.A. (2001) Some considerations on the validity of evidence-based practice in social work. *British Journal of Social Work,* 31: 57–79.

Webb, S.A. (2006) *Social Work in a Risk Society: Social and Political Perspectives.* Basingstoke: Palgrave Macmillan.

Weber, M. (1978) *Economy and Society: An Outline of Interpretative Sociology.* London: University of California.

Wenger, E. (1998) *Communities of Practice.* Cambridge: Cambridge University Press.

West, K. (2013) The grip of personalization in adult social care: Between managerial domination and fantasy, *Critical Social Policy,* 33(4): 638–657.

White, S. (2009) Fabled uncertainty in social work: A coda to Spafford et al. *Journal of Social Work,* 9: 222–35.

White, S., Fook, J. and Gardner, F. (2006) *Critical Reflection in Health and Social Care.* Maidenhead: Open University Press.

White, S., Hall, C. and Peckover, S. (2009) The descriptive tyranny of the Common Assessment Framework: Technologies of categorization and professional practice in child welfare. *British Journal of Social Work,* 39: 1197–217.

Widdowson, H.G. (1995) Discourse analysis: A critical view. *Language and Literature,* 4: 157–72.

Wilkinson, R. (2005) *The Impact of Inequality: How to Make Sick Societies Healthier.* Abingdon: Routledge.

Wilson, J. (1989) *Bureaucracy: What Government Agencies Do and Why They Do It.* New York: Basic Books.

Wilson, K., Ruch, G., Lymbery, M., et al. (2011) *Social Work: An Introduction to Contemporary Practice* (2nd edn). Harlow: Pearson Education.

Winnicott, D. (1965) *The Maturation Process and the Facilitating Environment.* London: Hogarth Press.

Wolf-Branigin, M. (2013) *Using Complexity Theory for Research and Program Evaluation.* Oxford: Oxford University Press.

Woodhouse, D. and Pengelly, P. (1991) *Anxiety and the Dynamics of Collaboration.* Aberdeen: Aberdeen University Press.

Woods, D., Dekker, S., Cook, R., Johansson, A. and Sarter, N. (2010) *Behind Human Error.* Farnham: Ashgate.

Yan, M.C. (2008) Exploring cultural tensions in cross-cultural social work practice. *Social Work,* 53: 317–28.

Yates, S. and Payne, M. (2006) Not so NEET? A critique of the use of 'NEET'in setting targets for interventions with young people. *Journal of Youth Studies,* 9: 329–44.

Yeung, H.W-c. (1997) Critical realism and realist research in human geography: A method or a philosophy in search of a method? *Progress in Human Geography,* 21: 51–74.

Yin, R.K. (2009) *Case Study Research: Design and Methods.* Thousand Oaks, CA: Sage.

Yip, K-s. (2006) Self-reflection in reflective practice: A note of caution. *The British Journal of Social Work,* 36: 777–88.

Youth Justice Board (2005) *ASSET– Risk of Serious Harm.* Available at: www.justice.gov.uk/downloads/youth-justice/assessment/asset-young-offender-assessment-profile/Risk Form.pdf.

iNDEX